More Speech, Not Less

MORE SPEECH,
NOT LESS

COMMUNICATIONS
LAW IN THE
INFORMATION AGE

Mark Sableman

With a Foreword by Paul Simon

Southern Illinois University Press

Carbondale and Edwardsville

140683

Copyright © 1997 by Mark Sableman
All rights reserved
Printed in the United States of America

00 99 98 97   4 3 2 1

Foreword by Paul Simon, copyright © 1997 by the Board of Trustees, Southern Illinois University

Library of Congress Cataloging-in-Publication Data

Sableman, Mark, 1951–
    More speech, not less : communications law in the information age / Mark Sableman; with a foreword by Paul Simon.
        p.   cm.
    Includes bibliographical references (p.).
    1. Mass media—Law and legislation—United States.   2. Press law—United States.
    3. Telecommunication—Law and legislation—United States.   I. Title.
    KF2750.S33   1997
    343.7309'9—dc21
    ISBN 0-8093-2071-1 (cloth : alk. paper)
    ISBN 0-8093-2135-1 (pbk. : alk. paper)   96-53449
                                                                                        CIP

Earlier versions of many of the essays in this book were previously published and appear herein with permission of the *St. Louis Journalism Review*, the *St. Louis Post-Dispatch*, the Missouri Bar, the American Civil Liberties Union of Eastern Missouri, and the Bar Association of Metropolitan St. Louis.

This book contains commentaries on legal subjects; it is not a substitute for legal advice. Readers who want or need legal advice should consult an attorney.

The paper used in this publication meets the minimum requirements of American National Standard for Information Sciences—Permanence of Paper for Printed Library Materials, ANSI Z39.48-1984. ∞

For Paul, Charlotte, and Brian,

beneficiaries and future guardians of "the Blessings of Liberty"

promised in our Constitution

[N]o danger flowing from speech can be deemed clear and present, unless the incidence of the evil is so imminent that it may befall before there is opportunity for full discussion. If there be time to expose through discussion the falsehoods and fallacies, to avert the evil by the process of education, the remedy to be applied is more speech, not enforced silence.

— JUSTICE LOUIS D. BRANDEIS

Contents

Foreword   xiii
     Paul Simon
Preface   xvii
Acknowledgments   xxi

1   First Principles   I
     The First Amendment and Its Purposes   I
     Freedom of Speech   3
     Freedom of the Press   6
     Hate Speech, Toleration, and "More Speech"   8
     The Scholarship of Press Freedom   II
     The British System   13

2   Censorship and Prior Restraint   17
     Textbook Censorship   17
     Arts Censorship   22
     Arts Censorship and Political Correctness   25
     Radical Feminist Arguments for Censorship   27
     Censorship Arguments   31
     Symbolic Speech   34
     Prior Restraint   38

3   News Gathering   41
     Access to Court Documents   41
     Court Protective Orders   44
     Access to Electronic Records   47
     Access to Electronic Statutes   50
     Access to War and the Military   52
     Access to Voters and Polling Places   55

140683

Access Rights (and Hazards) Abroad   57
Should Lawyers Talk to the Media?   60

4   Confidentiality and Sources   64
Confidentiality Promises   64
Waiver of the Reporter's Privilege   68
Media Subpoena Cases: Practical Concerns   69
Agreements with Sources   72
Interview Contract Lawsuits   74
Reporters Versus Sources   77

5   Libel   81
Fact and Opinion   81
Opinion in Critical Reviews   85
Privileges for Witnesses and Reporters   88
Trials and the Press   90
Constitutional Privilege   94
Fault, Semantics, and Altered Quotations   98
Libel and the Rehnquist Court   102
Reckless Disregard and the Westmoreland and Sharon Cases   104
Coals of Fire and the Alton Telegraph Case   108
Abuse of Libel Suits   112
Libel Reform Efforts   116
Defending a Libel Case   119

6   Privacy   123
The "Right of Privacy"   123
Journalists' Right of Privacy Primer   126
Right of Privacy and Gary Hart   133
Scandal, Victims' Names, and Ethical Limits   136

7   Lawbreaking, Negligence, and Unusual Claims   139
Reporter Deception and Lawbreaking   139
"Negligent" Publications   143
Failure to Publish   147
Threats to Publishing   150
Silly Media Lawsuits: Aberrations or Barometer?   153

8   Copyright and Protection for Ideas   157
Copyright Myths and Realities   157
Fair Use and the Salinger Biography   161
Copyright Lesson   163

The Nature of Copyright and Users' Rights   166
Parody and Fair Use   170
Rights in Ideas   173

9   Advertising   176
Comparative Advertising Regulation   176
Use of Trademarks in Advertising   178
Publicity Rights in Advertising   181

10   Broadcasting   185
Licensing of Broadcast Spectrum   185
Broadcasting and Press Freedoms   189
Political Television Commercials   193

11   Fair Trial, Free Press   197
Fair Trial Right: Impartial, Not Ignorant, Jurors   197
Fair Trial, Free Press in Practice   201
Cameras in the Courtroom   204

12   The Business (and Education) of the Press   210
Student Press Rights   210
Reporters as Professionals   215
Book Publishing Contracts   217
Distribution Rights   221

13   The Internet and Electronic Information   225
Information as Property   225
Price Tags on Information   228
Who Owns Information?   231
Law of Cyberspace Messages   235
Internet Jurisdiction   239
Facts and Promise of the Internet   243

Notes   251
Select Bibliography   273

Foreword

I first encountered Mark Sableman in reading one of the nation's liveliest and least-known publications, the *St. Louis Journalism Review*, founded by Charles Klotzer. Through its pages, I learned the views of a true champion of First Amendment rights.

History can teach us many lessons, and one is that freedom is not easily preserved. If there are not voices like Mark Sableman and others to remind us of our heritage, there will be a gradual erosion of our basic freedoms. The threats to freedom rarely come as ogres; rather the threats come packaged attractively, with labels of things all of us espouse. Mark Sableman believes that communications laws, which affect the basic freedoms of thought and expression, are too important to be left to the experts. His message is that by understanding and actively seeking to influence their direction, informed citizens can help preserve freedom as changing times bring new issues—and new threats—to the forefront.

Years ago I served in the U.S. Army and was part of the Counter Intelligence Corps, an entity that no longer exists. I quickly learned that some items were properly classified as secret, like the names and identities of those who provided information from the other side of the Iron Curtain. But there were also many things classified to which the public should have had access, including matters that would have embarrassed military authorities if the information had been made public. Individual citizens who solicited classified information, whether such status was justified or not, received the answer that national security required that matters be kept secret. And who would undermine national security?

It is easy to find excuses to restrict freedom when it is politically convenient. As I write this, U.S. citizens, with a few narrow exceptions, cannot legally visit Cuba. The reason: We do not want to help a dictator. I don't want to help dictators, but shouldn't American citizens be able to travel anywhere, as long as there is no threat to their physical safety, and learn what is happening in other nations? A government that advocates freedom should not restrict that movement of its people and their right to acquire knowledge and ideas.

What does the increasing concentration of media ownership do to the free flow of ideas in our nation? I cast one of six votes in the Senate against the Telecommunications Act that passed Congress in 1996 in part because it would open the door to huge concentrations of radio and television ownership. When that bill passed, Westinghouse, CBS, and Infiniti were the three biggest owners of radio stations in the nation. Within two years of the passage of that Act, all of their radio stations were gathered under one umbrella of corporate ownership.

The great concentration of newspaper ownership is likewise unhealthy, but there is little the federal government can do about it. We can do something about radio and television ownership, and yet we are not doing it, in part because of the entanglement between the ownership of radio, television, and newspapers and because lawmakers are reluctant to confront these corporate behemoths, which are capable of swaying public opinion. Again, the threats to freedom come in different wrappings at different times.

With the explosion of technology, difficult decisions will have to be made in the years to come. All of us soon will be able to possess genetic maps of ourselves. How do we move ahead with such issues, preserve privacy, and yet make information available for research? Will individuals have the right to give this information to employers and insurance companies? And if we can voluntarily provide it, will it cause discrimination against those who do not provide it? Where do media rights fit in all of this? Many of the new technologies will involve us in gray areas where lines must be drawn and redrawn with great care, and these crucial evaluations, distinctions, and decisions will be determined by which justices sit on the United States Supreme Court.

As we confront these and many other difficult policy choices, we need, more than ever, informed and active citizens who understand, care about, and seek to influence both our overall political direction and particular policy choices. We need to understand the issues, and we need to embrace the values of freedom.

Mark Sableman's pleas for understanding communications laws and policies, and for honoring First Amendment values, are pleas that we all should heed as we encounter ever more complex questions and enter ever more complicated times

Paul Simon

Preface

For almost twenty years, I have practiced the law of personal, business, and media communications, and for more than half of this period I have regularly set forth my observations in articles in the *St. Louis Journalism Review* and other publications. For this book, I have revised and organized many of those articles and essays into a guide, both descriptive and analytical, for interested citizens.

The articles have often been pegged to local and regional events and cases, but they discuss legal principles, policies, and trends that are common to the whole country. In the articles, I have attempted to examine, explain, and analyze legal principles and developments as they affect professional communicators (journalists, writers, and artists) and, just as important, communications recipients—the citizen readers, listeners, and viewers to whom media and other mass communications are directed.

Communication among humans is nothing new. It has been a defining characteristic of human society and has existed since the first cave men and women gossiped about their cave neighbors, criticized their cave leaders, and organized cave conferences and conventions. Human communication during the late twentieth century derives from the first cave talk but departs from it in many non-content-related ways. Communication has intensified, accelerated, and mechanized in astonishing ways. As with industrialism in an earlier century, communications in our time has experienced a kind of "takeoff" in media, messages, and modes (such as interactivity). The legal implications have followed; wherever there is growth in society, there is growth in law.

Communications law matured and expanded—and bedeviled those who sought either simple solutions or hard-and-fast rules—in the 1980s and 1990s. During these years, it became clear that our system had definitively rejected sweeping solutions on either side. Free expression advocates saw First Amendment absolutism (such as that advocated by Justices William O. Douglas and Hugo Black) fail in the 1960s, and in the following decades their hopes for an ever-expanding constitutional protection for expression were lost as well. But the throw-the-book-at-'em press critics and the extremists who sought to impose a government censor's heavy blue pencil on unorthodox expressions lost, too, as the 1980s and 1990s became a time of legal fine-tuning, not major constitutional backtracking.

In each of the many legal areas affecting communications (areas like libel, privacy, copyright, and advertising), intricate webs of legal *do*s and *don't*s, practical pitfalls and effective safe harbors, have been constructed. These rules and practicalities have developed through the cumulative effect of judges' decisions, legislative enactments, public opinion, technological advances, and (more significantly than most credit it) journalistic self-analysis and self-criticism.

To take but one example, American libel law today consists of a complicated patchwork of rules and practicalities, based on sources as disparate as English common law, First Amendment principles, empirical journalistic standards, and modern semantic understandings. The plaintiff-favored thicket of the old common law is gone, felled by Justice William J. Brennan Jr.'s eloquent and trenchant analysis in *New York Times Co. v. Sullivan*. But the sunny paradise of journalistic freedom predicted by many after the 1964 *Sullivan* ruling never came into being, either. The constitutional privilege of *Sullivan*, particularly as construed, limited, and factually tested in the 1980s and 1990s, is simply another *defense* to libel, not the near-perfect immunity that many press advocates once hoped for and even expected.

So in modern libel law, neither side is guaranteed a victory; both must confront and navigate the accumulated rules, principles, and practicalities. Are particular words sufficiently disparaging to be actionable? Go to the old common law rules, informed by modern semantics. Are *opinions* actionable or only statements of facts? It depends, according to the Supreme Court, which directs you to follow a difficult and somewhat counterintuitive analysis. Does the *Sullivan* defense, which was designed to protect discussion of public issues and public figures, apply in a particular case? That depends, too—though less on the issues or public figures involved than on how the journalist approached them. Does it matter what other journalists or the public think? Technically, it matters hardly at all; but in reality, journalistic practice and public opinion matter tremendously.

Legal issues pervade in almost all other areas of communications, as they do in libel. Freelancers and artists grapple with copyright issues. Advertisers and business promoters work around advertising regulations as well as trademark and publicity rights. Broadcasters and cablecasters deal with content, financial, and technical regulations. Book publishers, student editors, and musicians all struggle with agency-imposed rules, direct and indirect attempts at content regulation, and the threat of damage claims. And conduits, content providers, and users alike face legal problems as they use (and develop) the new electronic media of computer-based communications.

Law, and lots of it, is here to stay in the communications field. Communications professionals must understand the legal issues and govern their conduct accordingly.

But more than just knowing the rules is at stake. Since we have rejected the absolutes on either side, the policy choices that are made within the broad middle area are all-important. These policy choices are very much influenced by the attitudes, values, and priorities of those who, in one way or another, participate in the public debate on communications and free expression. Both communications professionals and informed citizens who care about what they read, hear, and learn must understand and influence the *direction* of the law. That is, opinion leaders and the public need to debate and understand the value of press freedoms, in the context of the (sometimes difficult and troublesome) practical situations in which new and groundbreaking issues arise.

No one can approach these subjects free of bias. My primary bias is a simple one—the preference for, in Justice Louis D. Brandeis's words, "more speech, not enforced silence" in all but the most extreme situations. The "more speech" formula is not legal doctrine. The preferences of Justices Black and Douglas for absolutely no restrictions on speech never made it as constitutional law. But the "more speech, not less" principle (as it is usually expressed today) remains alive as an instinct, a preference, and an influential point of view. This viewpoint is, admittedly, but one of many respectable positions or perspectives in the continuing debate over calls for limits on potentially harmful speech, imposition of responsibility on speakers (if such a thing is possible), and control over communications as a means of attaining social objectives.

The importance of this public debate is the reason why I have sought to turn a gimlet eye to, and share my observations on, communications law during this period of its development and maturity. In this field, the law is not just something that *happens*. It is something we all help *create*. It demands understanding and critical thinking by everyone who cares about the power of information and the magic of words and images.

Acknowledgments

Because this book describes ideas and principles that developed during an intellectual journey through communications law and policy, I owe thanks to those who have led, joined, and assisted on this journey. Among others, they include:

My mentors and colleagues in the discovery and practice of communications law, especially Lawrence Gunnels, James A. Klenk, and Charles J. Sennet.

Clients, including many media companies, and, even more important than the companies, the individual publishers, editors, writers, news directors, correspondents, producers, and artists whose work I have been privileged to defend.

Those who taught and worked with me in my journalism education at the Medill School of Journalism and in my journalism career at the *Clearwater Sun* and the *Washington Post*.

Webster University, which has given me the opportunity to teach communications law in its School of Communications.

The individuals who encouraged me to write these commentaries, especially Charles Klotzer, the founder of the *St. Louis Journalism Review* and its editor and publisher until 1996.

Of course, I acknowledge the patience and encouragement of my family, especially my wife, Lynn, who has indulged me in my popular writing avocation during my "free time" away from the practice of law (i.e., nights and weekends).

More Speech, Not Less

First Principles

The First Amendment and Its Purposes

IF THE CONSTITUTION WAS MEANT ''TO INSURE domestic tranquility," as its preamble asserts, then the First Amendment sometimes seems a little out of place.

Rather than tranquility, the First Amendment freedoms of speech, press, religion, petition, and assembly often seem to promote discord. This is particularly so as the First Amendment has been interpreted by the Supreme Court to allow protesters to burn the flag, citizens to sharply, even unfairly, criticize public officials, and fringe religious groups to pursue unorthodox practices and lifestyles. This is hardly a prescription for a "tranquil" nation.

But the tension that results from freedoms of conscience and expression is only a surface disturbance. These freedoms ultimately strengthen the nation and give it its distinctive vitality. That was the intention of the founders of the nation in 1789, when the Bill of Rights was passed by the first Congress and sent to the states for ratification. And it was behind the vote in the Bill of Rights' bicentennial year, in 1989, when the Senate rejected a constitutional amendment cutting back on First Amendment freedoms where the flag is involved. The Senate did not so much reject one expression of American freedom, the flag, as reaffirm another, the First Amendment. As Senator John Danforth, Republican of Missouri, noted when he changed his position and opposed the amendment, "Every country has a flag. But America has the Bill of Rights. And it is the crowning glory of our country."

The freedoms we know now as First Amendment rights were the most uniquely American contributions to the Bill of Rights. Many of the other parts of the Bill of Rights declared rights that had long been recognized in English law. The English Bill of Rights of 1689, for example, recognized the right to freedom from excessive bail and cruel and unusual punishment. Even earlier, English law had recognized rights of trial by jury, the writ of habeas corpus, and protection from double jeopardy.

In the areas of political and religious thought and expression, however, English law was less enlightened. By various means—taxation, licensing, grants of "official" status, and trials of those who departed from officially sanctioned lines—freedoms of speech, press, and religion were suppressed in colonial America. Printers in colonial America faced official licensing and taxation schemes as well as broad seditious libel laws that made any criticism of authorities risky. Religious freedom in most colonies was limited only to certain sects, and adherents of nonofficial sects were taxed to support the established church.

The independent-minded founders of the nation saw that the British authorities' suppression of dissenting beliefs and expressions had suppressed the strength of colonial society. Officially imposed orthodoxy promoted governmental arbitrariness and public dispirit and ultimately led to the American Revolution.

Thus, the founders attempted to give the United States the strength that came from freedoms of thought and expression. Most of the states' new constitutions, adopted immediately after the Declaration of Independence, granted broad protection for freedoms of speech, press, and religion. These freedoms were especially important to Thomas Jefferson, George Mason, and Patrick Henry, the three Virginians who led the movement for enactment of the federal Bill of Rights. Virginia's historic Declaration of Rights of 1776, primarily written by Mason, identified freedom of the press as "one of the great bulwarks of liberty." And Jefferson wrote and took great pride in Virginia's landmark "Bill for Establishing Religious Freedom" of 1779.

Jefferson recognized the social and political friction that would accompany these rights. "The declaration of rights," he wrote to James

Madison in 1789, regarding the newly proposed Bill of Rights, "is, like all other human blessings, alloyed with some inconveniences. . . . But the good in this instance vastly outweighs the evil." Two years later—shortly after he, as secretary of state, certified the final enactment of the Bill of Rights—Jefferson again explained the need to tolerate its "inconveniences": "I would rather be exposed to the inconveniences attending too much liberty than those attending too small a degree of it."

Today our courts and our wisest leaders recognize the need to tolerate the "inconveniences" of First Amendment freedoms. They understand that diversity in thoughts and voices is a strength, since it keeps us open to new ideas and safe from stifling official orthodoxies. Tolerance of diversity reminds us, as Judge Learned Hand eloquently explained in 1944, that "[t]he spirit of liberty is the spirit which is not too sure that it is right . . . the spirit which seeks to understand the minds of other men and women."

That spirit was alive when the federal Court of Appeals for the Eighth Circuit rendered a decision that effectively required a public official to suffer the inconveniences of a book critical of his actions. "We have decided," the court held, "that the Constitution requires more speech rather than less." The court recognized that a decision ignoring the claimed injury to the plaintiff's reputation was an "anomaly" at a time when individuals demand recompense for every injury. "But there is a larger injury to be considered," the court continued, "the damage done to every American when a book is pulled from a shelf, as in this case, or when an idea is not circulated."

For more than two hundred years, the First Amendment, while causing some discord and "inconveniences," including those associated with "more speech rather than less," has contributed to the nation's strength by protecting us from that "larger injury."

Freedom of Speech

The classic picture of free speech is easy to paint. It is almost pastoral in nature: an orator on a soapbox in the town square, holding forth on his political views to all who will listen.

Many modern free speech claims present a much different picture. Rather than a nostalgic Currier and Ives scene, they suggest the harsh designs and colliding colors of a Kandinsky painting. They involve at times unpatriotic acts, hateful demonstrations, and offensive music lyrics.

The framers of the First Amendment believed in free expression and wrote it into the Constitution in a few words of simple dignity: "Congress shall make no law . . . abridging the freedom of speech." They left it to the future—to lawyers, judges, and jurors—to put life into those words in particular cases. Contemporary society has sorely tested the free speech guarantee. Many of its celebrated free speech battles have involved messages and forms of speech that are disturbing—even profoundly so—to many citizens.

During the tumultuous era of the Vietnam War, protestors often sought the protection, broadly construed, of the First Amendment. Protests extended into new forms and kinds of expression, including display of attention-getting written messages that shock and disturb, and visible protests even in public school classrooms. These protests led to two key Supreme Court rulings that held that the First Amendment embraces and protects such activities.

Justice John Marshall Harlan, perhaps the Court's most conservative member at the time, wrote for the majority in the 1971 decision that upheld the right to use offensively worded public protest messages. The First Amendment protects not just intellectual but also emotional and even foolish arguments, he explained. So broad a right of free expression is nothing less than a "prerogative of American citizenship." Similarly, in its 1969 ruling that protests may extend into public school classrooms (so long as they are not disruptive), the Supreme Court based its decision on a view of free expression not as a disturbance but as an essential element of education for adult citizenship. Students, it held, have rights within the schoolhouse gates, and within a public school "they may not be confined to expression of those sentiments that are officially approved."

Even as the national scars of the Vietnam era healed, divisive and upsetting protests continued to challenge the limits of free speech. Most dramatically, in 1977 a small group of self-styled American Nazis sought to march in Skokie, Illinois, a community with a sizable Jewish population including many survivors of the Holocaust. Emotions and tensions rode high in Skokie for months. But courts upheld the right of the Nazis to march. Years later, the march and the Nazis are all but forgotten, but the principle of the incident—free speech for everyone, even those we despise—is proudly remembered.

Later, the flag protest cases of 1989 and 1990 tested the same principle. The cases began in Dallas, Texas, in 1984 when Gregory Johnson burned an American flag in public in protest of the Republican Party, certain Dallas corporations, and nuclear war. A Texas statute, similar to laws in effect in many states, made desecration of the American flag a crime. Johnson was arrested, prosecuted, and convicted. He appealed with free speech as his defense.

The case reached the Supreme Court in 1989, and the Court upheld Johnson's defense. Burning the flag in protest is a form of free speech, the Court majority held, and cannot be prosecuted. Justice William J. Brennan Jr. noted in the decision that protection of speech that most citizens would find offensive was not an aberration but a core purpose of the Bill of Rights. "If there is a bedrock principle underlying the First Amendment, it is that the Government may not prohibit the expression of an idea simply because society finds the idea itself offensive or disagreeable," he wrote.

A firestorm of public criticism ensued after the 1989 decision and its reaffirmation by the Court a year later. Congress twice came close to proposing a constitutional amendment that would—for the first time in history—carve out an exception (for flag desecration) to the Bill of Rights. The amendment was rejected, in recognition of the importance of an unblemished and unconditional Bill of Rights.

Even as core principles of free speech protests are settled, however, new free speech claims and controversies have continued to arise, and will continue to arise. In the decade of the 1990s, the decade of the 200th anniversary of the ratification of the Bill of Rights, many new (and sometimes disturbing) claims of artistic freedom of speech began to arise.

In 1990 in Ohio, a contemporary art museum that displayed artistic erotic photographs and its director were accused of obscenity. And in Florida the same year a popular rap band was accused of obscenity violations based on violent sexual images in its (barely understandable) song lyrics. In both cases, the artists raised free speech as a defense. In both cases, juries upheld those defenses by handing down verdicts of acquittal. Jurors in both cases explained later that they did not admire the particular photographs or lyrics involved, but they did not consider them obscene, and they respected the right of the artists to express their views, disturbing as they may be.

If 200 years of the First Amendment have taught anything, it is that free speech is not quiet, serene, or comfortable, but tumultuous, disturbing, and inconvenient. But because this tumult arises out of the underlying principle of liberty, our society for the most part accepts and even embraces it. It is, after all, part of the "crowning glory of our country."

Freedom of the Press

Modern America is a media and information society. We wake to the radio and eat breakfast with the morning newspaper and television shows. At work we read trade journals and newsletters and issue our own reports and news releases. At the end of the day, we relax with books, magazines, television, and movies.

Our eyes, ears, and brains are daily filled with input from communications media, print and broadcast—and, increasingly today, on-line. This is a fairly modern phenomenon. Yet all these modern media owe much of their existence and editorial freedom to a 200-year-old legal enactment: the First Amendment of the U.S. Constitution, which guarantees freedom of the press.

The "press" had a somewhat different meaning in the preelectronic age when the Bill of Rights was written than it does today. The framers of the Bill of Rights undoubtedly had in mind the press of their day: independent journals chiefly devoted to opinion, sprinkled with bits of news and advertising. These papers, often erratic in content and publication frequency, and produced laboriously using hand-set pieces of lead type and Gutenberg-era printing presses, were a far cry from modern communications media.

But the concept behind the First Amendment's free press guarantee—"Congress shall make no law . . . abridging the freedom . . . of the press"—was not restricted to the antiquated media of the 1790s. To the framers, freedom of the press was an integral part of the freedom of thought and expression that was necessary to developing informed and educated citizens and a free democratic society.

The story of freedom of the press in America during the last 200 years has thus been the story of this old core principle applied to the new issues and problems that have developed out of modern communications media. In short, it is the story of how the concept of freedom of the press has grown to meet the changes in technology and society.

What Media Are Protected. Is "freedom of the press" limited to the freedom to publish written material with a printing press? Not at all. The Supreme Court has held that it applies to all communications media, including radio, television, and movies. In one landmark case involving movies, the Court noted that "[m]otion pictures are a significant medium for the communication of ideas" and thus fully covered by the First Amendment. Movies, the Court noted, no less than other media "may affect public attitudes and behavior in a variety of ways, ranging from direct espousal of a political or social doctrine to the subtle shaping of thought which characterizes all artistic expression."

Content Controls. Courts have often recognized that the government should not control the content of what is published or broadcast by the media. Thus, for example, the state of Florida could not require newspapers to publish politicians' responses to critical articles or editorials. The choice of what to publish, the Court held, is solely for editors.

Some general content controls have been imposed on radio and television, on the theory that media that use the public airwaves can be required to serve the public. These controls have included public service broadcasting requirements and the *fairness doctrine*, which required broadcasters to air both sides of controversial issues. But many of these controls, including the fairness doctrine, have been dropped in recent years in attempts to give more press freedom to broadcasters.

Advance Censorship. Except in the most extraordinary cases, the government is prohibited from censoring a publication (or a movie or a television or radio show) in advance. Advance censorship (called *prior restraint*) is considered the worst kind of government interference with the press; it is the tool most often used in totalitarian countries by governments that wish to control the knowledge and thinking of their citizens.

Hence, when the *New York Times* and other newspapers obtained a top secret government report on the Vietnam War, the Supreme Court did not permit the Nixon administration to prevent publication of the report. Similarly, attempts by the government and private litigants to prevent publication of books, airing of television shows, or showing of films almost always fail.

Criticism of Public Officials. In England and pre-Revolutionary America, if freedom of the press was recognized at all, it always had a catch: it did not apply to *seditious libel*—that is, it did not apply if the newspapers severely criticized government officials.

Our modern press law includes no such catch-22. The Supreme Court in a key 1964 decision recognized that uninhibited debate on public issues "may well include vehement, caustic, and sometimes unpleasantly sharp attacks on government and public officials." Thus, the Court imposed special high barriers to libel and slander suits brought by public officials. Subsequent decisions have set other limits on libel and slander suits.

Access to News. For any news medium to be effective, it must have access to news, and in particular to government officials, proceedings, and documents. Both courts and legislatures have recognized this in case law and in statutes such as the federal Freedom of Information Act. For example, trials and other judicial proceedings must almost always be open to the press.

Student Press. In 1988, the Supreme Court ruled that the First Amendment does not give full press freedom to high school editors. Essentially, high school newspapers that are produced as part of the school curriculum are subject to control by school authorities like any other part of the curriculum. But even in this situation, the First Amendment still imposes limitations, for censorship by school authorities can only be imposed for legitimate educational reasons. Also, school newspapers prepared outside the official school curriculum have full press freedoms.

The principles outlined above make up much of freedom of the press as it now exists. But the media and the communications environment continue to change and evolve—and the meaning of press freedom will continue to change and evolve in response.

Hate Speech, Toleration, and "More Speech"

For all of our flag-waving about free speech principles, the fact is that most of us, at least on our initial instincts, wouldn't mind banning *some* speech. And we could feel *comfortable* banning speech, even in view of our long-standing recognition of the value of free speech, if we based the ban on some lofty principle.

Like, "no hate speech." That sounds pretty fair. Hate is bad, undesirable, harmful. Hateful words are only one step removed from hateful conduct. Hate serves no value, and cutting hate out of the national dialogue isn't going to cost us much in terms of great ideas or the advancement of arts, sciences, humanities, and civilization. The idea sounds even better in practice than it does in the abstract. Think of those who would be silenced: Ku Klux Klan. Neo-Nazis. Homophobes. Far right extremists. Religious zealots. The list can go on and on . . . *Oops!*

That's part of the problem, isn't it? The list *can—and will*—go on and on. Once the door is opened to banning speech based on judgments of the propriety of the speaker's message, the key to acceptability or nonacceptability becomes a content-based judgment about a particular speaker's hatefulness. Zionists—hateful to Palestinians? Radical feminists—hateful toward men? Editors of gay publications that specialize in "outing"—hateful toward closet gays? African American activists who seek reparations for slavery—hateful toward innocent whites? Socialists—hateful toward property owners?

Yes, the list can *and will* go on and on. Confident as we may be in the correctness of our own judgments as to hatefulness and nonhatefulness—or whatever other measure we intend to use for *allowable* and *nonallowable* speech—those judgments are just that—*judgments*—and others will, at times, come to different conclusions.

You may think we could handle this decision the normal democratic way. Let the majority decide. If the majority finds it hateful, it's banned. If the majority finds it acceptable, it's okay. But do we really want to rely on majority rule here? Majorities don't have the best record for judgment and toleration. Majorities couldn't be relied on to protect African Americans from the Ku Klux Klan when that group was a far greater threat than its motley current-day descendant. Indeed, most minorities get little comfort from the protection of majorities—especially when times gets tough and economic or other outside conditions strain tolerance and stir prejudices.

And we need to face the fact that historically minorities—even despised minorities who often seemed at odds with the most basic values of society—have often been right. Abolitionists were seen as radical and unworthy extremists in most of America, even the North, for much of the early nineteenth century; but they were right. Interventionists carried little weight with the majority in our insular post-World War I period; but they were right. Civil rights protestors and Vietnam war protestors— this list of minorities who were despised but who turned out to be right could go on and on, too.

So, even at first glance, there are some serious problems with banning some speech: The difficulty of making proper content-based judgments. The impossibility of having a majoritarian government fairly impose controls on content. And the danger of muzzling speech that is worthy. These considerations are at the heart of our Constitution's First Amendment.

But they may seem like negative and overly theoretical considerations. In that case, it is worth considering two more positive and practical reasons for free speech. Return for a moment to the basic instinct that leads one to consider any kind of a ban on speech. Some things are right, and some are wrong. It was wrong enough that in the shadows of the Civil War a group of hateful and misguided vigilantes called themselves the Ku Klux Klan and terrorized African American citizens. It is despicable that in today's enlightened age persons who certainly know better desire to carry on that dubious organization. The Klan is wrong and should be exposed as such.

But is a ban on the Klan's speech the only way to expose it as wrong? Hardly. As anyone knows, banning something simply gives it a mystique and makes it seem more desirable. Rather than silencing extremist speakers, a ban is more likely to create extremist martyrs and draw the curious and disenchanted to the extremist message.

There is another way to expose an idea as fallacious. That is to speak up against it—to drown out the hatefulness of the wrongful idea with rationality, facts, and human concern. This is the response of strength, not weakness. It says, *"We're not afraid of your ideas, because in any fair contest, ours will win and yours will lose."* This is the first positive answer that the First Amendment gives to those who would ban speech that appears bad. Speech isn't the problem; it's the solution. In the words of Supreme Court Justice Louis D. Brandeis, the remedy is "more speech, not enforced silence."

The second positive answer to the bad-speech problem is more subtle but just as important, and the Klan episode illustrates it, too. The Klan is a narrow-minded organization built on prejudice. It represents the antithesis of toleration and open-mindedness. The free speech principle of our Bill of Rights represents an ideology diametrically opposite to that of the Klan—open-mindedness, inclusion, and freedom of thought. Freedom even for the thought that we (the majority) hate, in Voltaire's famous phrase. Is there any better way to fight intolerance and hatefulness than with a *demonstration* of a system that thrives on inclusiveness and open-mindedness? And is there any better answer to a message of hatefulness toward minorities than our own action in holding tighter to our precious civil liberties that demand toleration for all?

No matter how appealing it may seem to ban speech, there are many reasons why we should not do so. Some of these reasons (which I have called the negative, or theoretical, considerations) relate to the difficulties, even impossibilities, inherent in content-based speech limitations—the difficulty of line-drawing, the dangers of majoritarian decisions, the likelihood of suppression of worthy ideas.

But even those who focus solely on the evil at hand—the advocacy of hateful ideas by groups such as the Klan—ought to recognize the practical and *positive* reasons why free speech is the only answer. Ultimately, only more speech—the inherent persuasiveness of truth, when it is aired in the open in opposition to falsity or hatefulness—can defeat a bad idea. And only a system that upholds toleration in all circumstances has the moral authority to stand up to falsehood, hatred, and intolerance.

The Scholarship of Press Freedom

Classic free speech theory derives from those glory days of Milton, John Stuart Mill, and the original New England town meetings. It holds that in an atmosphere of tolerance, when many different voices are heard and considered on matters of important social policy, thoughtful people will reach considered, wise judgments on those weighty issues. It seems like a wonderful, lofty ideal—and a somewhat simplistic and naive vision for today's world of nasty political campaigns, sensational and celebrity-oriented television, personality politics, and a cynical public.

But in one field—the area of scholarly debate of free speech principles—the theory is even followed. Scholars, advocates, jurists, and ordinary citizens regularly write and argue about free speech topics, passionate and secure in the conviction that their contributions to the debate will make a difference. And, remarkably, the participants in these debates even *listen to one another*, and to some extent critique, credit, and build on the theories, studies, and proposals propounded. American laws and practices have richly benefited from this debate.

Despite our frequently expressed doubts about freedom of speech and of the press, and whatever problems we have reconciling it with our political, social, and emotional needs from time to time, we Americans ultimately take free speech principles very seriously. Our leaders, our scholars, and our lawyers and jurists, for the most part, believe in free speech and want it to work for us. A monumental bibliography, *Freedom of the Press: An Annotated Bibliography*, edited by Ralph McCoy of Southern Illinois University, makes this clear. This work, which had its second

extensive supplement published in 1994, demonstrates this country's remarkable devotion to freedoms of speech and of the press.

McCoy's first volume, published in 1968, annotated articles, books,
and speeches on press freedom, ranging alphabetically from Clarence Ab-
bott's 1917 article on movie censorship to Sidney Zagri's 1966 monograph
on free press and fair trial, and embracing 7,541 entries. The work didn't
just list the articles but summarized and often quoted them, hence making the bibliography itself interesting and stimulating reading—a kind of
"best of" album for the free speech set.

One might have thought that McCoy had accumulated just about
everything worth saying about press freedom in his original volume.
Hardly. Ten years later, when the first supplement (covering 1968 to 1978)
was published, it was fuller even than the original. And for the second
supplement, covering 1978 to 1992, McCoy took a more selective approach in order to avoid excessive length and duplication of subjects and
ideas—but still the volume ran to 404 large-format pages and 4,153 entries. (McCoy vowed in the introduction that the third volume would be
his last.) The second supplement continues old themes (book censorship,
obscenity, libel, privacy, and the problem of conducting fair trials under
the glare of the media) and features current themes (artistic, school, and
library censorship, freedom of information, hate speech, and responses to
new technologies).

Given the length and breadth of McCoy's volumes, it is difficult to
do them justice other than to praise their usefulness to researchers. But
even a somewhat random perusal of the current and original volumes
prompts a number of thoughts and observations about free speech in the
United States, where it has been and where it is going.

The Warren Court's Leadership. In areas like libel, obscenity, and
broadcast regulation, among others, the law has changed considerably in
the past thirty years. The leader in many of these changes, without any
doubt, has been the Supreme Court in the Warren era (and to some
extent the Burger era as well), and, most particularly Justice William J.
Brennan Jr., whose First Amendment principles and doctrines have in-
spired much of the scholarly and professional thinking of this period.

Hundreds of the articles and books in the bibliography owe their topics or many of their ideas to the Supreme Court's pro-free speech initiatives of the 1960s and 1970s. Without the trailblazing policy-oriented decisions of politically active justices like Brennan, Douglas, Black, Fortas,
and others, our entire free speech literature would be far less complete

and less profound. (That should prompt concern as to the direction of free speech in the future, under a Supreme Court dominated by conservative legal technicians.)

Obscenity and Indecency. In practice, if not theory, the law of obscenity has undergone a drastic change. Free speech crusaders in the early and middle parts of the century had difficulty, and often lost, in defending writers like Dreiser, Joyce, and Arthur Miller. By contrast, in current practice, even the pornography industry faces few limits. It is not apparent why things have changed so dramatically, though undoubtedly the rationales of free speech advocates and leading jurists (including Justice Brennan in his 1957 *Roth* decision, which recognized that sex, "a great and mysterious motive force in human life has indisputably been a subject of absorbing interest to mankind through the ages") have influenced both judicial policy and administrative enforcement practices.

But while we have in recent years narrowed obscenity (the category of publications so vile they can be banned absolutely), we have focused more and more on issues such as exposure of children to nonobscene but indecent or inappropriate materials. Much of the current literature grapples with broadcast content controls, industry self-regulation, and other ways of protecting children from today's everything-goes atmosphere in literature, movies, and video. These are difficult issues, which have yet to be resolved, as many of the articles annotated by McCoy demonstrate.

Ideological Justifications for Controls on Speech. The special development of the last decade has been the growing demand from the political left for controls on speech to serve egalitarian ends. Many entries in the third volume discuss proposals to ban or limit "hate speech," which is deemed offensive or harmful to minorities, and pornography, which is deemed harmful to women. Given the extent to which these plans are being seriously proposed, considered, and debated, it is clear that the issue will persist for some time.

The McCoy bibliography highlights these and many other free speech issues. Both the researcher and the casual reader interested in freedom of expression will find the bibliography a stimulating sourcebook and an extremely helpful starting point for further reading and thinking.

The British System

According to one of Judge Learned Hand's most famous statements, deeply held convictions protect civil liberties more than constitutions, laws, or courts. "Liberty lies in the hearts of men and women," he wrote. "While it lies there it needs no constitution, no law, no court to save it." Well . . . cynical observers of human nature may wonder just how firmly some liberties—including freedom of the press—are implanted in the hearts of men and women.

One need only look to Great Britain, the source of much of our law, and a nation with similar convictions, to see that press freedom has no firm hold on the hearts of policymakers. Indeed, most of the differences between press freedom in Britain and America appear because of the different constitutional structures of the two nations.

As an example, in one brief period late in the Thatcher administration in Britain, Parliament considered new "right-to-reply" and "right to privacy" bills and pushed closer to approval of an amended official Secrets Act—all of which would be plainly unconstitutional here. Numerous existing British press laws also would not pass muster here. British libel law, for example, imposes heavy burdens on the press even where public officials are involved. A celebrated libel suit by novelist and Conservative Party leader Jeffrey Archer—who had admittedly paid a prostitute for her silence—would have been thrown out at the pretrial stage here. But Archer won almost $1 million against a London newspaper.

The differences in British and American press freedoms stem largely from the difference in constitutional systems. Britain's "constitution" is unwritten; it consists of a tradition of liberty dating back to the Magna Carta, together with all the relevant laws enacted by Parliament, which are subject to changes and reinterpretations by Parliament. The United States Constitution, by contrast, is a single written document, relatively unchangeable, which is interpreted by courts, not legislators. As a result, constitutional freedoms in the United States are further removed than British freedoms from the heat of the political process and the passions of elected legislators.

The proposed British "right-to-reply" statute vividly illustrates the import of these differences. The bill would have given every citizen who complained of press coverage an automatic right to an unpaid reply of equal size and prominence in the newspaper that published the original story. The bill was even broader than a Florida statute that granted a right to reply to political candidates who complained of newspaper coverage of their campaigns. The Florida law was unanimously held unconstitutional by the U.S. Supreme Court in 1974 in the case of *Miami Herald v. Tornillo*.

The right-to-reply bill was introduced in Parliament on an unusual procedural basis, by a single member of Parliament without government support. But it nonetheless garnered the support of a majority of members of Parliament. The debate on the bill highlighted how far the British press is from the freedoms enjoyed by its American counterpart. One press supporter, for example, argued as follows:

> A newspaper is more than a passive receptacle for news, comment and advertising. The choice of materials, decisions on size and content, the terms of discussion of public issues, public opinion and politicians, whether fair or unfair, constitutes the exercise of editorial control and judgment. I have yet to be convinced how government regulation of this crucial process can be exercised consistent with a free press.

The words were eloquent. They were also lifted, almost verbatim, from the U.S. Supreme Court in *Miami Herald v. Tornillo*. Those statements, settled law in the United States, were but unpersuasive debating points in Great Britain.

The bill was ultimately defeated by the British equivalent of a filibuster. But even defeat of the bill did not constitute a press victory, since the government in response to members' anti-press sentiment formed an independent government commission to review press conduct and laws. The threat represented by the commission was made explicit by one government minister, who explained, "Editors and publishers . . . are on probation. They have a year or two to clean up their act." If they do not "clean up," he stated, "Parliament will certainly return to this issue."

After the reply bill's defeat, Parliament still had before it a related right-to-privacy bill that would present an even greater nightmare for editors. The privacy bill would prohibit newspapers from reporting any news, including crime and accidents, without the express permission of the individuals involved. And its provisions designed to prevent media harassment would prevent many routine news-gathering techniques. The privacy bill was also expected to fail but remain a part of the legislation that may be revisited by the government's press commission.

Other parliamentary action around this time reinforced the relatively low legal protection for press freedoms in Britain. A few days before it debated the reply bill, Parliament considered a proposed new Official Secrets Act, a bill that would both particularize and strengthen the law that

is an important constitutional right; it guarantees freedom of conscience, thought, and belief, perhaps the most basic of all individual liberties. True, the concrete meaning of the constitutional protection for free exercise must depend to some extent upon the particular beliefs held—the Amish or Jehovah's Witnesses, for example, may obtain special protection such as exemptions from compulsory public education or from saying the pledge of allegiance because of the nature of their beliefs. So, theoretically at least, special protection could be extended under the free-exercise clause for those whose religion finds secular humanism offensive.

A viewpoint that uses the right to free exercise of religion as a launching base for a campaign of schoolbook censorship, however, is myopic and contrary to constitutional values. The First Amendment of the Bill of Rights is a charter of openness, not restriction. It was never intended to close off *discussion* and circulation of ideas. Indeed, toleration, and education of youth to understand different beliefs, are essential to protect all rights.

For many years now, attempts to censor, purge, or purify public school libraries and curricula have been escalating. Persons of practically every political, ethnic, and religious stripe have submitted their preferred list of banned books, including everyone from Shakespeare and Walt Whitman to Donald Duck, Snow White, and Batman. Some have even organized public book burnings, including one in Indiana in the early 1980s.

In court, the would-be censors have usually, but not always, failed. And as the Tennessee case illustrates, they have with each attempt refined their arguments and objectives.

The first recent wave of censorship cases, which reached the courts in the mid-1970s, seemed to concentrate on school library books. In various school districts, parents found or became aware of one or more books in the school library that they considered inappropriate or objectionable. They protested to school officials, with various results. School officials who stood fast and refused to purge the libraries often found themselves in federal court.

One leading library book case, *Minarcini v. Strongsville City School District*, arose out of objections by parents in Strongsville, Ohio, to works of Kurt Vonnegut and Joseph Heller. The U.S. Court of Appeals for the Sixth Circuit upheld the school board's refusal to take the books out of the library. A library, the court said, "is a mighty resource in the free market place of ideas." Although there is no constitutional compulsion to create a school library, once the library was established, it could not be censored solely because of "the social or political tastes of school board members."

In similar cases, some other federal courts took a less strict stand and deferred to the judgment of local school boards. Then, in 1982, the U.S. Supreme Court ruled in *Board of Education v. Pico*, setting down a rule (similar to the one in *Minarcini*) that prohibited library censorship whenever the intent was to impose a right orthodoxy on students.

In *Pico*, a challenge to nine books, mostly fictional and autobiographical accounts of ghetto life, the Supreme Court acknowledged the right of the school board to seek to "transmit community values" to school children. But students have First Amendment rights to read, think, and debate ideas, too, the U.S. Supreme Court noted; open access to ideas "prepares students for active and effective participation in the pluralistic, often contentious society in which they will soon be adult members."

Because of these concerns, derived from the First Amendment's guarantees of free speech and thought, the Court held that the school board could not restrict the content of school libraries "in a narrowly partisan or political manner" in an attempt to prescribe a standard orthodoxy in politics, nationalism, religion, or other matters.

The *Pico* decision did not end the school censorship debate; it merely shifted the battleground from library books to *textbooks*. The post-*Pico* wave of assault challenged school *curricula*.

Textbook challenges are not new, particularly in the South. But a new more forceful wave of challenges arose around the time of the *Pico* decision and focused on religious objections to standard school curricula. The Arkansas legislature, for example, passed a law titled the "Balanced Treatment for Creation-Science and Evolution-Science Act." Louisiana and several other states passed similar laws, all of which sought to require teaching of the biblical theory of creation science along with Darwin's theory of evolution. Federal courts struck down the Arkansas and Louisiana laws as unconstitutional insertions of certain religious teachings into the curriculum.

Similarly, in Tennessee, the plaintiffs in the *Mozert* case began in 1983 their challenges to several basic grammar school readers, which they claimed depicted witchcraft, idolatry, evolution, and humanism, and thus were objectionable to their religious beliefs. They objected to passages from Shakespeare, the stories of Cinderella and King Arthur, and even dialogue from the *Sesame Street* television show, among other things. U.S. District Judge Thomas Hull denied their claims in 1984. He noted that the allegedly objectionable books "are aimed at fostering a broad tolerance for all men's diversity, in his races, religions, and cultures. They intentionally expose the readers to a variety of religious beliefs, without attempting to suggest that one is better than another."

The objectors, fundamentalist Christians, objected to this message of toleration. Nonetheless, the court held that the First Amendment—which along with free exercise of religion also embraces free speech and expression and the right of students to receive information and ideas—guarantees only *neutrality* on the issue of religion; it does not guarantee that a student will never be exposed to ideas different from his own. Judge Hull concluded that nothing in the objected-to books directly interfered with the plaintiffs' religion. Only such a direct interference, he said, such as a school's teaching that one particular religion is right or that the student's religion is wrong, would constitute a free-exercise violation.

In 1985, however, an appeals court reversed Judge Hull's initial decisions, requiring hearings to determine the nature of the plaintiffs' beliefs, the severity of the conflict between the required school readings and their beliefs, and the school district's justification for the texts.

At the follow-up hearings before Judge Hull, the plaintiffs produced evidence that the reading material directly violated their religious beliefs—a conclusion Judge Hull conceded many persons would consider "inconsistent, illogical, incomprehensible and unacceptable" but which he nonetheless concluded the plaintiffs sincerely held. The court also found that the public schools could, if necessary, educate the students by using other nonobjectionable books, and he ordered that that be done.

In essence, the *Mozert* plaintiffs succeeded before Judge Hull because they convinced the court that it is not just toleration to which they objected, but specific literary passages that directly violated their religion. The trouble with that distinction, however, is that it confuses *exposure* to ideas with *endorsement* of ideas.

The U.S. Court of Appeals for the Fourth Circuit, however, reversed Judge Hull's ruling and drew a needed distinction between required *exposure* to other beliefs and forced *acceptance* of those beliefs. Indeed, the court noted, public schools are expected to teach "toleration of divergent political and religious views." Such teaching does not violate the constitution, in the absence of "the critical element of compulsion to affirm or deny a religious belief."

A similar case in federal court in Mobile, Alabama, developed parallel to *Mozert*. In early 1987 the trial judge in that case, District Judge William Brevard Hand, upheld religious objections to public school textbooks that included excerpts from classic works of literature and science. Judge Hand's decision in *Smith v. Board of School Commissioners of Mobile County* became the manifesto of the campaign against secular humanism. His ruling permanently prohibited use in Alabama of the offending textbooks—not just for the students involved in the suit, but for all students in the state.

But the federal Court of Appeals for the Eleventh Circuit gave short shrift to Judge Hand's analysis. The appeals court pointed out that the very passages that Judge Hand and the plaintiffs found objectionable—promoting toleration and analytical thinking—were proper and necessary subjects in education:

> The message conveyed is not one of endorsement of secular humanism or any religion. Rather, the message conveyed is one of a governmental attempt to instill in Alabama public school children such values as independent thought, toleration of diverse views, self-respect, maturity, self-reliance, and logical decision-making. This is an entirely appropriate secular effect.

The key flaw with the rulings by Judges Hull and Hand, as pointed out by the appeals courts, is they confused toleration of viewpoints with adherence to those viewpoints. Any court ruling prohibiting classroom discussion, and basing that ruling on the First Amendment, appears to make a fundamental mistake about constitutional rights. Exposure to different ideas, and discussion of them, is necessary, as the Supreme Court noted in the *Pico* case, to prepare students for "the pluralistic, often contentious society in which they will soon be adult members." Mere exposure to other persons' beliefs does not infringe on one's own beliefs, any more than does living down the street from, or working together with, persons of other beliefs. If there is any detriment at all, it is a small price for the benefits of a society that tolerates all beliefs.

Moreover, carried to their logical conclusion, such restrictive rulings would make public education impossible, by allowing every interest group in society to censor and "purify" the curriculum its children are taught. Today's textbook critics are reminiscent of Dr. Thomas Bowdler, the eighteenth-century censor whose heavy blue-penciling of the classic works of Shakespeare and Gibbons gave rise to the word *bowdlerize*. The possibilities for bowdlerizing school texts based on personal belief are endless.

Ironically, one of the initial effects of the trial court decisions in Tennessee and Alabama was to prohibit teaching (at least to the objecting students) of the poem of John Godfrey Saxe, based on the Hindu fable "The Blind Men and the Elephant"—the classic story of the blind men who feel different parts of an elephant and by their limited perspective are unable to see the whole picture. In part, the poem reads:

> These men of Indostan,
> Disputed loud and long,
> Each in his own opinion,
> Exceedingly stiff and strong.
> Though each was partially in the right,
> And all were in the wrong!

It is fortunate that through the appeals decisions the teaching of this poem will not be restricted. It contains a thoughtful lesson for those who wish to sacrifice discussion.

Arts Censorship

Years ago, a leading First Amendment lawyer noted that among all the arts, music, painting, and sculpture were "least molested" in the law. That may be changing. Visual arts were at the forefront of controversy in the late 1980s, and in many ways visual artists have found themselves and their work entangled in legal questions and legal issues. Speakers at two St. Louis seminars portrayed the visual arts as increasingly under attack.

Joyce Fernandes, director of exhibitions and events at the School of the Art Institute in Chicago, portrayed the visual arts as a target of "repression and cultural terrorism." The Art Institute was repeatedly attacked for controversial art displays.

The first Chicago incident occurred when a graduating student from the Art Institute School selected as his submission for a final seniors' exhibition a painting of the late Mayor Harold Washington of Chicago wearing women's lingerie. Within hours after the work was hung in a hallway at the school, a public uproar began. The city council debated the painting. The police "arrested" the painting and charged it with incitement of a riot. The Art Institute received eighteen bomb threats and numerous angry phone calls. The president and dean of the Art Institute met with aldermen, state legislators, and concerned citizens. Graduation at the school was conducted under tight security and "a pall of shock and hurt," according to Fernandes.

Following this incident, the Art Institute established a minority and multicultural task force. The task force recommended holding an exhibition featuring minority artists. But that exhibit in turn led to a second even more tumultuous controversy. One of the entries for the minority art exhibition was a three-dimensional art display consisting of a photo montage, a comment book on a ledge, and a large American flag placed on the floor, directly beneath the ledge and in front of the photo montage. Thus, the American flag was placed where it appeared likely to be walked on.

Soon after the display was set up, veterans, politicians, citizens, and camera crews showed up to protest, criticize, and film the exhibit and to taunt and provoke art students, Fernandes said. Opponents even obtained a temporary restraining order against the exhibit, which Judge Kenneth Gillis of the Circuit Court of Cook County promptly lifted. He held that "artistic and political freedom protected by the U.S. Constitution" was at stake, noting, "It is the role of the flag and the artist to communicate ideas and emotions."

Yet the effect of the exhibit and the controversy it engendered seemed to chill rather than promote artistic freedom, Fernandes said. The Illinois legislature drastically reduced funding to the Art Institute School and to an independent group that supported its claims to artistic freedom. And school officials, in reaction against the protests, eventually prohibited a later exhibition of the flag display because of fears involving the public's reaction.

Fernandes related the Chicago controversies to the national controversies over funding by the National Endowment for the Arts of controversial photographs by Andres Serrano and Robert Mapplethorpe. She concluded that as a result of these controversies and restrictions on artists,

140683

"We are living in a climate of real repression. The rift between the values of the American public and the artistic community is extreme, and it creates a risk of violence by people who have a self-interest in repressing ideas not their own."

Nadine Strossen, national president of the American Civil Liberties Union (ACLU), reached a similar conclusion—that recent attacks on artistic freedom are representative of a broader "war against independence of mind." Strossen, a constitutional law professor at New York Law School, characterized attempts to censor or deny government funding to particular artists and works of art as part of a broader conservative offensive against diversity and free expression. "What is at stake is not only artistic expression, but the whole constellation of civil liberties," she said, explaining that she believes many opponents of free artistic expression have a "larger agenda directed at the suppression of human freedom, individuality and diversity." She warned that artists and citizens who oppose arts censorship and funding restrictions must "organize our own counter pressure" to influence public opinion and policy makers.

Strossen admitted that many of the arts censorship controversies of recent years involve sexually oriented expression that even many civil libertarians find "hard to defend." Often, she noted, such works are attacked "both by right-wing moralists and by left-wing feminists." Such expression, however, is valuable and deserves protection not only in its own right but also as "part of a larger defense of human rights," she asserted. Erotic and sexually oriented publications serve important purposes in society, she said, by promoting diversity and nonconformist behavior. Those who oppose such expression, she warned, do so because they oppose social diversity and individuality.

Strossen identified threats to artistic freedom from four major areas: the Supreme Court, other government agencies, private pressure groups, and public opinion. The Supreme Court, she said, has become a "major threat to free speech in this country." She charged that the 1990 *Rust v. Sullivan* "gag rule" case, which allowed federal agencies to impose content-based speech regulations on recipients of government funds, had seriously eroded the long-standing First Amendment principle of viewpoint neutrality. And she pointed to the Court's 1991 nude-dancing regulation case, *Barnes v. Glen Theater*, as allowing curtailment of protected free speech solely on the basis of community standards of morality, even in the absence of any actual or imminent harm.

In addition to the erosion of important First Amendment principles, the two cases displayed a "class-oriented bias" in the Supreme Court, Strossen said. She noted that the Court's nude-dancing decision said that such dancing would probably have been allowable if performed at Lincoln Center. "This is the chablis theory of free speech," she said. "Apparently whether nude dancing is protected depends on what you are drinking when you are watching it. If you're drinking wine, it's protected. If you're drinking beer, it's not."

The Department of Justice's special obscenity unit also represents a major threat to artistic freedom, Strossen said. She charged that the suit has been employing "dirty tricks" and entrapment techniques in its "zeal to eradicate all sexually oriented publications—even those that do not rise to, or sink to, the level of obscenity." Overzealous prosecutions by this unit and by local authorities have sought, in some cases successfully, to prevent sale of nonobscene publications such as *Playboy* and *The Joy of Sex,* she said. In one case, prosecutors targeted a videotape with the suspicious title "Doing It Debbie's Way." Strossen noted: "It turned out to be an exercise tape featuring Debbie Reynolds."

Strossen identified private pressure groups and public opinion as the other threats to artistic freedom. She cited surveys showing that the public is not very supportive of First Amendment rights, particularly where controversial artistic works are involved. Strossen cited the struggle of Salman Rushdie, the British author who has lived for many years under a death threat from Islamic fundamentalists, as a symbol of the importance of artistic free expression. Rushdie's persecution, like the recent arts censorship and funding controversies in the United States, makes it clear that attacks on the arts "will follow us throughout the 1990s," she said.

Arts Censorship and Political Correctness

As a columnist who delights in revealing irony and exposing pompous silliness, Elaine Viets of the *St. Louis Post-Dispatch* must have loved the hide-the-painting controversy in 1993 at the University of Missouri-St. Louis (UMSL). The university, which owned a painting titled *Natural Rhythm: Thank You Jan van Eyck*, removed the painting from the lobby of Lucas Hall because of several complaints. The painting, done in the style of a fifteenth-century Flemish work, portrayed a noticeably pregnant black woman holding hands with a white nobleman.

Norman Seay, a university official and a civil rights leader, claimed the painting was racially offensive and didn't "show African-Americans in a positive vein." A few others also complained. After hearing the complaints, the university's Artwork Review Committee decided to remove the painting. The committee reported—in what Viets later characterized as "a stunning contradiction"—that "despite the artistic and social importance of the piece, it serves little, if any, constructive educational function in its current context."

If that were the only irony involved—that a university would hide rather than display a thought-provoking and controversial work of art—the incident probably wouldn't have caused much of a stir. But this incident involved a second, juicier, ironic twist. As Viets revealed in her *St. Louis Post-Dispatch* column, the artist, Robert Colescott, was himself an African American. His painting parodied a well-known van Eyck work, *Marriage of Arnolfini*.

As Viets's column explained, Colescott meant no racist message. As he explained to Viets, the painting is a "gentle nudge at art history." Among other things, the work tends to highlight how unusual it is to see a black person in European art. And it certainly portrays the white man less favorably than the black woman. Colescott, Viets reported, was offended (albeit to some extent amused) that his work would be hidden in a storeroom in the name of "protecting" his race.

Viets's column had an effect. A *Post-Dispatch* news report a few days later reported that UMSL's administration decided to bring the painting back and hang it in a different (though more remote) location, together with explanatory labels. Seay was quoted as saying he would be satisfied so long as the accompanying materials made it clear that the painting was not racist, but rather had an antiracist purpose.

Though the rehanging of the painting might seem an unqualified victory for free expression, it is really something short of that. After all, it was irony #2—the fact that the artist was black and intended an antiracist message—that compelled the university to permit the rehanging. One wonders if the painting probably would have emerged from storage if there were only irony #1—the university's hypocritical censorship in the name of a greater good.

And irony #1 is a serious problem these days. Forgetting that censorship is always justified in the name of higher values, many individuals and groups are seeking to censor whatever offends their own narrow interests.

The new censorship movements fly under many banners, including, quite often, those of racial, sexual, or ethnic sensitivity. Thought-purity proponents argue that particular social values (such as the need to respect minorities and show them "in positive vein") override the need to tolerate expression of "improper" viewpoints. This is the philosophical underpinning of the theories of procensorship feminists such as Catharine Mac-Kinnon and Andrea Dworkin who argue that erotic expression should not enjoy legal protection. It is the basis as well for extreme-hate-speech laws and campus codes that go so far as to ban all expression deemed insensitive to minority races and other protected groups. And it is becoming manifest in many other modern movements.

Those who fight against these new-fashioned censors have learned a sad lesson: free speech rarely wins on its own merit. On the plate of public preference, the abstraction of free expression goes over like brussels sprouts ("tastes terrible, but good for you") compared to the sweets of special-interest-driven, thought-purity censorship.

And so savvy free speech proponents often drop their classic arguments ("freedom even for ideas we hate") in favor of a new pragmatic approach ("free speech will better promote your special interest agenda"). In the *Natural Rhythm* case, for example, the painting was *rehung*, not because of an abstract commitment to free expression, but because the university was convinced that the painting was antiracist after all. Similarly, free speech advocates at a symposium on the feminist censorship controversy focused their efforts on showing that such censorship could *hurt* women more than it would *help* them.

These pragmatic approaches are fine for situations like the *Natural Rhythm* controversy, where the double ironies make apparent the silliness and counterproductiveness of censorship. But they beg the question of whether free speech can or should be defended in its own right.

Let's be honest with ourselves: the double-irony cases are the easy ones. It's nice that *Natural Rhythm* was put back on display. But this incident reveals little about whether the community will defend free expression in a truly difficult case.

Radical Feminist Arguments for Censorship

Comstockery. Bowdlerizing. And now, *MacDworkinism.* Something about sex in print seems to bring out the censor in the strangest people and, indirectly, to enrich the language with new words for crusades of extremist paranoia.

The activities of Dr. Thomas Bowdler, the English editor who, around 1820, rewrote Shakespeare and the Bible to delete their objectionable passages, gave our language its word for arbitrary expurgation, *bowdlerize*. The crusades of Anthony Comstock, the man whose raised eyebrows had the power to prevent booksellers from handling many books and magazines in nineteenth-century America, gave us *Comstockery*, a synonym for overzealous censorship.

A century after Comstock, we now confront a new set of censorship advocates, as fresh, committed—and extreme—as Bowdler and Comstock were in their days. The new censors-to-be are author Andrea Dworkin and law professor Catharine MacKinnon, the proud and strident exponents of an allegedly feminist procensorship philosophy sometimes disparagingly dubbed *MacDworkinism*. Their claim is that a very broad range of literary and artistic content, which they view as demeaning woman, can and should be outlawed.

MacKinnon, Dworkin, and their supporters characterize the matters to which they object as "pornography," but the targets of their theory are really broader than what most people view as pornography. Not unlike the last century's Comstock crusades, their movement seeks to significantly limit a broad range of publications touching on human sexuality.

The MacKinnon-Dworkin viewpoint, extreme as it is, cannot be easily brushed aside, for several reasons:

- MacKinnon and Dworkin are *feminists* who base their philosophy on protection of women. This makes their viewpoint attractive to many women and to liberals who otherwise might reject a procensorship position.
- The MacKinnon-Dworkin position feeds on many persons' natural discomfort with published portrayals of sex and sexuality.
- The feminist procensorship position appears to provide answers and solutions to some basic problems in society, as it ascribes sexual inequality, family problems, crime, and domestic violence to a broad range of objectionable literature. It is a "blame the messenger" theory, but a sophisticated one.

In America the usual test of a creative legal theory is simple: Will the courts accept it? Here the answer so far is a clear *no:* the courts haven't bought MacDworkinism. When the city of Indianapolis in 1984 adopted a MacKinnon-drafted ordinance equating pornography with sex discrimination, the ordinance was challenged by book publishers and librarians and was promptly struck down by the courts as unconstitutional. In other tests in this country, the MacKinnon-Dworkin theories have been rejected. First Amendment rules are clear—speech that falls outside the narrow category of legal obscenity cannot be banned.

But do our traditional First Amendment arguments really provide a persuasive answer to this new theory? The MacKinnon-Dworkin theory may be antithetical to the First Amendment, *but is it wrong?* Judicial rulings have usually skirted this key policy issue. As long as this question remains unanswered, the MacKinnon-Dworkin theory retains its potential appeal to public opinion and hence presents a serious threat to free expression.

This is where Nadine Strossen comes in. Strossen, national president of the American Civil Liberties Union, is a feminist and constitutional scholar of unquestioned standing. In her book *Defending Pornography: Free Speech, Sex, and the Fight for Women's Rights*, she takes on MacKinnon and Dworkin both as a free speech advocate and as a feminist. She directly addresses the legal, social, and feminist policy questions raised by MacDworkinism and does not skirt the important underlying issue of the role of sexuality, and portrayals of it, in the lives of women and men.

The focus of the book is a feminist response to MacKinnon and Dworkin—as Strossen puts it, "a women's rights-centered rationale for *defending* pornography," based on the MacDworkinite threat "not only to human rights in general but also to women's rights in particular." She argues that MacDworkinism, though clothed in the dress of modern feminism, actually represents a reversion to overprotectionism based on a belief in the inherent weakness of women. This "victim feminism" viewpoint, she concludes, ill serves women and, if accepted, would reverse many modern feminist gains.

Strossen gives multiple reasons for her feminist attack on MacDworkinism. One concern is that the MacDworkinite antipornography statute, as tried unsuccessfully in the United States and as actually implemented in Canada, sweeps so broadly that it becomes in practice "a powerful weapon that can be aimed at dissent," including feminist speech. She also suggests that schemes for censoring pornography ultimately undermine women's rights, in ways ranging from the outright suppression of feminist works to the denial of choices, the perpetuation of stereotypes, and the reinforcement of the existing male-dominated power structure.

Beyond its feminist focus (and as part of it, since Strossen assumes that women care strongly about free speech and argues that free speech is a bedrock of feminist activism), *Defending Pornography* is a brief for free speech. Strossen explains with admirable clarity how and why sexual speech came to be regulated as it is today. She gives the historical perspective on prior "dictatorships of virtue." She ably refutes the "blame the messenger" tactic by which MacKinnon and Dworkin attempt to blame speech and publications for long-existing social problems, including inequality of the sexes. She repeatedly points out that MacKinnon and Dworkin seek to control ideas through government coercion—not private persuasion, the method that time has taught us is the best means for controlling bad ideas.

And, perhaps most important, Strossen argues that free speech not only does but *should* extend into the sexual realm. Picking up from Justice William J. Brennan Jr.'s description of sex as "a great and mysterious motive force in human life . . . a subject of absorbing interest to mankind throughout the ages," Strossen presents several reasons why sexual speech deserves protection.

First, laws targeting sexual content are often really viewpoint-directed. In early American history, antiobscenity laws often targeted those who challenged the official political and religious orthodoxy. Even today, obscenity and indecency regulations and controversies usually revolve around social and sexual nonconformity—disturbing NEA art, nontraditional roles and conduct including homosexuality, and various aspects of feminism. The experience in Canada under a MacDworkin-modeled criminal obscenity law is no different; the speech suppressed has often been that of minorities and dissidents. In short, one cannot easily separate sexual speech from political speech; the two are often connected.

Second, sexuality is an important part of human experience that, like other aspects of life, can be better understood through speech, writing, and artistry. Strossen probes this issue in depth, drawing on historical and psychological sources and personal accounts, the great majority of which come from the point of view of women. In particular, she notes the close tie-in between women's rights and the struggle to disseminate basic information about sexuality and birth control in the early twentieth century.

Specifically, Strossen rejects the claimed dichotomy between protected political speech and nonprotected nonpolitical speech. She asserts, instead, that "sexual freedom and freedom for sexually explicit expression are essential aspects of human freedom." She examines the viewpoints of both readers/viewers (men and women who enjoy or learn from pornography) and authors/artists/participants (including women who work in the so-called sex industry in roles ranging from models to prostitutes). From both viewpoints she concludes that sexual expression is not much different from nonsexual speech: it can instruct or inspire, help identify desires and dislikes, and liberate, directly or vicariously.

Strossen suggests that just as movies were slow to be recognized as legitimate media for expression, expression relating to the sexual side of life is just as deserving as other speech and ultimately should be recognized as such.

Traditionally, liberals and minorities were viewed as friends of free speech. But every generation confronts new circumstances, and today some of the most dangerous attacks on expression, like the Mac-Dworkinite challenge, come in the name of preventing "hate speech."

The feminist procensorship viewpoint is a particularly sensitive one to challenge because it touches on many emotional issues—the status of women, the shadowy nature of pornography and other legal forms of sexual expression, the mysteries and intimacies of sexuality. Strossen has tackled these issues forthrightly, directly, and analytically. She has given feminists a lesson in free speech, free speech advocates an immersion in feminist concerns, and both a powerful brief against the Mac-Dworkinism.

With *Defending Pornography*, and her other ongoing activities, Strossen has taken the lead in the fight against MacDworkinism. *Defending Pornography* demonstrates that this is a worthy fight, based on the true interests of women, on the common interests of women and men, and on the conviction that readings, writings, and artistry about the mysterious realm of human sexuality are better left to personal choice than to a modern Comstockian censorship scheme.

Censorship Arguments

The scene in the legislative committee room in Jefferson City was almost comical. An advocate of state-mandated "warnings" of offensive rock music lyrics was testifying. In his testimony, he quoted at length from many of the song lyrics he considered offensive. As the speaker droned on, late at night in a crowded hearing room, the chairman fidgeted and finally interrupted him, asking him to wrap up his testimony. Immediately the witness took offense. "Are you trying to censor me?" he bristled.

ACLU spokesman Tom Blumenthal referred to the incident in his testimony a few hours later, pointedly noting, "No one likes to be censored." But though no one likes to be censored, many persons would like to censor. The issues change (for some time the hot issue was school textbooks; then it became music lyrics), but censorship battles seem unending.

Missouri became a major battleground in the music lyric censorship battle when a state representative, Jean Dixon, proposed a bill to require "warnings" on music recordings. At the same time, the Supreme Court took a new look at the permissible reach of state antipornography laws, and a report by the Missouri Coalition Against Censorship found that censorship attacks on school libraries and textbooks were continuing.

Though the participants on both sides rarely admit it, censorship battles are actually kind of entertaining. They revolve around current celebrated or scandalous publications, usually both outrageous and titillating. And even the arguments that dominate the debate can be amusing.

In most censorship battles, the debate rarely reaches first principles, such as the need for access to information and ideas, and the legitimate boundaries of protectable speech. Instead, participants argue, using the easier, more picturesque, and more entertaining "slippery slope" and "parade of horribles" arguments. These rhetorical patterns appear in almost every censorship dispute, in every forum, including the Supreme Court.

The slippery slope argument, a favorite of censorship opponents, attempts to demonstrate that the censorship law at issue will sweep so broadly that it will prohibit or penalize many time-honored valuable works of literature and art. The free speech advocates' similar parade of horribles argument usually focuses on actual rather than speculative objects of censorship. It includes a marching panorama of actual cases in which censors and censorship laws have targeted lofty and valuable books and works of art.

Advocates of censorship (like the witness in Jefferson City) have their own parade of horribles, with each float containing objectionable passages from the works they wish to outlaw. History's most extreme slippery slope argument was the list compiled more than 100 years ago by the writer Annie Besant (a defendant in a famous criminal obscenity prosecution) of 175 Bible passages that could be considered obscene.

Similarly, Shakespeare's work contains many highly suggestive passages, which can be used as an argument against censorship laws. In one case, attorneys attempted to use some of Shakespeare's bawdy passages for a slippery slope argument in a censorship case. But Shakespeare's writing, they concluded, might be too lurid for direct quotation in a Supreme Court brief. They took the safer course of giving citations for the passages, which inquisitive law clerks (or justices) could look up.

The parade of horribles arguments are favorites of Supreme Court justices. In the Court's most important schoolbook censorship case, *Board of Education v. Pico*, the Court majority listed the targeted library books—all classics of minority and antiwar literature—in order to show the misguided (and ideological) nature of the school board's censorship. The dissent, in turn, set forth in an appendix a selection of the most explicit passages from each of the ten books—thus giving those seven pages of the official Supreme Court reporter perhaps the highest concentration of objectionable material of any book in the country.

Similarly, Justice William J. Brennan Jr. in his dissent to the Court's 1990 decision upholding state laws against possession of child pornography, raised the slippery slope and asserted that the statute question was so broad it could embrace Michelangelo's *David* statue and "the depictions of nude children on the friezes that adorn our courtroom."

Against this background, it is no surprise that local censorship disputes are fought on the slippery slopes, as parades of horribles march by in both directions. The Missouri Coalition Against Censorship, for example, devoted most of its report on censorship in local schools to a list and exegesis of books that have been challenged—thus implicitly assuming that the best argument against censorship is the record of the books that have been attacked.

And in the fighting over Representative Dixon's music warning label bill, censorship opponents quickly selected the slippery slope as their major weapon. In one of their submissions to the legislature, for example, music industry lobbyists warned that the censorship law could be applied to a "vast range of musical forms," including:

- Operas such *as La Traviata, Madame Butterfly,* and *Carmen,* which deal with drinking, adultery, murder, and sex;

- Renaissance madrigals, which have sexual conquest as a recurrent theme;
- "Beer Barrel Polka," which deals with alcohol consumption;
- Cole Porter's "I Get A Kick Out Of You," which deals with alcohol and drug consumption; and
- Country music ballads, which tell stories dealing with murder, adultery, and drug and alcohol abuse.

The record industry lobbyists even provided the legislature with a two-page, single-spaced list of potential music censorship targets, including "Good Night, Irene" (which concerns suicide), "That Old Black Magic" (Satanism), and "Old Man River" (alcohol).

The slippery slope and the parade of horribles arguments will probably be around as long as "Old Man River"—not just because they're persuasive but also because they're entertaining.

Symbolic Speech

Irish American organizers exclude gay pride groups from their St. Patrick's Day parade in Boston. The Ku Klux Klan erects a symbolic cross in a Columbus park. Students in Los Angeles perform a mean-spirited "ugly woman" contest. And a lone protestor burns an American flag in Dallas.

These incidents are *actions*—actions that exclude, hurt, and frustrate many people. Not surprisingly, many people call for regulations, controls, and prohibitions on these actions. After all, why should not *actions that hurt* be legally controlled, as are negligent driving, discrimination, and other kinds of hurtful conduct?

The twist here, which makes these actions different from other actions, is that each of these actions carries a *message*—an expression of the actor's viewpoint on an issue he or she believes important. Messages and viewpoints enjoy, and deserve, the strongest protection of the First Amendment. Free speech protection adheres to messages regardless of their form—whether expressed in words, symbols, or symbolic actions.

From time to time almost everyone uses non-word messages (legally known as *symbolic speech*):

- A salute or a hand held over one's heart during a flag ceremony or the singing of the national anthem

- A handshake (or, occasionally, a refusal to offer one's hand)
- The wearing of religious, fraternal, or other special symbols

Apart from such common instances of symbolic speech—so much a part of daily life that we may not even think of them anymore as expressions of messages—we all recognize that actions may indeed carry forceful messages. As with abolitionist William Lloyd Garrison's dramatic burning of a copy of the Constitution in 1854 (to demonstrate his disdain for the continuation of slavery), symbolic actions are often key devices of protesters, who seek both expression and impact. Particularly in today's chattering world, the most effective political messages are often uttered with dramatic but silent symbols:

- A student wears a black armband to high school during the Vietnam War.
- Homeless people and advocates for homeless aid erect a makeshift tent city in a public park, timing it to contrast sharply with an elaborate nearby festival.
- Supporters of hostage or abduction victims blanket their neighborhoods with yellow ribbons and wear the ribbons on their clothing, as a visible reminder of the victims and their importance.
- Quilts, red ribbons, and other symbols are used in various messages of support, sympathy, and protest relating to the fight against AIDS.

Symbolic speech can be quiet, incendiary, or in-between. When a world leader lays a wreath at a graveyard at Omaha Beach, he or she need not say anything; the profound message of respect for soldiers killed in combat is implicitly understood, so much so that it may bring tears to many. If one were to set fire to a photograph of Saddam Hussein during the Persian Gulf War, the angry and strongly felt message of hate for Saddam would be just as readily understood, though the context and reaction would be quite different.

So it is no surprise that burning the American flag qualifies as symbolic speech, too, as the Supreme Court held in 1989 and 1990. Flag burning sends a clear message—"I hate America"—and it evokes swift and strong reactions precisely *because* the vehicle of expression so dramatically brings the protester's pointed message home.

Non-word messages *are* expression. Although the emotions involved cloud discussion and analysis, symbolic speech deserves and needs full constitutional protection. The Supreme Court's St. Patrick's Day parade case illustrates this point and suggests the danger of a flag-burning exemption from the First Amendment, such as came under renewed consideration in Congress in 1995.

The St. Patrick's Day parade case initially turned on the simple issue of whether a parade is symbolic speech. A coalition of gay rights groups in Boston had asked Massachusetts courts to allow them to march in the city's traditional St. Patrick's Day parade, which is organized and run by a private organization.

The parade organization objected to including the gay group. The parade organizers said, essentially, that it was their parade, and they had a First Amendment right to include, or exclude, whomever they wished. The gay coalition countered that the parade was an eclectic mishmash that did not express any particular point of view. Moreover, the coalition claimed that the parade was akin to a public accommodation; hence, under the Massachusetts public accommodations act, the parade organizers could not discriminate against gays, lesbians, and bisexuals.

Trial and appeals courts in Massachusetts sided with the gay coalition and labeled the parade as a nonexpressive public accommodation. But the U.S. Supreme Court unanimously reversed the lower courts. Justice David Souter's opinion stressed two points:

- That symbolic speech, including parades, is fully protected by the First Amendment, and
- That the government should steer clear from controlling the message that any speaker wishes to express, by words or by symbolic means.

Justice Souter expressed no hesitation in making the first point—that parades are a kind of symbolic speech and enjoy full First Amendment protection. He noted that "the Constitution looks beyond written or spoken words as mediums of expression" and recognizes that "symbolism is a primitive but effective way of communicating ideas." He found abundant precedent pointing to "the inherent expressiveness of marching to make a point," including decisions that recognized as protected expression a student's refusal to salute the flag, an armband protest, the display of a red flag, and a march in Nazi uniform displaying swastikas.

Additionally, Justice Souter held that the Boston parade, although admittedly eclectic, had a sufficient point of view; he likened the parade organizers' selection of the participating groups to a newspaper opinion-page editor's selections of the commentaries to be printed. Such selectivity, he held, "falls squarely within the core of First Amendment security."

Having thus identified the Boston parade as protected expression, Justice Souter went on to consider whether Massachusetts could control the selection of parade participants through its public accommodations law. It could not, he held, because controlling the groups to be included in the parade would interfere with the basic First Amendment right of a speaker to choose his own speech.

That is, the Court upheld a private speaker's rights as preeminent over even well-intended laws designed to promote desirable social goals (in this case, prevention of discrimination based on sexual orientation). This point undoubtedly delights conservatives who worry about liberal "political correctness" codes that could elevate egalitarian goals over private choice. But it ought to give pause as well to those who advocate a restriction on free speech (the proposed flag desecration amendment to the Constitution) because of their own social goals (to prohibit certain unpatriotic acts and messages).

Justice Souter wrote that it "grates on the First Amendment" if a restriction is imposed on speech in order "to produce thought and statement acceptable to some groups." This, he held, "amounts to nothing less than a proposal to limit speech in the service of orthodox expression."

These words deserve careful consideration. In the parade case, the Massachusetts law was used by gay and lesbian citizens to seek to limit the parade organizer's speech, all in the name of the official orthodoxy of inclusion of gays and lesbians. But similar restrictions on speech can come from the opposite side of the political spectrum. The constitutional amendment passed by the House in late June 1995 was designed to produce thoughts and statements acceptable to those who revere the flag. It was designed to make respect for the flag a new national "orthodox expression" and to limit free speech in the service of that official orthodoxy.

Free speech has survived and prospered in the United States because wise judges and policymakers have, on the whole, construed protected speech broadly and given it preeminence over the particular social goals of powerful political coalitions and majorities. As in the Boston parade case, courts have recognized the expressiveness of symbols, the breadth of every citizen's right of free speech, and the inadvisability of government controls on speech based on state-imposed orthodoxies.

Under the First Amendment, Justice Souter wrote, the government "is not free to interfere with speech for no better reason than promoting an approved message or discouraging a disfavored one." Legislators considering measures such as the ever-popular flag desecration amendment need to study and consider these words. A constitutional amendment that prohibits expression of an officially disfavored message would constitute a truly radical departure from our free speech jurisprudence.

Prior Restraint

Mike Pride, now editor of the *Concord (New Hampshire) Monitor*, wrote in a column some years ago about "the certainties in the haze of the morning magic"—those facts we are sure of even during the foggy transition from sleep to awakeness. Pride's number-one certainty: "I will never go over Niagara Falls in a barrel."

For some time—at least since the *Pentagon Papers* case of 1970—press lawyers have had their own Niagara-Falls-in-a-barrel certainty: A court cannot successfully enter a prior restraint against publication, in any except the most extreme situation. The *CNN-Noriega* case has now dispelled that certainty. In November 1991, for three weeks, Cable News Network was enjoined from broadcasting recorded prison telephone conversations of deposed Panamanian leader Manuel Noriega regarding his pending criminal case. Not only the substance but also the timing of the case served to dramatize it.

First, it followed a period in which *five* different trial courts, in a period of about six months, had entered orders enjoining various publications and broadcasts. Prior restraint orders have been considered anathema to the First Amendment under key U.S. Supreme Court decisions going back to 1931. Yet, three of these prior restraints were even issued by the *federal* courts that can generally be trusted not to ignore or misunderstand settled constitutional law.

Second, the *CNN-Noriega* case arose just as a group of experts were discussing the principles, authorities, and practices that should have made it impossible. At a November 1990 seminar in New York, attended by lawyers who regularly represent publishers and broadcasters, the speaker on prior restraint, Floyd Abrams, discussed prior restraint law and the recent prior restraint cases. Abrams, who successfully represented the *New York Times* in the 1970 *Pentagon Papers* case, reported that the recent cases were aberrations.

Abrams noted that even in those unusual cases where prior restraints were issued, the enjoined parties were able to appeal immediately to appellate courts, which promptly reversed the restraining orders. Thus, Abrams assured his fellow media lawyers that the rule against prior restraints was "secure in a rather insecure way."

But as Abrams spoke on Thursday, November 8, 1990, at the Communications Law seminar in New York, Judge William Hoeveler in Miami issued his injunction against CNN. On the following day, the seminar's moderator promised to announce updates on the progress of CNN's immediate appeal. But the expected update (an appellate order reversing the injunction) did not come that day—or ever. And the following days and weeks brought even more bad news.

On Saturday, the federal Court of Appeals for the Eleventh Circuit in Atlanta turned down CNN's appeal, allowing the trial court's injunction to stand. And when CNN sought immediate relief from the Supreme Court, with Abrams by this time assisting CNN's team, with support from amicus briefs from the ACLU, media trade groups, and publishing companies, the court on November 18 flatly turned down the appeal, with only two justices dissenting.

CNN then had no realistic alternative but to comply with the order. It submitted its Noriega tapes to Judge Hoeveler, who had a magistrate review them. Then, on November 28, three weeks after the dispute erupted, in a double anticlimax, Judge Hoeveler determined that the tapes were harmless and could be broadcast—and CNN decided that they weren't newsworthy and wouldn't be broadcast, after all. Eventually, CNN was fined for violating the court order, and its executives apologized for their actions.

All this leaves the prior restraint doctrine as something considerably less than a Niagara-Falls-in-a-barrel certainty.

At first blush, the Eleventh Circuit's decision could be read to suggest that the danger of prejudicial pretrial publicity may now be considered sufficient to justify a prior restraint. That decision, turning down CNN's appeal from the restraining order, was based almost solely on the right of a criminal defendant to a fair trial, and it practically ignored the First Amendment. The opinion explicitly suggested that press rights to publish should give way where they "conflict" with the defendant's fair trial rights.

But this position has been rejected by the Supreme Court, in *Nebraska Press Association v. Stuart* in 1975, which held that fair trials can be protected by many means short of media prior restraints, even where a great deal of publicity attends the case. Moreover, properly analyzed, First Amendment press freedoms and the Sixth Amendment fair trial right do not "conflict." Both are rights extending from the government to private parties, and the existence of one right cannot excuse abridgment of another.

On these grounds, litigants in future cases should be able to overcome the *CNN-Noriega* appellate court's use of fair trial considerations as a justification for prior restraints. The big unresolved issue from both the *CNN-Noriega* case and the five other 1990 prior restraint cases is whether prior restraints are somehow becoming *acceptable* tools of media regulation.

At the very least, the *CNN-Noriega* case seems to foreshadow a period where the principles and policies of prior restraint law, rather than being taken for granted as an absolute, will be probed and tested on a case-by-case basis.

This in itself is a major setback for the media. The rule against prior restraints has long been considered near-absolute. The Supreme Court's famous 1931 *Near v. Minnesota* decision suggested that exceptions would be warranted only in cases of imminent threats to national security such as "publication of the sailing dates of transports or the number and location of troops."

But the *Noriega* precedent now sends the message that many less extreme exceptions may be possible. This almost inevitably means that there will be more litigation, which itself can chill and burden press freedom.

The five 1990 prior restraint cases besides *CNN-Noriega* suggest how broad an area will be affected if prior restraint prohibitions are eroded or even more seriously challenged. In those cases, the enjoined materials included a corporate television advertising campaign, a book about the Israeli secret service, a television documentary about child abuse, an investigative exposé about a diet doctor, and an accounting newsletter's report of financial data from two large accounting firms.

The future will determine if the 1990 cases were aberrations, or if the long-standing near-absolute barrier against prior restraints has truly been broken. For publishers, broadcasters, and their lawyers, these cases have battered a familiar and comforting legal certainty.

3

News Gathering

Access to Court Documents

"A TRIAL IS A PUBLIC EVENT," THE U.S. SUPREME Court noted several years ago—a simple and seemingly unambiguous endorsement of judicial openness. Journalists often assume this as a truism—that the courts and what they do are the public's business, open always to public observation and scrutiny. But courts have their secrets, too. And court proceedings, including many of public interest and importance, can easily become hidden behind closed doors.

In early 1988, the *New York Times* noted the growing trend of secrecy in the courts: "In almost every high-profile case tried recently in the New York courts, judges have been sealing documents, holding secret hearings, curbing lawyers' out-of-court remarks or taking other actions to limit the access of news organizations and the public to sensitive information." The *St. Louis Post-Dispatch* described similar trends in local federal courts: in several important criminal, civil rights, and constitutional cases, the article stated, "Entire files have been closed without notice to the public, sometimes with no explanation. Some suits have been filed under seal, with no public knowledge of even who the plaintiffs or defendants are."

These articles brought to light an important reality—the cloak of court confidentiality orders that are routinely imposed in many court cases, out of convenience or perceived necessity. Orders for confidentiality in court proceedings come in many forms and affect many different aspects of the cases. But usually they are imposed for the narrow purposes of the parties to the litigation, with little thought of the interest of the press and public. And usually, unless the press speaks up, the orders are carried out unchallenged.

There are several causes for court confidentiality orders. First, such orders usually satisfy needs of the parties to the litigation. In business litigation, confidentiality orders and sealed files are frequently and routinely imposed in order to protect trade secrets or other business confidences. This happens routinely in civil cases, usually with all parties' consent, even in some cases involving media companies.

Second, courts usually do not consider the interests of the press and the public in having open files because no one in the litigation asserts those interests. And usually no media organization intervenes to keep the case open. Third, the Supreme Court has yet to settle clearly the constitutional or common law rights of the public to access to court proceedings. And its decision in 1989 in *Gannett Co. v. DePasquale*, which permitted closure of an important pretrial hearing in a criminal case, though cut back by subsequent decisions, still suggests to many lower courts that closure can be easily imposed and justified.

In this context, it should not be surprising that confidentiality orders are often entered. A case highlighted by the *St. Louis Post-Dispatch* articles, in which the *Post-Dispatch* intervened in order to challenge some broad confidentiality orders, illustrates one kind of confidentiality problem. The case was a civil suit filed in federal court in St. Louis challenging Missouri's abortion law. One of the plaintiffs was a woman who alleged that the statute interfered with her right to have an abortion. At her request, in order to protect her confidentiality, and with the defendants' consent, the court file was sealed shortly after the case was filed in January 1987.

The order sealing the file went unchallenged for a year. During that time, the entire file was closed to any reporter who asked for it and all court hearings were closed. Ironically, the court's rulings on several major motions were promptly published in the official law reports, which are available at all law libraries. These published orders were probably the most newsworthy occurrences in the case, but since the original court file itself was closed, the *Post-Dispatch* and other news organizations apparently did not realize the rulings were publicly available.

When the *Post-Dispatch* intervened in the case in January 1988, requesting to open the court file, the court reconsidered the original closure order and concluded it was broader than necessary. In his ruling, federal District Judge George Gunn recognized a qualified public right of access to court files in civil cases, based both on the First Amendment and the common law. He concluded that closure could be justified only for an "overriding interest" such as the need to preserve the woman plaintiff's confidentiality. On February 5, Judge Gunn opened the entire file, except three documents that would reveal the identity of the woman plaintiff.

A few days prior to the ruling, the *Post-Dispatch* inveighed against court closure with an editorial titled "Stop the Secret Trials," suggesting that closure orders indicate that federal judges "may come to think of the entire judicial system as their own" and have been displaying a "preference for closed proceedings." In reality, rather than demonstrating any deliberate shielding of judicial action from public view, this case illuminates what happens when litigants and courts do not focus on the values of open proceedings—and when the press does not promptly and vigorously insist on openness.

Here, although the confidentiality order was imposed for honorable reasons, it became unnecessarily broad. As Judge Gunn's order indicates, far more was kept sealed than was necessary to satisfy the parties' objective of protecting the woman plaintiff's anonymity.

Local news organizations, moreover, apparently stood silent for most of the year during which the closure order was in effect. When the *Post-Dispatch* did challenge the order, it was able to open most of the file with relatively little effort. Our adversary system depends on parties asserting their rights; this case shows that the press, too, must assert its rights.

Not all court confidentiality disputes are as easily resolved. Sealed proceedings, and parts of proceedings kept from the press, are a real problem in many instances. The orders mentioned by the *New York Times* article reflect a serious damper on the flow of information coming out of some important criminal cases. In contemporaneous cases, for example, a newspaper was denied access to material in Ivan Boesky's pre-sentence report, and wiretap evidence in a political leader's corruption trial was sealed and kept out of the press.

Another serious problem for the press is court rulings excluding re-porters and the public from whole parts of judicial proceedings or whole areas of information. Pretrial discovery materials in civil suits, for in-stance, are often kept from the press, even in cases where the materials might be of wide interest. For example, tobacco companies sued in civil wrongful death cases have fought to keep materials discovered in those cases out of the public domain. A federal court in Boston ruled in one case involving pretrial materials that press access to court records "has never been unfettered" and hence records could be withheld from the press for a variety of compelling reasons.

Similarly, when reporters have sought the right to attend pretrial depositions in civil cases, this has usually been refused. A federal court ruling in Washington, D.C., acknowledging a press right to attend civil deposition was one of the first press victories in this area. And broadcast news organizations are still encountering many special problems when they seek access to video and audio tapes that are used as part of court proceedings. Often, courts treat audiovisual material in court files dif-ferently than written materials, to the great disadvantage of broadcasters who need access to such materials.

Some of these access problems may be solved by more explicit Su-preme Court rulings on the rights of the press and public to pretrial and audiovisual materials. Other cases rest inevitably on a balancing of the public's access rights with privacy or fair-trial rights of litigants and thus depend on the wisdom of the judge who does the balancing.

But as the St. Louis experience indicates, the essential ingredients of every access case—and perhaps the ones most essential to ensuring an open judicial system—are reporters and editors who seek to keep the sys-tem open to public scrutiny.

Court Protective Orders

Journalists and lawyers are often portrayed as natural adversaries, and it is sometimes even suggested that each side possesses a set of "rights" that are supposedly at war with the "rights" of the other. These legal-journalistic clashes include the alleged "conflicts" between the rights of fair trial and free press and between the need for confidential sources in reporting and the demands of the legal system for every person's evidence.

Another legal-journalistic "battleground" might involve court secrecy orders. Lawyers, after all, generally desire to protect their clients' secrets by keeping confidential documents and materials out of public view. Journalists, by contrast, view skeptically court orders that shield activities of public interest from full public scrutiny.

If this simplistic picture were all there were to the court secrecy issue, the "clash" scenario might have some validity here. But in this dispute, there is a wild card—a powerful and influential group of lawyers who for their own reasons want to limit court file secrecy. Plaintiffs' lawyers— lawyers who take on the claims of injured persons in return for a percentage portion of any eventual recovery—object to tight limits on court files. Like reporters, they recognize that court files contain much valuable information, which they would like to be able to review and use. In particular, the plaintiffs' bar desires access to court files in environmental, products liability, "toxic tort," and financial fraud cases—essentially, those complex cases where the files in earlier cases may be significantly useful to lawyers in subsequent cases.

As an example, let's take the fictitious case of Joe Blow and his co-workers who sued MegaChemicals over injuries they allegedly received while manufacturing "Sicklygloop" at Mega's Illinois plant. Blow and his co-plaintiffs hired plaintiffs' lawyer Mike Shrewd. Shrewd and his partners researched the issues, filed suit, reviewed thousands of MegaChemical documents, took scores of depositions, hired experts on chemistry and medicine, and after five years of work finally took the case to trial. For our purposes, it doesn't matter whether Blow won, lost, or settled. Whatever the outcome, the court file in *Blow v. MegaChemicals* was a gold mine of information on Sicklygloop.

As soon as the *Blow* case concluded, investigative reporter Woody Stein and lawyer Jim Trendy (who represents consumers who claim injury from Sicklygloop) visited the courthouse and placed calls to Shrewd. Both Stein and Trendy were disappointed. The court clerk told them that except for some basic procedural files, the exhibits and other case files were under seal and not open for public inspection. And Shrewd explained to the reporter and to his plaintiffs' lawyer colleague that he was bound by the court secrecy rules and could tell them little of the volumes that he knew about Sicklygloop. In fact, he explained, he was in the process of returning all of his MegaChemical files to the company, pursuant to the terms of the court secrecy order.

The restrictions on the *Blow v. MegaChemicals* file were typical of

such cases. Early in the case, MegaChemicals sought and obtained the secrecy order, to protect from public disclosure all of its trade-secret formu-
las and processes and its confidential corporate policies and communications that came out in the litigation. Mega listed most of the documents
and testimony in the case in these categories, and the court permitted that
classification. That meant Stein and Trendy couldn't get much information at all from the *Blow* case file. If they wanted to recreate the information it took Shrewd five years to assemble and assimilate, they would
have to use their own funds and legwork.

Stein quickly gave up and returned to writing features about Baby
Boomers. Trendy pursued the consumers' case for a while, but he couldn't
afford a Shrewd-like five-year litigation offensive, and eventually his clients accepted a low settlement offer from MegaChemicals. The story of
Blow v. MegaChemicals—somewhat exaggerated but generally illustrative
of the effects of court secrecy rules in major injury cases—ends here. Or
at least it and similar cases would end here, under traditional court secrecy
rules.

The rules on court confidentiality orders have usually been framed
solely from the perspective of the litigant with confidential information
to be protected. (The name used in court rules—*protective order*—reveals
the orientation of the rules.) Courts usually considered confidentiality a
matter of right or at least a matter to be left to the litigants themselves,
and judges rarely insisted on keeping court files open.

Because of real cases similar to the *Blow* hypothetical, however, plaintiffs' attorney groups have sought to revise and reform rules on court secrecy. These are significant efforts, for the plaintiffs' bar's American Trial
Lawyers Association is a powerful and skillful lobby, with friends in many
legislatures.

Florida and Texas changed their rules and statutes concerning protective orders to accommodate objections from the plaintiffs' bar. A Florida
statute, known as the "Sunshine in Litigation Act," prevents protective
orders that would have the effect of stopping disclosure of information
on broadly defined "public hazards." In California, the legislature passed
a similar bill that would limit protective orders in cases involving defective products, environmental hazards, and financial fraud, but Governor
Pete Wilson vetoed it.

In more than fifteen other states, legislatures or state supreme courts
have considered laws to narrow court secrecy rules or to broaden the rights
of citizens to public records and files. On the federal level, a Senate com-

mittee has investigated court secrecy, and President Clinton has supported greater access to federal court files. Finally, although it is difficult
to generalize as to the actions of many different courts addressing many
different fact situations, there seems to be a new willingness on the bench
to closely scrutinize requests for secrecy orders, and more judges seem to
be resisting routine, broadly worded protective orders.

There is still much to be done before cases like *Blow v. MegaChemicals* are history. Media and journalistic organizations, in particular, need
to become more involved in the lobbying and the important court cases
to ensure that their interests, which are different in some ways from those
of the plaintiffs' bar, are heard. But meanwhile, observers might take note
of the unusual interests and alliances that, in this case, are helping to bring
about changes important to the news media. What is happening here may
challenge that old simplistic model—lawyers versus reporters, courts versus media—by which media legal issues are so often viewed.

Access to Electronic Records

A new kind of reporter is being seen in the modern newspaper news-
room. Instead of the traditional messy desk piled high with old note-
books, yellowed newspapers, and unread reports, this new reporter's desk
features a personal computer and stacks of computer discs and printouts.
Instead of the traditional journalist's inability to operate advanced mechanical devices such as adding machines, microfilm viewers, and the like,
the new reporter can not only operate his computer but is even fluent in
the arcane language of computer software.

But there is one way this new-tech journalist is just like the old-
fashioned reporter: He has problems getting the information he needs
from government agencies. Paralleling the recent growth of computer-
assisted reporting has been the development of computer-related excuses
and exceptions to government disclosure laws. Important new legal issues relating to media access to government computer records are being
fought out in court.

Coverage. The threshold issue—whether government computer records are *covered* by freedom of information laws—has for the most part
been won by the press. Several federal court decisions, including one written by Supreme Court Justice Anthony M. Kennedy when he was on the
federal Court of Appeals for the Ninth Circuit in San Francisco, have
acknowledged that the federal Freedom of Information Act (FOIA) ap-

plies to computer tapes to the same extent as it does to other documents. Similarly, most state public records laws explicitly list computer tapes and databases as among the records covered.

Records Format. Reporters using computers need access to copies of government computer tapes. But in many cases, agencies have refused this and offered only information in a nonelectronic format. By one report, a state agency in New Hampshire once refused to provide a computer tape costing $35 and required instead that a researcher obtain the same information from 35,000 printed cards. Many similar stories abound.

Unfortunately, however, some courts initially narrowly interpreted access laws to only require some disclosure of information—not necessarily disclosure in a convenient and useful form. A leading federal case, for example, allowed an agency to refuse to produce computer tapes when the same information was available on microfiche. Despite these rulings, there are also contrary authorities, including a strong statement by the congressional committee with oversight over the FOIA that access must be regarded as a "dynamic concept" requiring not just disclosure of *content* but also disclosure in a useful and meaningful format. Congress eventually overruled the narrow rulings in the Electronic Freedom of Information Act Amendments of 1996, which mandated production of records in electronic format wherever possible.

Search Responsibilities. In order to have effective access to computer records, reporters often need government agencies to isolate particular data from computer files. Agencies sometimes claim in response that records laws do not require them to write and carry out search programming. (Most records laws do not require agencies to make new records just to satisfy a requester.)

Congress and most courts have sided with the press on this issue. The legislative history of the FOIA states that agencies must make reasonable computer searches of computer records, just as they must reasonably search manually for traditional documents. Several leading court decisions have reaffirmed this. These holdings make sense, since searching for computer-stored records is usually easier than searching for manually maintained files.

Confidential Information. Public records laws almost uniformly require that documents containing some confidential information should be produced to the extent possible with that information redacted. That is, the presence of some confidential information cannot be used as an excuse for a total refusal to produce anything.

Computerization of records should generally aid redaction of confidential data. Instead of the manual blacking out so familiar to FOIA recipients, a few keys punched on a keyboard can often serve to exclude all confidential segments in a document.

In practice, reporters have often had to litigate in order to get the benefit of the computer's data-segregation capabilities. Many such disputes become hung up on whether confidential and nonconfidential information really is "reasonably segregable"—the applicable FOIA test. One of the leading pro-press cases was written by Justice Kennedy, while he was on the appeals court. In that case, Justice Kennedy held that even Internal Revenue Service files could be disclosed so long as the computer could ensure deletion of all confidential personal taxpayer identification information.

Information Rearrangement. The broadest expression of agencies' duty to produce data with confidential materials deleted could lead to a major expansion in the amount and kind of data available to the press and public. Currently available computer data-rearrangement techniques allow data laden with confidential information to be rearranged in a way that can be disclosed without breaching confidentiality.

For example, under the data-rearrangement technique called *compacting*, a computer would take files containing specific confidential information (e.g., names, incomes, criminal charges, etc.) and assemble, or *compact*, them into broader categories (e.g., numbers of persons, income ranges, and categories of crimes). The resulting nonconfidential compacted information would never have been available without computers.

The most prominent court decision so far that considered those techniques has refused to require their use, reasoning that such techniques involve creation of new documents, which the FOIA expressly does not require. This decision may not be the last word, however. As more journalists (and academic and commercial researchers) seek greater use of government computer records, the pressure is bound to mount for a more expansive reading of the agencies' duties to utilize their computer capabilities in a way that maximizes the amount of information made public. In coming years, Congress and state legislatures will probably have to specifically decide whether to require use of such data-rearrangement techniques.

These are just a few of the legal issues raised by computer-assisted reporting. Many of them reflect old-fashioned conflicts between the press, as an advocate for disclosure, and agencies and others who resist disclosure. The characteristics of computer records, and their potential uses and abuses, attract attention and stimulate emotions on all sides. The job of the media in these cases will be to show the need, usefulness, and lack of undesirable effects of allowing practical and effective access to computer records.

However these issues are resolved, disc drives and databases, not card files and cabinets, are likely to be a leading subject matter of the access law of the future.

Access to Electronic Statutes

The laws of Missouri are public records of Missouri. That doesn't seem like a very startling conclusion, but it took more than a year of litigation to establish that principle in a Missouri trial court.

The case in issue, *Deaton v. Kidd*, involves an important emerging legal issue—the extent to which members of the public may share access to *electronic* government records on the same terms as apply to *paper* records. And the case takes as its subject matter perhaps the most basic of all state records—its statutes.

For several years, the Revisor of Statutes, an employee of the general assembly, has had the statutes available on a computer in the Missouri House of Representative's computer center. These data, which exist in standard ASCII format, can be readily transferred to a $10^1/_2$-inch reel of $^1/_2$-inch magnetic tape (costing $29) in about one hour, at an actual cost of less than $100. Once copied, the data could be readily adapted to diskettes or a CD-ROM for use on personal computers, where the data can then be readily and easily searched. Thus, the electronic statutes have the potential for making the laws of the state readily accessible to any citizen equipped with a personal computer.

You might assume that state officials would embrace and encourage such accessibility. Not so. Acting under legislative direction, the revisor has refused to make copies of the electronic statutes available to the public at anything near that relatively low cost of copying. Rather, the revisor's office has entered into contracts with two legal publishers, giving them the exclusive right to sell the electronic statutes, in return for a hefty fee. The publishers, Compass Data Systems and Missouri Lawyers Weekly (MLW), each paid the state more than $10,000 for the right to the electronic statutes.

Compass and MLW in turn sell the statutes to lawyers, libraries, and others. Their prices ranged from $150 to $300 for a single user to about $2,000 for one hundred users. In their contract with the state, the firms agreed to remit a portion of each sale to the state.

Patrick Deaton, a lawyer in Springfield, Missouri, challenged in Cole County Circuit Court the state's claim that the electronic statutes were not covered by the state Sunshine law, which directs that all public records be made available to the public at "the cost of copies and staff time required for making copies." The state hired an outside firm in Jefferson City and fought Deaton's claim. Circuit Judge Thomas Brown III ruled in Deaton's favor and held that the statutes must be made available at reasonable copying cost.

Judge Brown's decision noted, among other things, the special usefulness of electronic statutes. The electronic records obviate the need of searching through several volumes of updates. Moreover, Judge Brown noted, they "allow the user to search all volumes in seconds by key word, phrase, or statute number. The user is no longer limited by the index or his knowledge of where to look in the Revised Statutes to find particular topics."

Judge Brown quickly disposed of the revisor's arguments that he was not a state agency, that the statutes were not public records, and that the fee charged was reasonable. On the public record point, Judge Brown noted, "It is hard to think of a more important public record than the general laws of the state." Finally, Judge Brown found the revisor's position a clear and purposeful violation of the Sunshine law and awarded Deaton a modest fee for his efforts.

Judge Brown's decision established that Missouri's electronic statutes should be readily accessible to its citizens at reasonable cost. Judge Brown's decision, important as it is, is but the initial stage in the battle over access to electronic government records. Lurking behind the somewhat simplistic definitional issue in the *Deaton* case are broad policy issues concerning whether citizens should have ready and inexpensive access to state electronic records or whether state officials may use electronic records as a source of revenue.

Judge Brown's decision, based on the Sunshine law's directive for release of electronic records at copying cost, applies only the Sunshine law as so phrased. Some legislators have sought to explicitly exempt the statutes from the Sunshine law, and any such change would set a precedent that would likely affect how other potentially "profitable" state databases are handled.

Deaton convinced Judge Brown and, later, an appeals court that electronic records must be readily and reasonably accessible to citizens of the state. But the issue will not be settled until the public and, even more important, a majority of the legislature become convinced that such access truly is good public policy.

Access to War and the Military

One news report relating to the Persian Gulf War was guaranteed to strike a cord of disbelief with the public. It described the suit by *The Nation* magazine and other publishers to open up direct media access to the fighting. You can almost hear the conversation in the living rooms of Mr. and Mrs. Middle America: "Those crazy media people! They want to go to the front lines and interfere with our troops. And they're even trying to make a federal case out of it!"

It was, admittedly, an unusual suit. People sometimes go to court to keep out of war but rarely to put themselves into the middle of one. And because of the undertones of interference with the war effort, the case raised sensitive issues, which the mainstream media had been hesitant to raise in court. But access to the war is not at all a silly issue. There is extensive support for the media's position that reporters have a constitutional right to see the war, up front, on their own.

The particular issue of media access to the front lines has never been decided (though it was briefly raised after the 1983 Grenada invasion in a suit brought by *Hustler* magazine publisher Larry Flynt). However, the general principle of media access to news is well established through scores of decisions, most of them in the past decade.

Ironically, one of the early statements of support for media access to news came from a Supreme Court decision decided against the press. In that 1973 decision, the Court majority denied the media's claim for a privilege against revealing confidential sources. But the Court acknowledged that, at least in principle, freedom of the press embraces some protection for news gathering: "Without some protection for seeking out the news, freedom of the press could be eviscerated."

While that lone sentence established no law, it foreshadowed a line of cases that began in 1980, in which the Court upheld media claims of rights of access to particular kinds of court proceedings. All of these court-access decisions involved quite narrow issues, such as press access to a criminal trial, to the jury selection period of a civil trial, and to certain pretrial proceedings.

But Justice John Paul Stevens noted in his concurrence in the landmark 1980 *Richmond Newspapers* case that despite the unremarkable factual setting of these cases, the principle established was truly revolutionary: "This is a watershed case. . . . Never before has [the Court] squarely held that the acquisition of newsworthy matter is entitled to any constitutional protection whatsoever."

Subsequent decisions have taken this principle far beyond the courtroom setting. Various decisions recognize the right of access to administrative hearings, local government meetings, and even areas beyond police lines at crime and accident scenes.

The legal rationale behind these decisions is that press access should be allowed where the areas in question have been traditionally open to the press and where press access to these areas furthers the purposes of the First Amendment, by helping inform citizens about the workings of their government. Thus, when media organizations litigate access issues, courts usually ask whether there is a tradition of openness and a public need for the information that would become available through the requested press access.

Many cases have even held that the press not only enjoys a right of access to these news-gathering locations but also is entitled to *preferred* access—for example, a seat in the first row of the spectator's section at trials or access to areas beyond police lines. This special access is also a sensitive issue, since many media people are rightly concerned that they will lose public support, and maybe some important rights, if they characterize First Amendment rights as belonging especially to them rather than broadly to the public. In many reporter-access cases, however, the press often *must* argue for special access if it is to have any realistic access at all. As a practical matter, the only way to give the public access to many events is to grant special access to the reporters who serve as the public's "eyes and ears." Former Chief Justice Warren Burger acknowledged this in the *Richmond Newspapers* case: "Instead of acquiring information about trials by first-hand observation or by word of mouth by those who attend, people now acquire it chiefly through the print and electronic media. In a sense, this validates the media claim of functioning as surrogates for the public."

All this indicates that there is a firm legal foundation for the position asserted by *The Nation* and other media organizations that the media are entitled to some special access to the troops and even the front line fighting. One of the key complaints of the plaintiff media organizations was that the military in Operation Desert Storm, by imposing movement and travel restrictions on reporters and by insisting on "pool" reporting, had improperly restricted the amount and character of war reporting. The "pool reporting" system, in particular, represented a significant barrier to access to the news for most media organizations. The system grew out of a post-Grenada study commission as an attempted solution to the needs of the media. In its actual workings, the pool system presented many problems. Initially, the media must depend on the military to notify them to put together a pool for a certain news mission. Pools often do not get to important missions or get there too late. The military determines pool size (how many print reporters or television photographers, for example) and that necessarily affects the reports that result. And the pool system obviously means that many reporters are left out altogether.

To effectively challenge these restrictions, the media will have to demonstrate to the court that fewer restrictions on war reporting are traditional and that greater access is necessary to give citizens the full and complete coverage they need. Finally, the military's obvious needs to maintain war secrets will be factored into any decision, and the press plaintiffs will have to demonstrate that greater access can be allowed consistent with maintenance of true military secrets.

Challenging the military when the country is at war is never popular. But how the war is reported is too important an issue to be left unresolved. The suit by *The Nation* raised significant issues in the evolution of the right of the media for access to the news.

As it turned out, however, somewhat like the Iraqi Republican Guards in the final battles of the Persian Gulf War, advocates of greater press access to the war got caught in a squeeze play. The suit, filed only days before hostilities began, was dismissed before a decision was ever reached. Judge Leonard Sand dismissed the case shortly after the war's successful end.

Judge Sand specifically did *not* refuse to rule because the end of the war made the issues moot. He acknowledged that similar situations may arise in the future, and by the nature and swiftness of modern warfare, a strict application of the mootness doctrine could keep the important issues from ever being decided. In situations like this, courts generally rule

anyway, for although the current dispute (over Persian Gulf War coverage) is moot, similar disputes (over coverage of future wars) will arise in
the future.

But after acknowledging all this, Judge Sand nevertheless refused to
decide the case. He first noted that it raised difficult and important issues
for which there were few direct legal precedents. And with the war over,
the issues would be presented "in a highly abstract form." The situation,
he ruled, was just too uncertain to support the making of new constitutional law. In essence, the decision left media advocates of greater war
access in a legal no-man's-land—with a case too "moot" to be decided on
the facts, too "abstract" and important to be decided on the legal principles. General Norman Schwarzkopf could not have planned a better
victory for the Pentagon.

Access to Voters and Polling Places

Political polls discomfort self-respecting voters. Polls carry the sub-
liminal message that voters really do not have free will—that the collec-
tive selections citizens make in private voting booths can be accurately
predicted like any other foreordained phenomenon of the physical world.
Because polls demean us, we secretly hope that they will fail, or we publicly try to stop them from being taken or published.

The center of the stop-polls campaign is the effort to prevent "exit
polls"—polls taken on Election Day of voters leaving their polling places,
which are publicized either immediately after the election or on television
before Election Day is over (and before some voters have even voted).
Several states enacted laws designed to prevent the media from taking
exit polls.

Florida, for example, which held its key presidential primary on "Super Tuesday" beginning in 1988, amended its law on soliciting at polling
places in 1987 to prohibit anyone from "soliciting . . . any . . . opinion . . .
for any purpose" within 150 feet of the front door of any building in which
any polling place is located. Although exit polls were not mentioned in
the statute, its clear intent and effect was to prohibit exit polls from being
taken. A Washington state law was even more explicit. It made it illegal
for anyone, within 300 feet of a polling place, to "conduct any exit poll or
public opinion poll with voters."

Both laws were challenged by media organizations, and both were struck down as unconstitutional infringements of the media's First Amendment right to gather the news. Both cases were heard and decided on expedited schedules so that decisions were reached prior to the important 1988 presidential primaries. In the Florida case, for example, CBS and several other media organizations brought an emergency challenge to the Florida statute shortly before the March 9, 1988, "Super Tuesday" primary. A federal district court in Miami ruled, only a week before the primary, that exit polls could go ahead.

Both courts analyzed the statutes as effective prohibitions of exit polls, even though they only affected certain areas around polling places and the Florida statute did not even mention exit polls. Moreover, both courts readily found that the broad prohibitions of the two statutes interfered with television and newspaper reporting of elections.

In the Florida case, federal District Judge Stanley Marcus noted that exit polls have become "a prime source of data for political contests and scholars" and a "priceless resource in the study of voter behavior and elections." Moreover, for exit polls to be effective, Judge Marcus noted, they must be taken close to the polling place. If reporters and poll takers must stay far away from polling places, they will not be able to determine for sure whether the persons they interview have actually voted. Thus, Judge Marcus found, a 150-foot no-polling zone "would destroy the ability to conduct exit polls."

Based on those facts, Judge Marcus held that exit polls and journalistic interviews of voters leaving the polling place are protected by the First Amendment's guarantees of free speech and free press. He noted: "Without the ability to collect information, viewpoints and opinions from voters, the right to report and publish political news would be left with little means of fulfillment."

Similarly, in the Washington state case, a three-judge federal Court of Appeals panel concluded that exit polling is a part of the news-gathering and dissemination process protected by the First Amendment. Each court, after recognizing the constitutionally protected nature of exit polling, held that it could be abridged only on a showing of compelling state interests, which could not be satisfied by any less restrictive regulation.

Florida officials offered two "compelling interests" to justify the statute. First, they claimed the statute was necessary to create a "zone of privacy for voters" and to protect "voter sanctity and electoral decorum." The court found, however, that the 150-foot zone around the polling place was open to many persons and many disruptive activities and, moreover, exit polls were no more disruptive than many of the permitted activities. Also, the so-called privacy zone did not really create any privacy because the 150-foot radius around most polling places included public streets, sidewalks, and parks.

Florida's second rationale for the statute was that private groups that donated their property for use as polling places might not do so if they were going to be bothered by exit polling. But this rationale did not hold up to scrutiny, either, Judge Marcus held. State officials could not offer any evidence of polling place owners who had been upset by exit polling, and exit polling (which only occurs at a few sample polling places, anyway) is less disruptive than many other activities outside polling places.

The Court of Appeals in the Washington state case rejected similar rationales offered by state officials for the Washington exit-poll ban. Moreover, that court directly confronted what is probably the real reason why many persons wish to prevent exit polls—the feeling that poll results should not be available for broadcast on Election Day, when they might influence those who have not yet voted. Washington state officials, while denying that this was the real reason for the exit-poll ban, defended this justification. They claimed that broadcasting of poll results affects voting behavior, and the state has a "significant interest" in preventing this influence on voting behavior. The court firmly rejected this argument.

The First Amendment prohibits any ban on speech "on the basis that (the speech) might indirectly affect the voters' choice," the court held. Just as with Election Day editorials and other publications, the media have the right to publish information that may affect voters. Exit polls, like other parts of our electoral process, may be disliked, but they are here to stay.

Access Rights (and Hazards) Abroad

The reporting of the rise and repression of China's short-lived democracy movement in 1989 illustrates an increasingly common phenomenon—American journalists operating subject to hostile and unpredictable foreign law.

Foreign correspondents are known for their resourcefulness, and for the most part those stationed in China managed to find the news and file their stories even in martial-law Beijing. But every day in a foreign country often presents special legal obstacles to American reporters. The re-

strictions imposed in Beijing are typical of controls regularly imposed by
many foreign governments.

Access Limits. The simplest and most frequent way foreign governments control news coverage is by limiting reporters' access to the news.
Ironically, the students' dissent in China initially received quite broad
news coverage because the Chinese government was allowing some liber-
alized reporting by its own media and initially allowed many extra foreign
correspondents into China for a historic showpiece Sino-Soviet summit
meeting.

As a result, arrangements made for the summit meeting, such as satellite linkups allowing live reporting from China to the United States,
served the unintended purpose of increasing worldwide coverage of the
dissent. Once the summit was over, the Chinese government reverted
to the traditional news policies of governments under attack and began
clamping down on those channels. Live satellite linkages were eventually
banned, and the U.S. television networks were forced to use less dramatic
and reliable telephone communications. And as the government in early
June 1989 cracked down on the student dissent, it also imposed stringent
access restrictions on the foreign press. Among other things, the government's martial-law decree banned reporting of the student demonstrations and the military activities.

The correspondents' reaction was disarmingly simple. According to
the *New York Times*, reporters concluded that under Chinese martial law
it was illegal to be a reporter but perfectly proper to be a tourist. Suddenly,
reported *Times* correspondent Nicholas Kristof, one saw self-described
American tourists going about Beijing with pens and notepads, asking
questions such as, "So are the soldiers there from the 38th Army, and are
they ready to fight with the 27th Army?" Radio and television reporters
similarly took precautions such as concealing their equipment or using
tourist-type video cameras.

The reluctance of Chinese citizens after the imposition of martial law
to speak to foreign reporters was an indirect access limitation, also. But
the phenomenon of news sources who fear retaliation if they speak to the
press is not unique to foreign correspondents; it is familiar to every reporter who has ever covered an American city hall.

Expulsion. Another legal tool often used by foreign governments
against foreign correspondents is expulsion. Since journalists stay in the

country by virtue of visas issued by the governments, the visas can be readily revoked if the foreign government disapproves of the reporter's dispatches or other activities.

This, too, occurred in China: three Western reporters were expelled shortly after martial law was imposed, and the threat of expulsion undoubtedly caused reporters to take extra caution. In some cases, the reporters' home nation can attempt to fight expulsions either by diplomatic pressure or retaliatory evictions against the foreign nation's journalists here. But in situations like the recent Chinese martial law, little, if anything, can be done.

Censorship. Censorship is another common tool by which foreign governments control reporting, although little censorship occurred in the Chinese situation. The general openness of communications during the May 1989 visit of Soviet Union leader Mikhail Gorbachev, and the number of Western reporters in China, made it difficult for the Chinese officials to impose censorship.

Censorship, in any event, is rarely effective in situations short of open warfare. Usually reporters can make arrangements to transmit their reports out of the country. Modern audiotapes and videotapes, for example, can be hidden, taken out of the country, and then instantaneously transmitted to the home country, where they provide a remarkably complete news report from within the area supposedly governed by censors.

Similarly, censors often allow so many different small pieces of information to get through the censorship barrier that the outside world can piece together a fairly full picture. One of the classic instances of reporters outsmarting censors occurred several years ago during the Israeli incursion in Lebanon. Reporters sent identical videotapes by satellite from both Damascus and Tel Aviv, expecting that both Syria and Israel would censor only the favorable portions, thus allowing the full story to emerge.

Other Restrictions. Many other measures have been used by foreign governments in restricting reporting, ranging from mild harassment to threats, arrests, and even killings. When formal legal charges are brought against reporters, the entire proceedings are governed by the foreign nations' laws. Thus, Soviet trials of several American reporters (including the trial of *New York Times* reporter Craig Whitney for libel and the trial of *U.S. News and World Report* correspondent Nicholas Daniloff for espionage) not surprisingly have resulted in convictions. The only way out was payment of the fines (in Whitney's case) and diplomatic action (in Daniloff's case—the trade of Daniloff for a Soviet spy in U.S. custody).

Even in Western countries friendlier than the Soviet Union, moreover, correspondents can face hostile legal action. British and Canadian laws on state secrets and gag orders are serious legal hazards, which have trapped American reporters on several occasions.

Prospects for Change. The plight of an American correspondent subjected to hostile foreign law is unlikely to change in the near future. Ironically, while international agreements and laws are increasingly making the world safe for new American business ventures abroad, these agreements rarely protect the press, which has had foreign correspondents abroad for many decades.

Neither are international organizations helping the press. Rather, Third World nations, working though the United Nations Educational, Scientific, and Cultural Organization (UNESCO), have been promoting a system of international press accreditation that would be tied to obligating reporters "to serve the social, political, and economic objectives of those who are responsible for the quality of life in a given country." This, of course, would effectively increase rather than lessen the power of foreign authorities over reporters and is unacceptable to the Western press. Foreign correspondents, thus, are in little danger of losing either the legal hazards or the swashbuckling traditions of their job.

Should Lawyers Talk to the Media?

Every journalist has met at least one lawyer, if not many, who has a two-word answer for everything.

What is your client's defense? "No comment."

How do you intend to respond to the charges against your client? "No comment."

What explanation do you have for your client's associates, employees, and customers? "No comment."

When can we expect to see your client's position? "No comment."

Many reporters probably conclude that there is a standard course in law school titled "Telling Reporters 'No Comment.'" But in fact "no comment" is not the only response a lawyer can make to a reporter's inquiry, and there is an increasing school of thought among lawyers that they actually have the *duty* to speak to the press and to seek to convey their client's position to the public.

The innate reluctance of many lawyers to speak to the press stems from two concerns. First, not too long ago legal advertising was prohibited, and bar associations were known to investigate and reprimand lawyers who in any way sought or facilitated publicity about themselves. Second, most lawyers know from experience the truth of the warning given to all criminal suspects: "Anything you say can and will be used against you." Lawyers trained to be cautious frequently conclude that the safest thing to say in public is nothing.

The combination of those two concerns has sent a clear message to lawyers: Stay out of the newspapers (and off of radio and television) and you will stay out of trouble. That lesson, however, was probably always simplistic and overdrawn. It is even more suspect today given the speed and pervasiveness of modern communications. Silence in some instances can be damning. Lawyers should know this because there is even an evidentiary rule to this effect.

Consider a lawsuit alleging corporate misconduct. The corporation may be charged with putting a defective product on the market; with polluting the environment; with dealing unfairly with its employees; or with improperly seeking to influence government action. These serious allegations are naturally publicized in great detail. In response, usually, the corporation's lawyer or spokesmen is quoted as stating: "We have no comment at this time." Or, perhaps, he is bold and states: "The company intends to defend the case vigorously but has no further comment." What does the reader, listener, or viewer conclude from this? Most likely, that the company is guilty as charged; that it offered no specific answer to the charges because it *had* none.

The "no comment" lawyer may justify his failure to comment on the grounds that the trial is supposed to occur in a courtroom, not the news media. This is true but only part of the picture. With today's communications, one cannot expect publicity about a lawsuit to await the suit's conclusion. Corporations and public persons today are subject to intense and pervasive public and media scrutiny and publicity, which does not await the conclusion of formal legal proceedings. Such publicity affects reputations, the conduct of business, and public perceptions of corporate citizens and public persons generally.

Publicity about legal proceedings need not be one-sided, however.

Contrary to the view of the "no comment" school of lawyering, litigation does not require silence on the part of the party charged and lawyers. Rather, today's counselor is entitled to act suitably within today's communications system. In many cases, the need to win the case in the courtroom is only one of the client's needs. Conscientious counsel should recognize and attempt to satisfy other objectives. He or she should consider all the ways in which the case and publicity about it affect the client, including all of the following concerns:

The "Trial" in the Public Forum. Many public controversies undergo two trials: the legal one in the courtroom and the public debate in the media. For major corporations and public figures, it can be catastrophic to win the case in the courtroom but lose it in the public debate. The Ford Motor Company case concerning the allegedly defective Pinto gas tank and the Agent Orange controversy, for example, are controversies where the defendants lost the public debate even though they won most of the courtroom battles. If the defendants had good answers to the charges against them, to their own disservice they failed to convey them to the public.

Timely and Effective Disclosures. Many lawyers undoubtedly feel that they will "set the record straight" concerning their client after the trial or resolution of the case. This may have been possible in the days of slower communications, but today it is delusory to rely on such after-the-fact disclosures. After the case is over, especially if (like most cases) it concludes with a whimper rather than a bang, the result will be buried on page 18-E and not even merit mention on radio or television. If the original charges were on page one and the evening news, the *delay* in setting the record straight really constitutes a total failure to set the record straight.

Education of the Public. Publicity can educate the public concerning what the law requires and how the legal system works. Today's public is, by and large, well educated and interested in legal issues. The public is able and eager to consider and debate issues such as the scope of corporate liability, environmental protection, safety and job protection standards, and government regulation of business. For a fuller, better understanding of the issues, the public needs to hear all sides to a legal controversy disclose and explain their positions.

Prevention of Bias and Misunderstanding. The lawyer who refuses to talk to the press increases the chances that the case and his client's position will be misunderstood. Reporters rely on interviews with experts and participants in news events; if they cannot get the story from the participants, they are less likely to get it straight. Lawyers who have a good story to tell should be willing to discuss and explain it to the press, to help ensure that their story is told accurately, fully, and properly. This will both aid public understanding and help prevent the prejudice that often results from ignorance and misunderstanding.

In short, "no comment" is not the lawyer's only available answer when a reporter calls. In many cases, a lawyer's duty to represent his client may *require* him to discuss cases with the press in order to help bring before the public, in a timely and effective manner, the facts and positions of his client's case.

Lawyers can fulfill this duty without turning their press interviews into either unseemly displays of self-promotion or admissions giving away their client's secrets and strategies. Rather, they can handle press interviews in a way that explains and furthers their client's position and, in so doing, makes them helpful, useful participants in the process of reporting and debating legal developments.

4

Confidentiality and Sources

Confidentiality Promises

A WASHINGTON POLITICAL REPORTER WRITING a story about the 1988 presidential race reportedly traveled to Iowa to sample grassroots political feelings. After arriving in Des Moines, the reporter drove north, deep into Iowa's isolated farm community, where, safe in the midst of the true rural grassroots, he approached a farmer in a field and asked about political issues. "Well," the farmer began cautiously, "on deep background . . ."

The story illustrates a truth of modern journalism. Reporting regularly involves confidential sources and interviews conducted under "background," "off the record," "not for attribution," or other restrictive guidelines. Even persons who are not regular or professional news makers, like the Iowa farmer, often treat confidentiality as an essential part of the news-gathering process.

Confidentiality, in its origin, is a journalistic concept, not a legal concept. It is a reporting technique born out of the dual needs of reporters and their sources—the sources' need for confidentiality so they can give the story without incurring retaliation or other unwanted consequences and the reporters' need for stories or information that would otherwise be unavailable.

Nonetheless, many do perceive "legalities" with respect to journalistic confidentiality. These really operate on two different levels. The first level at which the journalist and source work out the agreements is sometimes colored with quasi-legal understandings. In some areas, such as political reporting in Washington, this level may contain elaborate, almost scholastic, distinctions among various categories of confidentiality (such as "background" versus "deep background"), each carrying different consequences as to how information can be used or disclosed. No legal mechanism enforces these arrangements and responsibilities. In a few cases, sources have sued reporters for allegedly breaching confidentiality arrangements, but the courts usually refuse to entertain such suits.

Thus, the issues of whether and how confidentiality is used by a journalist, what a particular confidentiality agreement requires, and how a journalist should attempt to protect his or her confidential relationships are largely matters of journalism ethics, not law.

But on another level, civil courts deal with disputes as to journalistic confidentiality. This occurs when someone seeks a court order requiring a journalist to disclose information, documents, or identities that he or she believes should be kept confidential. When this happens, confidentiality often presents a difficult issue for the courts. Courts understandably are protective of their ability to compel evidence, and thus most courts look skeptically on claims of privilege exempting journalists from the civic responsibility of giving testimony.

Moreover, journalistic confidentiality embraces a wide variety of circumstances. The confidential matter can be information, documents, or the individual source's identity. The confidentiality agreement may be explicit or implicit. Or protection may be required even in the absence of any confidentiality arrangement because compelled disclosure would hamper the journalist's further effectiveness. Judges are accustomed to narrow, predictable concepts; hence, many jurists are put off by the broad, variable concept of journalistic confidentiality.

Nonetheless, most courts have recognized the practical need for some protection for journalistic confidentiality. Within the last forty years, courts began to grapple directly with journalistic confidentiality. In a celebrated case in 1958, entertainer Judy Garland sued columnist Marie Torre for libel and demanded that Torre identify a television executive who made allegedly disparaging remarks about Garland. A federal appeals court rejected Torre's claim of journalistic privilege and ordered her to reveal the source.

Litigation over journalistic confidentiality escalated by the early 1970s. In scores of cases, lawyers attempted to subpoena, sue, or prosecute reporters to compel their testimony as to the sources and information they used in researching and writing their stories. In 1972, the U.S. Supreme Court heard three cases presenting claims of journalists' privilege and, in a landmark 5–4 decision, rejected the reporters' claims to a special constitutional privilege, at least in the context of a subpoena from a federal grand jury.

The decision, *Branzburg v. Hayes*, did not end the controversy, though. The Court was closely divided, and the crucial concurring opinion of Justice Lewis Powell recognized the need to strike "a proper balance" between the needs of the courts for evidence and the needs of reporters to gather news. Justice Powell's concurrence, together with the four-justice dissenting opinion favoring a journalist's privilege, laid the groundwork for a constitutional privilege protecting journalists' confidentiality according to a "balancing test."

Most, although not all, of the post-1972 decisions have followed this constitutional privilege, using three factors:

- Is the information requested relevant to an underlying substantial legal proceeding?
- Is the information requested *essential* to the party requesting it?
- Have all alternative ways to meet the requesting party's needs been exhausted?

Under the balancing test, disclosure of confidential sources or information will not be compelled unless all three of those questions can be answered affirmatively.

Although this qualified constitutional privilege was initially resisted by some judges, it is becoming increasingly well established. Indeed, the privilege has been expanded to cover scholars, researchers, and professional expert witnesses. These decisions help demonstrate the practical and social need for an evidentiary privilege for professional information gatherers.

About half of the states have protection for journalistic confidentiality in addition to the constitutional privilege, in the form of reporters' "shield" statutes. Shield laws vary in their coverage. Some are near absolute in the protection afforded, while others essentially adopt the three-part balancing test under the constitutional privilege. Some have extra limitations, too.

Until recently, for instance, the Illinois shield law did not apply in libel cases, and in a widely publicized case in 1985, Richard Hargraves, a former editor of the *Belleville News-Democrat*, was imprisoned for contempt for not revealing in a libel case his confidential sources. The sources eventually revealed themselves and Hargraves was released. Later that year, the Illinois Legislature amended the shield law to apply in libel cases.

Overall, the constitutional privilege and state shield laws provide a significant, but limited, measure of legal protection for journalistic confidentiality. Results in any confidentiality case depend on many practical factors.

First, the legal context in which the case arises is extremely important—that is, whether the information is sought for a criminal prosecution or defense, a civil lawsuit, a grand jury investigation, or some other proceeding. Courts give greatest weight to claims that disclosure of a reporter's sources is needed for a grand jury investigation or a criminal case. Similarly, in libel suits, courts are sometimes skeptical of confidentiality claims asserted by reporter-defendants. Thus, reporters must take particular care when dealing with information that may be material to a criminal investigation or prosecution or when working on stories about persons who may be inclined to file libel suits.

Second, the reporter is most likely to prevail where he can demonstrate a persuasive need for confidentiality. If possible, reporters should use confidentiality agreements only when necessary; this will help demonstrate a real need for protection. Similarly, narrow, explicit confidentiality agreements are more likely to be protected than broad or implicit agreements. Also, confidentiality is more likely to be upheld as necessary when it is used in sensitive investigations rather than routine noncontroversial stories.

Third, the precedents and statutes in the particular jurisdiction play a role. One of the earliest and strongest decisions recognizing the protection of the reporter's privilege involved former St. Louis mayor Alfonso J. Cervantes's libel suit against *Time* magazine. In *Cervantes v. Time*, Cervantes attempted to compel disclosure of the sources of Denny Walsh, one of the authors of the *Time* article. Cervantes claimed he needed to have the sources revealed to make out his libel case. The trial court and the Eighth Circuit Court of Appeals, however, refused to compel disclosure, holding that Cervantes had not shown the compelling need required under the constitutional reporters' privilege.

Ultimately, legal protection for confidentiality depends on the circumstances of the confidentiality arrangement and the legal challenge. Thus, reporters can enhance the likelihood of obtaining legal protection for their confidences in two ways, first, by adopting sound, consistent, and ethical practices that clearly merit legal protection and, second, by vigorously asserting the journalist's privilege in court whenever compelled disclosure is attempted.

Waiver of the Reporter's Privilege

Lawyers (and judges) love "waiver" arguments. They have an obvious appeal, for they tell a litigant that by his *own* actions he has given up the very rights, privileges, or entitlements that he is asserting. So when reporters encounter a claim of "waiver" in court, they had better watch out. The reporter's privilege case involving Linda Wheeler of the *Washington Post* illustrates the dangers of the waiver doctrine bluntly applied to a reporter's privilege claim.

A lawyer representing District of Columbia policemen subpoenaed Wheeler and sought disclosure of the source who told her in advance of a police drug raid. She refused. District of Columbia law firmly supported her claim of reporter's privilege. So the lawyer dug out the old waiver argument and claimed that Wheeler waived the privilege because she allegedly told her fiancé and another person the identity of her source.

In the context of the attorney-client privilege, which lawyers and judges deal with frequently, disclosure of confidential communications outside the confidential relationship *is* a waiver. That privilege, after all, is based on a desire to promote disclosures solely within the confidential attorney-client relationship. Some persons would like to automatically apply the waiver doctrine developed for the attorney-client privilege to *all* evidentiary privileges. This is simple and appealing—and wrong.

The reporter's privilege has a different purpose altogether than secrecy-oriented privileges. It does not exist to promote *confidential* communications but rather to encourage *disclosure of information* via news media. Confidentiality is not the purpose of the reporter's privilege. Rather, it is part of an agreement between the reporter and the source (which often does not require strict confidentiality from all others), which is a *means* to serve the purpose of disclosure of information.

Where promoting confidentiality is the purpose for the privilege, as with the attorney-client privilege, it makes sense to construe any disclosure to third parties as a waiver. But where limited disclosure to third parties will *not* interfere with the purpose of the privilege, as with the reporter's privilege, a strict waiver doctrine makes no sense at all. A number of courts have recognized this distinction and rejected various arguments that reporters "waived" their privilege to keep sources or information confidential.

In the Wheeler case, however, both the trial and final appeals courts in the district tacked the strict waiver doctrine from the secrecy-oriented privileges onto the disclosure-oriented reporter's privilege and ordered Wheeler to disclose her sources. If nothing else, the Wheeler case illustrates the unresolved nature of the reporter's privilege in our law. It is, quite clearly, a privilege that courts and journalists often understand differently in purposes, scope, and nature.

Media Subpoena Cases: Practical Concerns

In the interaction between journalists and the legal system, one of the key issues is the extent to which the law will protect a reporter's sources, notes, and source materials from involuntary disclosure.

The generally accepted rule is that there *is* a legally recognized—but "qualified"—reporter's privilege that protects against forced disclosure of a reporter's sources except in the most extreme circumstances. In practice, however, the application of the privilege is anything but certain and depends greatly on the factual situation presented, public opinion at the time, and pragmatic judgments by media organizations as to how far they will attempt to enforce their rights.

Two roughly contemporaneous cases in 1992—the Senate leak inquiry concerning its Clarence Thomas investigation and the Los Angeles federal prosecutor's subpoenas for film and photographs of the riots following the verdict in the first prosecution concerning the beating of Rodney King—are illustrative.

The Senate's Clarence Thomas inquiry, at first blush, had everything that it takes to overcome the reporter's privilege. Although the factors considered in reporter's privilege cases vary by jurisdiction and the kind of proceeding involved, in general, the party seeking to subpoena a reporter must show that the information sought is central to a nonfrivolous legal proceeding and cannot be reasonably obtained from other sources.

The Senate's inquiry appeared to be a serious nonfrivolous governmental proceeding. To hear some members of the Judiciary Committee tell it, the fate of representative government rested in good measure on the ability of congressional investigating committees to do their work in confidence. And information about reporters' sources was certainly central to the proceeding. The focus of the inquiry was how information about Anita Hill's sexual harassment charges against Clarence Thomas were leaked to Nina Totenberg of National Public Radio and Timothy Phelps of *Newsday*.

Finally, Senate special counsel Peter E. Fleming Jr. attempted unsuccessfully to get the information from other sources. After interviews with senators and staff members, he failed to determine who leaked the information to either of the reporters. This left the reporters as the only possible sources of information.

But Fleming didn't succeed in getting the information from Totenberg or Phelps. The reporters and media organizations involved took a firm stand. The case went to the heart of the reporter's privilege—the need to protect sources who disclosed information under a promise of confidentiality. So lawyers for Totenberg and Phelps not only argued strongly for application of the privilege but also took the offensive, portraying the Senate inquiry, essentially, as an attempt to make the media the scapegoat for the whole Clarence Thomas affair.

Fleming, who would have had to go to court to enforce his committee's subpoenas, obviously concluded that he faced problems if he pursued the matter. He may well have determined that neither judges nor the public would look sympathetically on senators ganging up on two reporters who, in essence, embarrassed the Senate by digging up facts that the Judiciary Committee initially suppressed. Fleming decided not to even attempt an enforcement action and simply concluded his inquiry with a report that the leaks could not be located.

The Los Angeles subpoenas present a much different picture. Indeed, on a factor-by-factor analysis, the authorities might appear to confront many difficulties in overcoming the reporter's privilege and enforcing the subpoenas.

To begin with, the Los Angeles subpoenas were basically part of a general fishing expedition. The subpoenas were not narrowly tailored but rather directed *each* of the Los Angeles television stations to produce *all* of its film of the riots. Although nonfrivolous criminal cases were involved in Los Angeles, the individual prosecutions at stake were mostly for garden-variety offenses, the sort that normally do not require abrogation of privileges rooted in the First Amendment. And there were many alternative sources about offenses committed during the riot—shop owners and employees, noninvolved witnesses, and police officers, to begin with. Law enforcement officials even had their own off-the-air tapes of most of the riot television footage and their own video cameras filming some of the riot.

Yet despite these factors—the fishing expedition nature of the subpoenas, the relatively minor offenses involved, and the existence of many alternative sources—the Los Angeles subpoenas met with better success than the Senate subpoenas. Media organizations in Los Angeles did not resist the subpoenas absolutely. For one thing, promises of confidentiality to sources were not involved because the subpoenas sought film of events occurring in public.

Moreover, in a case like this, there was little sympathy for the media among the general public and the criminal court judges who would hear subpoena disputes. If a confrontation developed where it appeared that the media were standing in the way of prosecution of rioters, the media would lose. Media executives and lawyers recognize this. Thus, rather than risk a difficult confrontation that the press loses and that sets a bad precedent, Los Angeles broadcasters attempted to compromise. A variety of compromises are available in such situations; for example, broadcasters could agree to give up their original tapes of the riot (which have better resolution than off-the-air tapes) in return for the prosecutor's agreement not to seek nonbroadcast film footage, known as *outtakes*.

Important as the reporter's privilege is to journalists, neither the applicable legal rules nor the level of the media's support in public opinion and the courts allow the media to take an absolutist stand in every battle. Like Kenny Rogers's "Gambler," media executives need to know when to hold 'em and when to fold 'em. Their pragmatic judgments as to when and where to take a stand influence not only particular disputes but also the development of the law.

The Clarence Thomas privilege, despite some surface problems, was clearly one to hold. The Los Angeles riot privilege, despite considerable merit under the applicable legal standard, was almost as surely one to fold.

Agreements with Sources

Press cases that make it to the Supreme Court always seem to bring surprises when they are decided. The case of *Cohen v. Minneapolis Star and Tribune* may make reporters think twice about their promises. The case began as a breach of contract claim based on a broken promise of confidentiality. In the end, however, the Supreme Court's decision in *Cohen* involved something different—maybe significantly different.

In the case, the plaintiff, Dan Cohen, while working for a Republican organization, had tipped off two reporters about minor past wrongdoings by the Democratic candidate for Minnesota lieutenant governor. Both reporters agreed in advance with Cohen that they would protect his confidentiality. But both of their editors decided to break the promises and publish the story of the attempted smear campaign.

Cohen won big at trial. And he also prevailed in the first appeals court. While that court cut down Cohen's award somewhat, it had little sympathy for the newspapers and rejected their substantive arguments. The Minnesota Supreme Court, however, handled the case in a way that truly transformed it.

First, the state supreme court, without relying on the First Amendment or any federal law, concluded that contract remedies were just not meant for a reporter-source agreement and, thus, Cohen had no basis for his breach of contract claims. If that were all the Minnesota court had done, it would have ended the case. The Minnesota Supreme Court had the final word on Minnesota contract law, exempt even from review by the United States Supreme Court.

During oral argument of the case, however, a judge on the Minnesota Supreme Court suggested an *alternative* noncontract legal theory for Cohen. That legal theory, usually applied in commercial situations, holds that if you make a promise to someone and that person relies on it and gives some benefits to you, you may be held liable if you don't keep the promise. The rule applies even if you and he have no enforceable contract. By accepting the benefits induced by your *promise*, you are *estopped* from reneging on the promise. Hence, the doctrine's name, *promissory estoppel*.

In its decision, the Minnesota high court, after deciding the contract issue favorably to the press, went on to explore the promissory estoppel theory. Applied literally, promissory estoppel seemed to fit Cohen's case. After all, Cohen had given the newspapers valuable information in reliance on their promise of confidentiality, so it seemed only fair to estop the papers from reneging and to hold the papers liable for breaking their promises.

But should this theory—designed, for example, for situations where someone has performed services in reliance on a promise of payment—apply to a reporter's promise of confidentiality? On this point, the Minnesota court split, and the majority concluded that the First Amendment prevented application of the theory in this context. That First Amendment ruling was important. It was, of course, an immediate victory for the newspapers. But it also set the newspapers up for eventual defeat because the ruling on the First Amendment invoked the jurisdiction of the U.S. Supreme Court.

The U.S. Supreme Court took the case, decided the issue of whether the First Amendment barred promissory estoppel claims against the newspapers, and ruled that it did not. It is now the law of the land that the First Amendment imposes no barriers to promissory estoppel claims against the press.

The twists of the *Cohen* case alone make for a surprising story. Since Cohen sued for breach of contract, and the Minnesota high court killed that theory, Cohen essentially lost the case he brought. But thanks to the free legal guidance he got from a Minnesota Supreme Court judge, Cohen's case led to a U.S. Supreme Court landmark ruling on a broader theory that he never raised.

The question that remains is whether the case is just an aberration or whether it will lead to more claims based on reporters' broken promises. Several similar cases have raised the theory. In a decision just a month after the U.S. Supreme Court's *Cohen* ruling, the Eighth Circuit U.S. Court of Appeals held that the promissory estoppel theory could be raised by a news subject who claimed that *Glamour* magazine broke a promise to obscure her identity in an article in which she was quoted.

If applied literally to relationships between reporters and news sources or subjects, the broad and pliable promissory estoppel theory could create problems. Not just promises of confidentiality (as in the *Cohen* and the *Glamour* cases) are at stake. Other promises—or remarks that news sources and subjects take as promises—could become subject of promissory estoppel suits.

For example, a subject of a feature story might claim that he consented to an interview only if certain subjects (his personal life, for instance) were kept out of the resulting story. He might be able to sue, under a promissory estoppel theory, if he thought the resulting story broke that promise. Reporting on prominent news subjects (such as financier Carl Icahn) who condition interviews on some control over their own quotations could also present problems. If it is interpreted to extend this far, the promissory estoppel theory would give legal significance to the informal oral agreements usually reached in these situations.

Until recently most suits over broken reporter promises (often brought by prisoners who were dissatisfied with stories resulting from their jailhouse interviews) were given little credence. The *Cohen* decision suggests that these cases may become more serious.

Interview Contract Lawsuits

Reporters, are you ready for your next interview? Be sure to take all of your essential interview tools—pen, notepad, and, of course, a contract lawyer.

Only a few years ago, agreements between journalists and news sources were rarely considered enforceable. But *Cohen v. Cowles Media*, a case decided by the U.S. Supreme Court in 1991, has helped to change that. Journalistic breach of contract cases are proliferating. Let's see if you are prepared for the new era of contract journalism.

Interview Conditions. Are you ready to negotiate the interview conditions before the interview begins? Don't be surprised if your source asks for this, particularly if he or she tends to one of the political extremes. News subjects who perceive the media as antagonistic may seek to control the circumstances of the interview.

Spike Lee's demands in an appearance at the University of Missouri–St. Louis (UMSL) are illustrative. He insisted that all television cameras be excluded from his talk to UMSL students, and he reportedly attempted to limit coverage to certain African American reporters. Given that UMSL is a quintessential public forum, it's doubtful that Lee had the right to exclude any one or any cameras. But where public forums are *not* involved, subjects like Lee *can* bargain for who will cover them and what journalistic tools will be used.

Bargained-for restrictions occur all the time. One source won't talk while a tape recorder is running. Another refuses to talk while caught on the street but agrees to give an interview in the controlled situation of his lawyer's office. So preinterview conditions can, and will, become the subject of bargaining and agreements between reporters and sources.

Restrictions on Use and Dissemination of the Interview. Your contract negotiations aren't over once you get your foot in the door. The interviewer may bargain for restrictions on how the interview can be used.

This issue first arose when a crafty freelancer managed to obtain an interview with the Reverend Jerry Falwell and then sell that interview to *Penthouse*. Falwell didn't like seeing his name on the cover of *Penthouse* and his interview sandwiched between photo spreads of nude women. He sued *Penthouse* but lost because he had had no understanding with the interviewer as to limitations on where the interview could be published.

Falwell's loss in the *Penthouse* case taught him, and some colleagues, a lesson. Another religious right activist, the Reverend Donald Wildmon, began conditioning his interviews on a written contract with a "no publication in *Playboy, Penthouse*, or *Hustler*" clause. Wildmon's interview contract in turn led to his suit over the documentary *Damned in the USA*.

Damned in the USA was a British filmmaker's look at morality and arts censorship in America. The producers sought an interview with Wildmon, head of the Tupelo, Mississippi-based American Family Association. And they agreed in writing as a precondition to the interview not to use "the contents of the interview" in "any other media presentation" besides the planned documentary on Britain's Channel 4. The completed film included both Wildmon's comments (fairly portrayed) and some of the photographs and artwork to which he objected. When Wildmon saw it, he objected to the film's "graphic content" and sued to prevent its distribution in the United States.

The contract proved difficult to interpret. Did it prohibit any showing of *Damned in the USA* outside of the original British broadcast, as Wildmon contended? Or did it only restrict the producers from allowing others to use their raw interview footage, as they asserted? The court ruled that the film could be shown. But it was no First Amendment victory over contract law. To the contrary, the court held that the contract was fully enforceable and simply agreed with the film producers' interpretation, not Wildmon's.

Wildmon and other like-minded news subjects will presumably write better contracts next time—meaning that we will be seeing more suits of the *Damned in the USA* variety.

Let's say you satisfy the preinterview conditions and get an interview you can use in the publication or medium of your choice. What other contract issues do you need to tie down?

Discretion to Reveal Source. In *Cohen v. Cowles Media*, the Minneapolis and St. Paul newspapers were successfully sued for breaching their reporters' promises of confidentiality to their sources. So if you think you or your editors might want to backtrack on a promise of confidentiality, as the editors did in *Cohen*, you had better make that clear to your source.

Although the Minnesota courts in *Cohen* refused to recognize breach of contract claims, they did recognize claims for promissory estoppel, which isn't really much different. The promissory estoppel legal theory permits courts to enforce promises made even where there is no enforceable contract if the other side has relied on the promise and other circumstances make enforcement of the promise fair.

Concealment of Source's Identity. Even if you attempt to honor your confidentiality agreement with your source, you had better make it clear what exactly you are promising and make sure you honor the promises.

In one noted post-*Cohen* suit, *Glamour* magazine published a story about sexual abuse victims. One Minnesota woman told her story on the condition that she would not be identified or identifiable in the story. After the published article mentioned several facts that tended to identify her as the victim described in the article, she sued. Eventually she lost, on the ground that the promise of making her "unidentifiable" was just too vague to be enforceable under the promissory estoppel theory on which she sued. But in a different context—or a different state—such promises could be actionable.

Other Promises. Given the breadth of contract and promissory estoppel law and the ingenuity of lawyers, just about any promise involving any material aspect of an interview or publication can lead to a lawsuit.

So should you take your lawyer to your interviews after all? Not quite. The contract cases *should* teach journalists to be more careful in making promises—and to use lawyers when dealing with those rare news subjects who insist on written contracts.

But so far, except in the *Cohen* case, which involved an unusual departure from the journalistic tradition of keeping confidentiality promises, contract cases have not led to any serious media liabilities.

Most courts are likely to recognize that the primary promise a reporter makes to a news subject is fair treatment. If a reporter acts fairly, any breach of contract claimant is likely to have an uphill fight. So although plaintiffs are finding it easy to enter the courthouse with their trendy new breach of journalistic contract claims, they may nonetheless find it hard to exit with any kind of a victory in hand.

Reporters Versus Sources

When courtroom closings began occurring several years ago, news organizations gave their reporters wallet-sized cards printed with the statement to read when a closure occurred, to preserve media rights to a prompt hearing. Now, some new wallet cards for reporters may be needed. The new cards would contain warnings similar to Miranda warnings and would be called "McGinniss Warnings."

A McGinniss Warning might go like this:

> I am a reporter and you are a news source. Everything you say to me is on the record. Anything you say to me can and will be used against you.
>
> If you are a politician, you may lose your reelection campaign as a result of what you tell me.
>
> If you are a criminal suspect, you may lose your case, or your appeal, or otherwise be exposed, as a result of what you tell me.
>
> If you are a business person, you may lose customers, or find yourself a target of a government investigation, as a result of what you tell me.
>
> You have the right to consult your criminal, corporate, or bankruptcy attorney before you talk to me.

Sure, this recital may chill a few reporter-source interviews. But it would have saved Joe McGinniss $325,000.

McGinniss is the symbol of the reporter as confidence man. The story of his travails unfolded like the Russian dolls that each open only to reveal another doll within. There are about four levels to the McGinniss story-within-a-story.

The story began with McGinniss's reporting of the trial of Jeffrey MacDonald, a North Carolina physician accused of the murder of his wife and children. In a written contract, for the right to MacDonald's inside story, McGinniss agreed to give MacDonald a portion of his advance and royalties. During the trial, McGinniss participated as a writer and an official part of the MacDonald defense team. But eventually McGinniss became convinced of MacDonald's guilt. So did the jury, which convicted MacDonald.

McGinniss never told MacDonald that he thought he was guilty. Rather, McGinniss kept encouraging MacDonald to cooperate with him—and not to cooperate with other reporters. Even after the trial, McGinniss, in his correspondence and talks with MacDonald, led MacDonald to believe that he was his friend and supporter. That ended when McGinniss's book *Fatal Vision* was published. The book, which became a best seller and a television movie, portrayed MacDonald as a homicidal maniac.

Then the second story began: MacDonald, the convicted murderer, sued McGinniss for breach of contract, alleging that McGinniss had fraudulently induced MacDonald to cooperate with him and had violated his contractual agreement to write the book in a way that preserved the "essential integrity" of MacDonald's life story. When the breach of contract case was tried, it resulted in a hung jury, but little comfort for McGinniss. Five of the six jurors were ready to give MacDonald the multimillion dollar verdict he requested. Before any retrial, McGinniss settled by paying MacDonald a reported $325,000.

The third level of the story unfolded when the *New Yorker* magazine published a two-part article by staff writer Janet Malcolm, which portrayed the McGinniss-MacDonald relationship as a paradigm of the reporter-source relationship. Malcolm later published the articles as a book, *The Journalist and the Murderer*.

In the articles, Malcolm wrote that a reporter such as McGinniss is necessarily a kind of "confidence man," who must deceive his news subject into believing that his intentions are kind and friendly, when in fact they are antagonistic.

The Malcolm story raised a controversy. Few reporters relish a "confidence man" self-image. And there was yet another unusual twist—a fourth story within the story. Malcolm, it developed, had herself been accused of the same kind of conduct as McGinniss. She had even been taken to court by a subject of a book she had written, who claimed that she had misrepresented her intentions and feelings in her interviews with him.

Considering all these permutations, the MacDonald-McGinniss-

Malcolm saga might aptly be called "Three Wrongdoers Pointing Fingers at Each Other." MacDonald, the convicted-murderer-turned-civil-plaintiff, is an unsympathetic figure. And a reader of Malcolm's piece quickly develops a distaste for the conduct of McGinniss—only to find, in reading *about* Malcolm's article, that she may have acted very much as McGinniss did.

Thus, the Malcolm piece, far from illustrating a regular problem of journalism, describes instead a most unusual problem. While there may be some element of insincerity in the reporter-source relationship, Malcolm certainly goes too far when she claims that reporters are necessarily confidence men who actively seek to mislead and deceive their sources. Particularly in daily beat reporting where reporters depend on the trust and confidence of their sources, McGinniss-like behavior would not work and is not the norm.

And even most reporters who specialize in one-time investigative books and articles are mindful enough of their own reputation and self-esteem so that they do not use deception as their primary news-gathering technique.

Indeed, the Malcolm thesis is far overstated, even for those instances when a reporter knows that his article will portray the source unfavorably. Sources often feel a compulsion to speak and will give their story even to potentially antagonistic reporters without any deceitful encouragement. Reporters can usually get interviews and information from such persons simply by asking neutral questions, without actively encouraging the source to feel that the reporter is his advocate. The skill of maintaining and conveying a sense of neutrality is one of the basic working tools of a good journalist. The McGinniss approach (or is it the Malcolm approach?) is probably limited to a very few reporters and a few unusual situations.

Moreover, few journalists face the potential legal liability that occurred in McGinniss's case. McGinniss entered into a special business arrangement—a written contract—with MacDonald. In that contract, he agreed to write his book in a way that "maintained the essential integrity" of MacDonald's life story. No wonder he encountered problems when he surprised his business partner MacDonald with his harshly critical book.

The deceived-source suit against Malcolm was different, and was dismissed before trial because she, like most reporters, had no such special written contract with her source. (Other claims in that suit, alleging libel, raised serious issues and led to a Supreme Court ruling and two trials.)

The typical journalistic interview situation, by contrast with the McGinniss and Malcolm situations, includes neither a written contract nor a reporter inclined to deliberately deceive the source. So, luckily, most reporters probably won't have to carry McGinniss Warning cards after all. But Joe McGinniss, and perhaps Janet Malcolm, still ought to consider carrying the card. Although it will set their interviews off to a rocky start, it may save them a lot in legal fees.

Libel

Fact and Opinion

"AMERICANS HAVE BEEN HURLING EPITHETS AT each other for generations," a federal judge noted some years ago.

The sharply worded opinion, the critical commentary, and the uninhibited point-counterpoint are woven into the fabric of our national life. They define part of what it is to be an American: "It's a free country, and I'm entitled to express my opinion."

Each period of our history has seen its own opinions and epithets, as the federal judge quoted above noted: "From charging 'Copperhead' during the Civil War, we have come down [in the 1960s] to 'Racist', 'Pig', 'Fascist', 'Red', 'Pinko', 'Nigger Lover', 'Uncle Tom', and such."

The discourse of the latter part of the twentieth century has its own distinctive kinds of name-calling and opinion:

- "Sleaze bag," said of a sports agent in Louisiana who allegedly "kind of slimed up from the bayou"
- "Con artists" who were "part of an international network of medical quackery," said of certain physicians in Chicago

- "Barbarian," "lunkhead," "dictator and Nazi," said of a police officer by a citizen
- "Sleazy dealings" and "sleazy sleight-of-hand" said of a St. Louis attorney and politician
- "Card cheat," an accusation made as part of a quarrel among bridge players in St. Louis County
- The claim by an opponent of sex education in Missouri public schools, that an Independence, Missouri, teacher "derives probably a very secret sort of sexual gratification" from teaching that subject

The list could go on and on. Colorful and sharply worded opinions are part of our local and national discourse.

And most courts that addressed the issue between the mid-1970s and the late 1980s concluded that opinions are outside the reach of libel law. Libel, they concluded, deals only with false statements of fact. Thus, opinions, which are not fact and cannot be proven true or false, cannot be the basis of a libel claim. But the United States Supreme Court never ruled directly on that issue until 1990, in the case of *Milkovich v. Lorain Journal*.

The plaintiff, Michael Milkovich, was a high school wrestling coach whose team was declared ineligible for a state tournament because of a fight at a wrestling match. A sports columnist for the local newspaper, the *Willoughby (Ohio) News Herald*, covered the hearing at which Milkovich and his school superintendent, H. Don Scott, testified. The writer didn't believe the two officials' testimony and said so, writing in his column, "Anyone who attended [the meet at which the fight occurred] knows in his heart that Milkovich and Scott lied at the hearing after each having given his solemn oath to tell the truth."

Scott and Milkovich both sued for libel. Eventually, the Ohio Supreme Court ruled in Scott's case that the statement, properly analyzed under all the circumstances, was an assertion of opinion, not fact, and therefore not actionable as libel. A lower court followed that ruling in the *Milkovich* case and dismissed that suit, too. The rulings by the Ohio courts in these cases were fairly standard, consistent with the way most state and federal courts had handled "opinion" issues for many years.

For a number of years, most state and federal courts analyzed commentaries like this as opinions, not fact, based on their wording, context, and overall feel. Accordingly, libel suits based on such commentaries had been dismissed, often at early stages in the litigation, on the principle that libel requires a false statement of fact, and opinions can never be false.

Most courts, including the Missouri Supreme Court in an often-cited 1985 opinion, recognized and considered many different factors as bearing on the issue of whether something was fact or opinion. The particular words used—like "liar" in the *Milkovich* case—were not determinative. This "totality of the circumstances" test tended to protect columns and editorials, which are known by their nature to involve opinions.

As support for this rule, most courts cited a nonbinding statement made by the Supreme Court in 1974: "There is no such thing as a false idea. However pernicious an opinion may seem, we depend for its correction not on the conscience of judges and juries but on the competition of other ideas." But that Supreme Court "dictum" (a comment made in passing that was not essential to the decision at hand) had been, in the eyes of the Supreme Court in 1990, significantly misinterpreted by lower courts.

When the *Milkovich* case reached the U.S. Supreme Court, that Court laid down a new federal constitutional rule concerning liability for opinions: The more outrageous your opinions, in style and content, the more likely they are to be protected.

This is an oversimplification, but not by much. The Court's ruling in *Milkovich v. Lorain Journal Co.* divided up the universe of opinion, a field that had been afforded nearly complete protection from libel laws. Commentary that uses concrete words and facts and understated expression—the kind that really makes you think—after *Milkovich*, can, for the most part, subject the speaker to a full-fledged multimillion-dollar libel suit. But overstated and grossly exaggerated rhetoric—even when it uses highly charged words like "blackmail," "treason," and "rape"—remains fully protected.

In the sports column at issue in *Milkovich*, the writer suggested that a local high school coach involved in a controversy about a fight at a wrestling meet misled a court as to what had really happened. It was a formula column along the lines of "Mr. Big got away with something."

The Supreme Court, in its decision written by Chief Justice William Rehnquist, rejected a broad scope for protection of opinion as a matter of federal constitutional law and adopted a narrower one, focusing on whether a commentary contains specific factual assertions, explicit or implicit. Under the new rule, only pure opinions that can never be proven right or wrong (like "Reagan was our greatest president") and inflated rhetoric (like "You're a traitor for not supporting the flag amendment") are exempt from suit.

The Court's decision created some serious problems, not just on the editorial page, but also in businesses, schools, and other institutions.

Participants in today's information-based society need the ability to communicate freely and effectively and to influence the resolution of important issues. Decision makers frequently depend on low-key, thoughtful, and fact-based opinions and analyses. Commentators in newspapers, magazines, and books, in particular, need to be able to express opinions in order to give readers what Walter Lippmann described as "a picture of the world upon which men can act." Factual reporting alone cannot create a complete picture; commentary gives the picture the colors and shapes it needs in order to have real meaning.

As Justice William J. Brennan Jr. noted in his dissenting opinion, "Conjecture is intrinsic to the free flow of ideas." Justice Brennan gave some examples in his opinion:

> Did NASA officials ignore sound warnings that the Challenger Space Shuttle would explode? Did Cuban-American leaders arrange for John Fitzgerald Kennedy's assassination? Was Kurt Waldheim a Nazi officer? Such questions are matters of public concern long before all the facts are unearthed, if they ever are. Conjecture is a means of fueling a national discourse on such questions and stimulating public pressure for answers from those who know more.

On the opinion issue, the seven-member Supreme Court majority in *Milkovich* may have been out of line with the thinking of most state and federal judges. Most lower courts readily embraced a broad constitutional protection for opinion, not only because it made sense as public policy but also because it winnowed out many needless libel suits.

The Supreme Court's ruling in *Milkovich* is binding as a matter of federal constitutional law. But it did not necessarily mark the end of the matter. State courts under our system have the power to grant greater protection for opinion under their interpretations of their respective state constitutions. In light of their own prior decisions, recognizing the social importance of commentary and opinion, several state courts have taken up this task and essentially reinstated the broader pre-*Milkovich* rule in their own jurisdictions.

New York State's highest court, for example, shortly after *Milkovich* ruled that the old pre-*Milkovich* opinion doctrine reflected sound policies that could be traced back to many New York precedents, including several celebrated cases involving James Fenimore Cooper. That court therefore adopted the broad immunity for opinion as a matter of *New York* constitutional law. Several other states, including Utah in 1994, have reached similar conclusions and adopted the broad opinion doctrine as a matter of state constitutional law.

By taking these steps, these leading state courts have not only reinstated a sound and workable rule in libel cases. They have also begun the important job of making the bills of rights and free speech guaranties of state constitutions not merely echoes of the federal Bill of Rights but meaningful substantive sources of liberties in their own right.

Opinion in Critical Reviews

A court decision:

- inhibited free speech and debate
- misunderstood journalistic standards
- "played 'chicken' with the First Amendment"
- neglected "long and rich cultural traditions"
- "failed to understand" the critical genre
- "wreaked havoc on the law of defamation"
- was just plain "misguided"

There goes the press, you suppose—overreacting again to some court ruling on libel or privacy.

Not this time. Some of the comments above were indeed from press criticism of a federal appeals court's decision in *Moldea v. New York Times*, a libel suit based on a critical book review. But most of them came from a different source—*the appeals court itself*, in its startling decision, reversing its prior decision. In its revised decision the court held, contrary to its initial decision, that the *Times* book review in issue was, after all, constitutionally protected as opinion. This kind of judicial *mea culpa* doesn't happen very often.

The case involved a book review, in the *Times*'s regular Sunday book review section, of Dan Moldea's book *Interference: How Organized Crime Influences Professional Football*. The review concluded that Moldea's book contained "too much sloppy journalism," revived "discredited" claims, drew unwarranted inferences from facts, and generally just "warmed over" old information.

Moldea sued for libel. He claimed the review falsely disparaged his competence as an investigative journalist, discouraged sales of the book, and effectively ended his journalistic career. More than four years earlier, the case would have been quickly dismissed. At that time, and for more than a decade before, lower courts had developed strong protection for all statements of "opinion." If allegedly libelous language was comment or opinion, not a factual assertion, the case was usually dismissed.

The Supreme Court changed that in 1990, ruling in *Milkovich v. Lorain Journal* that not all statements of opinion are protected. Statements couched in terms of opinion that *imply defamatory facts* can be libelous, the court held. At the other extreme, statements that are clearly *only* opinion, like overcharged and exaggerated rhetoric, remain protected as opinion. That ruling left lower courts, after 1990, with the task of distinguishing between two kinds of opinion—opinions that are just vehicles for making factual charges (which can be sued on) and opinions that everyone knows are only opinions (which can't be sued on).

The distinction made by the Supreme Court in *Milkovich* is not difficult to understand, at the extremes. After all, one can imply defamatory facts even while using the format of an opinion. A classic case is an assertion such as, "I think my neighbor is an alcoholic." Any reasonable listener would assume the speaker had observed facts—like excessive drinking or drunken behavior—that supported that conclusion. If the statement is false, the speaker can't use the words "I think" to shield himself from a libel suit.

At the other extreme, some statements of opinion are obviously so overdrawn, exaggerated, or rhetorical that they are never reasonably understood as factual claims. Example: An irate citizen at a city council hearing claims that a developer is engaging in "blackmail" and "extortion" because it won't make landscaping concessions unless it is guaranteed a zoning variance.

Between the two extremes, however, it isn't so easy to distinguish opinion-as-implied-fact from opinion-as-opinion. That's why the *Mol-*

dea case was difficult for the court. To oversimplify somewhat, and focus solely on the key allegation involving the "sloppy journalism" phrase, the court had to decide if that phrase was an implied assertion that Moldea was an incompetent journalist or merely an overstated way of saying that the reviewer disagreed with his judgments and conclusions.

In its initial decision, the court's two-judge majority concluded that "sloppiness" implied factual, measurable, critical journalistic shortcomings. Then—critically—the court ruled that unless the review set forth true facts proving that Moldea committed those shortcomings, the review was actionable. This put the *Times* in a practically untenable position— it had to prove its reviewer correct, on matters (like interpretation of the significance of incidents relayed in Moldea's book) that the reviewer and *Times* considered *judgment calls*, not black-and-white truth or falsity.

In its rehearing petition, the *Times* hammered hard on the impracticality of the court's analysis, in the context of a critical review. If the test is reader understanding of the statement as a fact or opinion, the *Times* urged, then the *context* of a critical review ought to be considered. In a review, readers don't expect opinions backed up by *proven facts*; they expect as backup only *reasonable judgments*. Hence, the *Times* argued, in the case of a review, opinions should not be found to imply defamatory facts when the review reveals some *reasonable judgments*—not necessarily provable facts—in support.

The *Times* position on rehearing was strong, cogent, and reasonable. But rehearing requests rarely succeed, and it was remarkable that this one did. Judge Harry Edwards of the U.S. Court of Appeals for the District of Columbia Circuit, who wrote the initial decision and the later self-reversal, acknowledged error and adopted the *Times*'s standard for assessing opinion in the context of a critical review.

The new *Moldea* rule held, in essence, that if a statement of opinion in a critical review implies defamatory facts, it is nonetheless nonactionable if the review reveals judgments, supportable by the book under scrutiny, that could reasonably support the reviewer's opinion. Though the decision was confined to critical reviews, it may be extended in future cases to articles of commentary and other traditional forums for opinions.

Along with his own *mea culpas*, Judge Edwards agreed with the *Times* on the critical point that in reviews readers *expect* opinion, and hence analysis of whether a charge implies defamatory facts is somewhat different in a review context and another context. Following the Supreme

Court's policy direction in *Milkovich* hence requires more sophisticated tools of analysis than the Supreme Court laid out in that decision.

Judge Edwards's second decision also indicated—as lower courts recognized in many of their pre-*Milkovich* rulings—that often the fact/opinion distinction rests on policy issues and judgments as to whether to afford free speech extra "breathing space" in close-call situations.

The court's stunning reversal in this case highlights the interpretative difficulties involved in libel suits based on statements of "opinion," particularly in the case of critical reviews. To a lesser extent, it shows that distinguishing between *fact* and *opinion* is no simple mechanical task; it truly involves judgment and, to some extent, policy determinations.

Not surprisingly, for many, this incident only increases the yearning for those good old days when *most* opinion, not just *some* opinion, was protected.

Privileges for Witnesses and Reporters

Denise Sinner, a young woman on trial in St. Louis in 1988 for embezzling funds from a prominent St. Louis law firm, desperately tried to create a defense or excuse for her actions. First, she claimed that she was dying of cancer. But the authorities checked that story out and found that it was a fabrication. Then she made another claim—that the senior partner of the firm, the late John Shepherd, had had an affair with her and permitted her to steal the money. That story had many holes in it, too. The St. Louis Circuit Court jury didn't believe her and found her guilty beyond a reasonable doubt.

End of story? Not quite. Shortly after the trial, Shepherd was nominated by President Reagan to become deputy attorney general. And the charges made by Sinner—wild, unproven, and discredited though they were—became centerpieces in the national press's reporting on Shepherd.

Indeed, Sinner, despite her history of lies and her embezzlement conviction, became a fifteen-minute national celebrity, appearing on *Good Morning America* and in *Time* magazine. And Shepherd eventually chose to decline the nomination rather than subject himself to more of Sinner's accusations.

Realistically, Sinner's accusations against Shepherd were false. St. Louis Circuit Judge Thomas Mummert characterized Sinner when he sentenced her as a "pathological liar," and an examination of her background by the *St. Louis Post-Dispatch* provided much evidence to support this conclusion.

Does this mean that Shepherd could have sued either Sinner for the damage she caused to his reputation or the local media that publicized her allegations? After all, false accusations that damage someone's good reputation are the essence of libel and slander.

No. Two privileges in defamation law cover the situation and allow such statements, and reporting of them, to be made without fear of liability.

The first privilege is that of a witness in a judicial proceeding. A witness who testifies at a trial is given an absolute privilege to speak freely, without fear of later being sued for slander. The privilege also applies to judges, attorneys, jurors, and parties to litigation. The reason for this privilege, as explained by the Missouri Supreme Court in a leading case in 1942, is that in such cases "it is to the public interest that one should be permitted to speak freely and fully without being brought to account for injuring another's reputation in doing so."

Judicial proceedings, therefore (such as the Sinner embezzlement trial, where she made her accusations against Shepherd), can be conducted in the most thorough and complete manner in order to achieve justice. The privilege promotes this end by letting trial participants know that they can speak and testify freely, without fear that they will be sued by persons they offend in the course of the trial.

The privilege for participants in judicial proceedings is a broad one and has only a few exceptions. For example, a Missouri court has held that even *perjured* testimony is privileged; the witness can be prosecuted for perjury for it but not sued for slander because of it. In order to be privileged, a statement need only to be made in the course of a judicial proceeding and must be pertinent to that proceeding. Statements made in pretrial phases of litigation, as well as at trial, are usually covered by the privilege, although this varies a bit from state to state. And "pertinence" is usually viewed broadly; even many statements that eventually are ruled not relevant or admissible evidence at trial will be covered by the privilege because they are generally pertinent to the matters being examined in the case.

About the only real exception to the privilege is that one cannot institute a judicial proceeding for the sole purpose of attempting to defame someone under the shield of the judicial proceeding privilege. Thus, Sinner's accusations against Shepherd, even though false and defamatory, could not become the basis for a slander suit because of the judicial proceeding privilege.

The *reporting* of Sinner's accusations falls in a somewhat different category. The press is not covered by the privilege that protects witnesses, judges, attorneys, and jurors. Rather, the press relies on the "official report" or "fair report" privilege, which protects reporting of official government proceedings.

Reporters rely daily on the official reporting privilege. Any day's newspaper or news broadcast will include many items—defamatory but not actionable because of the official report privilege—reporting statements made in the course of trials, legislative debates, government briefings, and reports of official investigations.

The official report privilege, like the judicial proceeding privilege, is based on considerations of sound public policy. Just as it is important for trial participants to speak freely, it is important for reporters to be able to report freely on trials and other official proceedings—even when the reporting is of defamatory statements.

In order for the official report privilege to protect a news report, the news report must be a fair and accurate account of the official government proceeding. This does not require a bland "he said . . . she said" summary of the trial; it is permissible, and expected, for the press to report only those matters it deems of interest (such as Sinner's accusations against Shepherd). The press is liable only if its news account significantly distorts or goes beyond what was said in the official proceeding.

In short, the Sinner case was a textbook example of two defamation privileges at work. Sinner was permitted to testify freely at her embezzlement trial, without fear of a suit by Shepherd. And the press was similarly free from defamation liability for its accurate reporting of that testimony.

These privileges obviously permit many unfounded and unfortunate allegations to be aired. But they reflect the preference in our law for thorough, fair trials and for public knowledge and discussion of all matters relating to the administration of justice.

Trials and the Press

According to the popular folklore, the media usually lose libel cases at trial but ultimately win them on appeal. Two decisions in 1987, in libel suits against the *Washington Post* and the *Belleville (Illinois) News-*

Democrat, provided a test of this folklore. The two cases had some similar elements:

- Plaintiffs were a "public figure" and a "public official," subject to the most stringent constitutional hurdles in libel suits.
- Both cases went to trial, unlike the great majority of libel cases that are dismissed or settled before trial.
- Both plaintiffs primarily sought vindication, but both initially won huge money judgments.
- After trial, both news organizations put their hopes in the appellate process.

The decisions, both announced in March 1987, were good news for the *Post*—complete reversal of a $2.05 million judgment—and mixed news for the *News-Democrat*—affirmation of the judgment, but reduction of its amount from $1.05 million to $200,000.

In the *Post* case, conducted in the federal courts in the District of Columbia, William Tavoulareas, president of Mobil Corporation, and his son Peter, sued the paper over an investigative report by *Post* staffer Patrick Tyler. In the article, Tyler wrote that Tavoulareas had "set up" Peter in an international oil shipping business.

The *Post* story was essentially correct and had been carefully researched and edited. William Tavoulareas had helped to establish oil shipping arrangements that benefited his son, transforming Peter Tavoulareas from a $14,000-a-year clerk to a majority owner of a lucrative international venture. Tavoulareas claimed, however, that he was not guilty of legal or corporate misconduct and that the article was false in some details and in its overall implication of wrongdoing.

Legally, Tavoulareas had a heavy burden. Under constitutional libel law, he had to prove, among other things, that the story was *substantially false* and that the *Post* published it with either knowledge of falsity or serious doubts as to its truth. Moreover, the latter point (the issue that is sometimes known as "constitutional malice") had to be proven with "clear and convincing evidence"—the heaviest burden of proof in the civil law.

The case was tried in July 1982 and seesawed throughout its course:

- First, the jury found for Tavoulareas against the *Post*, awarding $2.05 million in damages.
- Next, the trial judge set aside the verdict.

- Third, a three-judge appeals panel, in a 2–1 decision, reinstated the verdict. This decision, joined in by Judge Antonin Scalia before his elevation to the Supreme Court, took the extreme position that a newspaper's penchant for investigative reporting can constitute evidence of "reckless disregard for the truth."
- Then, after a rehearing, the full appeals court (in a 7–1 decision) reversed the panel decision and reinstated the trial judge's decision.

In essence, the final ruling held that the *Post* article meant what it said, that Tavoulareas "set up" his son and was correct about that. Moreover, the *Post* could not be liable for the defamatory *implications* charged by Tavoulareas because the article never made those implications. Finally, the court held one aspect of the story false (the accusation that Tavoulareas initially brought Peter into the deal) but said the evidence was clear that the *Post*, after extensive research, had a basis for this statement and believed it. Thus, the majority held, there was no constitutional malice.

Neither a penchant for investigative reporting nor "adversarial stances" taken by reporters (what the dissent called an "antagonistic mindset") evidence constitutional malice because neither is inconsistent with the newspaper's belief in the truth of its report, according to the majority opinion.

One obvious conclusion from the *Post* case might be that the folklore is right: juries are bad for the press in libel cases. The jurors in the *Post* case apparently decided the case on their emotions, sympathizing with Tavoulareas, a man criticized in print for helping his son. There is good evidence, from posttrial interviews of the *Post* jurors, that they never understood the complex and heavy legal burdens on Tavoulareas. Instead, they followed their own inclinations and reversed the burdens of proof, treating the *Post* as if it were a public prosecutor in a criminal case.

Indeed, Judge Ruth Bader Ginzburg (who participated in the appeal before her elevation to the Supreme Court) noted in her concurring opinion that in libel cases jurors "can easily misunderstand more law in a minute than the judge can explain in an hour." She devoted her opinion to discussing the need for new techniques to make constitutional libel law understandable to a jury.

If juries are the problem, however, does that mean judges are the solution? Perhaps not. In the *Post* case, the judges, who unlike the jury understood the law, nonetheless differed on the wisdom and scope of the constitutional protections for the press. The two judges who would have ruled against the *Post* (including Justice Scalia) reflect a growing minority position that would cut back on press protections. The constitutional malice doctrine created by the Supreme Court in 1964 must be *interpreted* to be applied, and as the *Post* case shows, the very same evidence that liberal judges (the majority in the final *Tavoulareas* decision) view as journalistic carefulness may be seen by conservative judges (the minority) as reportorial recklessness.

For a view of a libel case decided only by judges, we can examine an interim ruling, handed down the same month as the final *Tavoulareas* decision, in the libel case brought by Jerry Costello against the *Belleville (Illinois) News-Democrat*. The suit, filed when Costello was St. Clair County Board chairman, complained of an editorial that accused him of lying by failing to keep a campaign promise that he would vigorously oppose new taxes.

The editorial opened with the sentence, "Jerry Costello lied to us," and went on to criticize Costello harshly for not preventing the establishment of a new taxing district. The *News-Democrat* editorial charged that Costello had broken "his most sacred campaign promise" and concluded that "we've got two more years of the Costello brand of lying leadership."

In his suit, Costello claimed that he did oppose the new tax district but that as county board chairman (without a vote on the board) he could not have prevented it. The *News-Democrat* asserted that Costello could have done more to stop the tax and, anyway, the newspaper was only fulfilling the classic role of a newspaper editorial—expressing an opinion about the area's leading political figure.

Costello, as a public official, had the same heavy burden as Tavoulareas—indeed, greater, because the Illinois courts required him to prove both constitutional malice and falsity by "clear and convincing" proof.

Initially, Costello's complaint was dismissed by the trial judge on the grounds that the accusation "liar" was not defamatory. The Illinois Appellate Court reversed this, requiring a trial. Both sides then submitted to a bench trial, and in March 1985, St. Clair County Associate Circuit Judge Roger M. Scrivner ruled against the *News-Democrat*, awarding Costello $1.05 million in damages. Then, in a 2–1 decision written by Appellate Justice Charles E. Jones of McLeansboro, the Illinois Appellate Court affirmed the judgment but reduced damages to $200,000.

As in the *Post* case, the issues were the meaning of the allegedly defamatory language, the truth of what was published, and constitutional malice. Even without a jury, however, and even after the initial appeal, the *News-Democrat* was the loser.

The appeals court majority and the trial judge both rejected the newspaper's argument that the editorial expressed constitutionally protected *opinions*, not defamatory *facts*. On this crucial issue, the appeals court refused to adopt an absolute protection for opinion. The majority also interpreted the editorial as a charge that Costello single-handedly could have prevented the new tax and thus found it false.

In a very brief discussion, the appeals court found that Costello had overcome the difficult constitutional malice barrier. The court, again relying on the distinction that Costello's powers on the St. Clair County Board were such that he could not have prevented the tax, concluded that the editorial writers knew their accusations were false. Finally, the appeals court reviewed the $1.05 million damages judgment, found it excessive, and reduced it to $200,000.

Judge Robert J. Steigmann, a trial judge from Decatur, Illinois, specially sitting on the appeals court, wrote an impassioned fifty-page dissent on the opinion issue, arguing that the *News-Democrat* editorial was classic constitutionally protected opinion, especially considering "the high purpose criticism of government serves in a democracy."

The folklore that appeals courts and judges are on the media's side obviously failed in the *News-Democrat* case at the trial and initial appellate levels. Why? Perhaps the folklore is just that—a useful but imperfect generalization.

The split appeals court in *Costello*, and the majority's limited view of the protections for editorializing, demonstrate that the media cannot always count on appellate reversal, even of results that some (like Judge Steigmann) view as shocking and outrageous. The *News-Democrat* ultimately won its battle, in the Illinois Supreme Court. But as the *News-Democrat* and the *Washington Post* learned in March 1987, and throughout their long cases, once a newspaper loses a libel trial, it has a long and difficult road to travel to vindication.

Constitutional Privilege

"When *I* use a word," said Humpty Dumpty in Lewis Carroll's classic *Through the Looking-Glass*, "it means just what I choose it to mean—

neither more nor less." Humpty Dumpty's theory of word meanings explains much about one of the most confusing phrases in law—the phrase *actual malice* that is used in libel law.

Ask any hundred persons what *malice* means and most will give answers like "spite," "ill will," "hatred," "meanness," "intention to injure," and "evil motives." For hundreds of years, the word *malice* was used in libel law in just that way. But when libel law was revolutionized by the United States Supreme Court in 1964, a totally different definition of *malice* was created. And libel law has been bedeviled by misunderstanding of malice ever since.

An excellent example of that bewilderment, which even courts face, is the libel suit brought by Jerry Costello against the *Belleville (Illinois) News-Democrat*. After an eight-year journey through the court system, involving two separate trips to appellate courts, the *News-Democrat* won the suit. The grounds for the newspaper's final victory were that it acted without "actual malice"—even though two lower courts, examining the same evidence, were convinced that there *was* malice.

The best place to begin this story is with the days when "malice" meant "malice." Malice in the sense that we normally understood it was an important concept in the early development of English law. In libel law, the presence or absence of malice—in the ordinary sense of ill will— was often important on issues such as privilege and damage.

For example, many privileges in libel and slander law historically protected speech only when the speaker or writer lacks malice, in the ill will sense. Thus, many routine business communications were privileged and could not support a libel or slander suit unless they were motivated by spite or ill will. This sense of malice became known as *common law malice*, since that was the sense in which the word *malice* was used in the common judge-made law of England.

In America, as English law was adopted and modified, malice in the sense of ill will continued to play an important role. But American courts, perhaps following moralistic impulses, ultimately refined and expanded legal doctrines of malice and came to distinguish among *degrees* of malice, ranging from common ill will, to intention to injure, to the highest form of malice, sometimes known as *actual malice*, which involved the most culpable and intentional wrongful conduct.

Courts then applied these different degrees of malice in different situations. In libel law, different states used different malice definitions, and a few of them created special privileges to protect speech about public officials except when the speaker acted with the knowing culpability that those courts were calling "actual malice."

Enter the Supreme Court. In 1964, in the landmark case of *New York Times v. Sullivan*, the United States Supreme Court injected *constitutional* defenses into libel law. The Court, in *New York Times*, desired to limit libel suits by public officials. To accomplish this, the Court needed to set a legal standard. The standard chosen—regrettably from the viewpoint of clarity and understanding—was the requirement derived from some state law precedents of proving that the speaker made his statement with the high level of knowing culpability called *actual malice*.

New York Times imposed a rule that public officials (later expanded to public figures, too) could not recover in libel or slander unless they proved that the reporter acted with, in the Supreme Court's words, "actual malice—that is, with knowledge that it was false, or with reckless disregard of whether it was false or not."

At this point, Humpty Dumpty's process was complete. The usage of malice had gone from the common definition of the word to a definition—knowledge of falsity or reckless disregard of truth or falsity—that practically *no one* would naturally associate with the word. As one forthright federal judge has noted: "When the Supreme Court uses a word, it means what the Court wants it to mean. 'Actual Malice' is now a term of art having nothing to do with actual malice."

Even the Supreme Court has now acknowledged (in a 1991 decision) that the phrase "actual malice" is an "unfortunate" choice of words, one that "can confuse as well as enlighten."

That is where the law of libel stands. Public officials and public figures cannot prevail in libel or slander suits without proving this special kind of actual malice. But *what is* actual malice? Does it embrace or suggest or relate to the common definition of malice? Is it a fancy way of describing negligence or recklessness or some other more familiar liability standard?

In fact, it is *none* of those, but a standard unique to libel law, requiring the highest form of culpable conduct—knowing falsehood—before liability can be imposed. It is a *subjective* standard, relating to what the defendant himself believed about what he said or wrote. It is not governed, for example, by what it would be reasonable for someone to believe.

Not only reporters, editors, and public figures but also lawyers and judges are frequently confused by this standard. The *Costello* case is a graphic example. In 1983, Costello, then the newly elected St. Clair County board chairman, took offense at a *News-Democrat* editorial that accused him of reneging on a campaign promise. He sued for libel. The *News-Democrat* raised, among other defenses, the *New York Times* actual malice defense.

The first two courts that examined the evidence at trial found that there *was* sufficient evidence of actual malice by the *News-Democrat*. The trial judge essentially concluded after trial in 1985 that the *News-Democrat*, in holding Costello responsible for a tax increase, made a "woeful and inadequate" check into the facts and may even have been "maliciously predisposed" to defame Costello. This, he found, constituted actual malice. A two-judge majority on the Illinois Appellate Court in 1987 found actual malice for a somewhat different reason—that the *News-Democrat* must have known that Costello opposed the tax increase the editorial said he condoned.

However, the Illinois Supreme Court ultimately unanimously concluded that actual malice had *not* been proven, and both lower courts had misunderstood the standard. Although both lower courts had avoided confusing actual malice with ill will, the state supreme court found that they had nonetheless erred by equating it with recklessness and unreasonable conduct.

Actual malice does not mean *malice* and it does not mean *recklessness*, either. Rather, either prong of actual malice—knowledge of falsity or reckless disregard of the truth—requires proof, in the U.S. Supreme Court's language from a 1968 decision, that the defendant "in fact entertained serious doubt" as to the truth of his statements.

The evidence showed that the *News-Democrat* editors never doubted the thrust of their editorial—that Costello had condoned a tax increase and broken his campaign promise—so actual malice had not been shown. The facts on which the lower courts relied, indicating that the editors *should have known* differently and *should have checked* more carefully, were simply irrelevant to the editors' actual beliefs, and hence to actual malice.

By virtue of the Illinois Supreme Court's ruling, Costello's libel case, which lasted almost his full eight-year term as St. Clair County board chairman, was over. But the confusion about and misunderstanding of actual malice, which have troubled thousands of litigants and cases, are likely to persist and to present more litigants and courts with the problems inherent in an unusual and confusing use of words.

Fault, Semantics, and Altered Quotations

Topics that are ideal for seminars on journalistic ethics may be less than ideal for Supreme Court decisions. After all, provocative seminar discussions are just that—discussions. Review by the Supreme Court of provocative issues can lead to something more significant and long-lasting—new constitutional law.

That, together with the conservative composition of the Supreme Court in the 1990s, is why the press was concerned about the case of *Masson v. The New Yorker*. As the case wound its way through the lower federal courts and the Supreme Court, and two trials, it raised uncomfortable and provocative issues. Among them:

- Should the First Amendment protect publication of deliberately altered or manufactured quotations that harm a public figure's reputation?
- Should deliberately fabricated quotations be excused, and considered not harmful, when the subject made other provocative or bombastic remarks?

The case concerned articles written by Janet Malcolm for *The New Yorker* magazine, concerning psychoanalyst Jeffrey Masson, who had been involved in a dispute with board members of the Sigmund Freud Archives. The articles contained numerous purported quotations of Masson. The trouble is that Masson claimed he never said many of the quotations that were attributed to him. And although Malcolm tape-recorded many of the interviews of Masson, the disputed quotations did not appear on any of the recordings.

To top it off, the alleged misquotations were pithy, colorful grabbers. At one point, Malcolm quoted Masson describing himself as an "intellectual gigolo." At another, he was quoted as planning to turn the scholarly Freud Archives into a place of "sex, women and fun." The final twist is that Malcolm, the author, had written a celebrated piece on journalistic ethics in which she suggested that journalists doing investigative profiles (like her piece on Masson) often and even necessarily deceive their subject-sources. All of these facts seemed to make *Masson v. The New Yorker* the press's nightmare of a Supreme Court case.

In the initial stages of the case in federal trial and appeals courts in San Francisco, Malcolm prevailed on a key legal issue. These courts ruled that even if Masson was misquoted, the misquotations were not so far off as to demonstrate that Malcolm published a knowing or reckless falsity.

Under the well-known rule of *New York Times v. Sullivan* and its progeny, such a high degree of fault (knowing falsity or reckless disregard of truth or falsity; sometimes known as *constitutional malice*) must be proven in any libel suit by a public figure like Masson. In public figure libel cases, it is always difficult for the plaintiff to prove this high degree of fault. It was *meant* to be this way, since the whole purpose of the *New York Times v. Sullivan* doctrine is to give journalists "breathing space" to write about newsworthy persons.

One of the most troublesome issues relating to this standard, however, is *how* constitutional malice is proven. In *Masson v. The New Yorker*, the plaintiff essentially argued that significant alteration of quotations, by itself, demonstrated that the reporter acted with knowing falsity or reckless disregard of the truth. He claimed that any adjustment of quotations by the reporter beyond those necessary to correct syntax evidenced constitutional malice.

The lower courts rejected this contention, after careful consideration of the facts of the case. They found that Malcolm's quotations of Masson, even if altered somewhat, were for the most part true to the *sense* of what he told her in the interviews or at least within the realm of *arguable interpretation* of his statements.

When Malcolm quoted Masson as saying that Freud developed a theory out of "moral cowardice," for example, she fairly portrayed Masson's thinking, since he had explained that Freud "lost his courage" and "didn't have the courage to stick with the things that he knew were true."

Even the "intellectual gigolo" and "sex, women and fun" quotations, though denied by Masson, were judged by the lower courts to be fair summaries of the substance of other admitted quotations in which he described himself and his plans for the Freud Archives or at least rational interpretations of things that he admittedly said. For these reasons, lower courts concluded that the allegedly altered quotations did not demonstrate knowing or reckless falsity.

There was, however, one significant qualification to Malcolm's victory in the court of appeals. While her position won the support of two of the three judges on the appeals panel, the dissenter was Judge Alex Kozinski, a well-respected and intellectual conservative. Kozinski's spirited dissent argued that altered quotations were prima facie evidence of knowing falsification. He characterized the defendant's position as arguing for "the right to lie in print," and he concluded that Masson should have been allowed to take his case to trial.

Not surprisingly in light of Kozinski's dissent and the troubling issues raised by a ruling that essentially exculpated limited fabrication of quotations, the U.S. Supreme Court decided to hear the case.

In its 1991 ruling, the Supreme Court, with Justice Anthony Kennedy writing for a seven-member majority, held that the significance of altered quotations must be judged against the traditional libel doctrine of substantial truth. Prior to reaching this conclusion, Justice Kennedy rejected simplistic rules offered by both sides.

The plaintiff's suggestion that reporters' quotations should be held to strict accuracy, excepting only corrections of grammar and syntax, was found unrealistic, given the realities of journalist-source dynamics and the frequent need of a reporter to reconstruct a source's statement from sketchy notes. Justice Kennedy noted: "The existence of both a speaker and a reporter; the translation between two media, speech and the printed word; the addition of punctuation; and the practical necessity to edit and make intelligible a speaker's perhaps rambling comments, all make it misleading to suggest that a quotation will be reconstructed with complete accuracy."

Similarly, the court majority rejected the appellate court majority's position that quotations were all right so long as they represented a "rational interpretation" of something the speaker said. This view, Justice Kennedy wrote, ignores the reality that readers give weight to quotation marks; they view purported quotations not as the writer's personal interpretation but as a more authoritative "direct account" from the speaker's mouth. Most graphically, Justice Kennedy held, "quotations may be a devastating instrument for conveying false meaning"; a self-condemnation in quotation marks carries far more weight with the reader than a condemnatory opinion in the writer's own narrative.

Based on these realities of journalism, language, and understanding, Justice Kennedy rejected both the plaintiff's approach and that of the court of appeals, for one that focused on a comparison of the core understanding of the quotations at issue with the underlying facts. This comparison is the heart of the long-standing substantial truth doctrine of libel law.

That doctrine holds that even a statement containing some minor inaccuracies may be permissible if the overall substance or essence of the statement—its "gist" or "sting"—is accurate. Justice Kennedy held that substantial truth was the test for determining constitutional malice based upon Malcolm's allegedly fabricated quotations. Deliberate alteration of quotations, he wrote, "does not equate with knowledge of falsity for purposes of *New York Times v. Sullivan* . . . unless the alteration results in a material change in the meaning conveyed by the statement."

If, due to reconstruction of incomplete notes, grammatical and syntactical infelicities, or other problems, the quotations in issue were inaccurate in some details—but nonetheless true to the speaker's basic message—then the alteration does not evidence constitutional malice. If, however, the quotations are so materially different from what the speaker said so as to leave a different effect on the mind of the reader—a different gist, sting, thrust, and substance—then the alteration may be used as evidence of constitutional malice.

Measured against this standard, the Supreme Court determined that five of the six statements in issue at that point in *Masson v. The New Yorker* could, if proven to have been altered, constitute evidence of constitutional malice.

The Supreme Court's ruling in *Masson v. The New Yorker* fully pleased neither Malcolm nor Masson. The ruling allowed Masson to get to trial on his libel claims and to submit the allegedly altered quotations to the jury as evidence of knowing or reckless falsity by Malcolm, but his first trial ended in a mistrial and he lost the second trial. Malcolm ultimately prevailed in a formal sense, but her journalistic credibility took a pounding, which even her posttrial discovery of long-lost notes may not effectively rehabilitate.

The audience beyond the litigants, however, ought not to be displeased with the ruling. The Supreme Court managed in *Masson v. The New Yorker* to navigate successfully the treacherous rapids where journalistic ethics and legal liability rush together. It did so by employing a sophisticated focus on how readers understand words and semantic devices, by taking note of the realistic exigencies of the craft of journalism, and by fashioning a legal test consistent with the two and with the purposes of libel law and free speech. Not a bad resolution of a seminar-perfect sticky issue of journalistic ethics and legal policy.

Libel and the Rehnquist Court

The Supreme Court of the 1980s and 1990s—the Rehnquist Court, for it has been led since 1986 by Chief Justice William Rehnquist—has been a conservative court, by nature unfriendly to the media and their pleas for expansive First Amendment rights. But its decisions have shown that while it intends to chip away at press liberties, and certainly not build them up, it also intends to leave the foundations of modern press freedoms in place.

Indications of this trend have surfaced for years and are particularly well reflected in the opinions of Chief Justice Rehnquist. For years, Rehnquist was the court's most conservative member (and frequent dissenter) on press freedoms. His views remained relatively constant, but as court personnel changed, they eventually came to represent those of the majority of justices.

Under the leadership of Justice William J. Brennan Jr., who retired in 1990, the Court in the Warren and early Burger years developed expansive First Amendment protections for the press. The keystone of these protections, of course, was Brennan's landmark 1964 decision in *New York Times v. Sullivan*, which put severe limitations on libel suits by public officials (later expanded to also include public figures).

But constitutional press freedoms did not stop with *Sullivan*, at least under the Brennan-influenced thinking of many judges and scholars. The "chilling effect" of libel suits, recognized in *Sullivan*, was considered to warrant a number of different protections for the press, including special solicitude for the press as to procedural issues like jurisdiction (where publishers and broadcasters could be sued) and pretrial motions (how readily judges should dismiss media defendants before trial). Rehnquist, who joined the court after *Sullivan* was established law, championed the opposite view—that the *Sullivan* rule alone (that public figures can prevail in libel suits only by showing knowing or reckless falsehoods) is sufficient to protect the press from the dangers of the "chilling effect." No other precautions are needed or appropriate, he has stated.

In 1984, for example, the Court confronted—and rejected—a rule accepted by many lower courts, that the First Amendment limited the ability of libel plaintiffs to sue media owners in states distant from their home base. Rehnquist wrote the decision for a unanimous court, calling such injection of First Amendment considerations in the jurisdictional analysis "double counting." His point was simple and obvious: the press enjoyed the protection of *Sullivan*, and that is all the protection it needs.

Rehnquist next squared off against an expansive view of press liberties in connection with the "opinion" exemption from libel that was readily adopted by most federal and state courts in the 1980s. In a dissent from a procedural vote in 1985, he sharply criticized the "opinion" exemption as a "meat axe" approach applied to "a very subtle and difficult question." Sure enough, when the "opinion" issue finally reached the court, in 1990, Rehnquist wrote the majority opinion, rejecting any broad exemption from opinion. He pointedly referred to *Sullivan* and other decisions as "adequately" securing press freedoms. By denying special protection for opinion, Rehnquist claimed to be "holding the balance true."

Similarly, in 1987, when the Court ruled on the unusual "emotional distress" case brought against *Hustler* magazine by the Reverend Jerry Falwell, Rehnquist wrote the decision and managed to decide in favor of the magazine without explicitly creating any blanket exemption from such creative tort theories. His approach, as might be expected, was to apply *Sullivan* (awkwardly, since *Sullivan* by its terms applied only to libel cases), treating it as the one and only constitutional protection for the press.

The oddest thing about Rehnquist's repeated focus on *Sullivan* as the sole constitutional protection for the press is that he quite obviously does not like the *Sullivan* decision. In a number of decisions, he has fought with Brennan, *Sullivan*'s author, as to its meaning, scope, and application to particular factual situations.

This tends to make press supporters uncomfortable. Having constitutional press freedoms narrowed down to *Sullivan*, and having Rehnquist and like-minded jurists as the chief interpreters of *Sullivan*, is a little bit like having the fox as the guardian of the chicken house. But so far the indications are that Rehnquist and the Rehnquist Court *will* stand guard behind *Sullivan*, even as they whittle away at, or reject, other constitutional protections for the press.

For all of the chief justice's criticism of many Warren Court landmarks, he has not chosen to make a frontal attack on *Sullivan*. Indeed, somewhat ironically, his own writings over the years have tied him fairly strongly to the position that *Sullivan* is the essential bedrock decision protecting press liberties. For that reason, it seems likely that the crucial press freedom protections recognized in *Sullivan* will withstand even the winds of change on the strongly conservative Rehnquist Court.

Reckless Disregard and the *Westmoreland* and *Sharon* Cases

A reader of Renata Adler's book *Reckless Disregard*, about the Westmoreland and Sharon libel trials, should not expect an objective account of those two celebrated trials or a fair critique of libel law in operation.

In one of the ironies that often occur when one journalist writes about another, Adler's account, which attempts to indict *Time* magazine and CBS News for poor reporting, is itself one-sided, overdrawn, and unreliable. The book will appeal to those who are inclined to criticize *Time* and CBS or who feel that American libel law gives the media an unfair advantage. But it does not provide a fair account of those two cases, or a fair insight into libel law. The two trials analyzed in *Reckless Disregard* were significant and unique.

General William Westmoreland's case put CBS's documentary "The Uncounted Enemy: A Vietnam Deception" on trial. In the documentary, CBS attempted to describe and document a "conspiracy" at the highest levels of U.S. military intelligence to deceive the president and the nation about the size of the enemy in Vietnam.

Israeli general Ariel Sharon's case, against *Time*, complained of a rather opaque passage in the magazine, characterizing a secret appendix to an official Israeli inquiry report, which (at least in Sharon's reading) accused Sharon of encouraging conduct that led to a massacre in Lebanon.

By coincidence, both cases went to trial at about the same time in the same federal courthouse in New York City in the winter of 1984–85. The jury ultimately ruled against Sharon, though it did find that *Time*'s article concerned Sharon and was false. Westmoreland dropped his suit against CBS only a few weeks before it would have gone to the jury.

Undeniably, the two trials present a fascinating case study—an opportunity to explore not only their subject matter but also the significant issue of how the plaintiffs, the press, and the courts fare when libel cases go to trial.

It is a shame, therefore, that Adler's account is so one-sided. Consider, for example, her initial analysis of the two news reports in issue.

As to CBS: "the thesis that underlay [the documentary] was, of course, preposterous." As to *Time*: "every element of the story is totally and self-evidently preposterous." From this starting point, she goes on to use practically every deprecatory adjective in the dictionary to describe the witnesses, lawyers, and legal strategies for *Time* and CBS. Thus, the book is not so much a journalistic account, as an advocate's remaking of the trials—attempting to make in print the case that the plaintiffs' lawyers failed to achieve in the courtroom.

Adler's advocate's approach colors everything—her conclusions about *Time* and CBS, her assessment of libel law, and even her reporting of the attorneys' trial tactics and strategies. For example, Adler seems to resent the skillfulness of the defendants' attorneys, and she frequently makes excuses for their adversaries. When one of Westmoreland's lawyers fails to succeed on cross-examination and abandons a point, she explains that he was too honorable to destroy a witness. By contrast, when CBS's lawyers abandon a point, she deems this proof that their argument was "implausible" and untenable.

By the same token, it is one of her major themes that *Time* and CBS compounded the dispute by vigorously defending themselves, never conceding an inch. But she never questions whether the plaintiffs, too, are at fault for mindlessly pushing the litigation and refusing several compromises that could have mitigated the supposed harm to their reputations. (Westmoreland, for example, turned down an offer of free air time by CBS.)

Witnesses, like attorneys, also wear either black or white hats in Adler's book. In analyzing defense testimony, Adler gives the melodramatic phrase "a simple yes or no" a workout that it probably hasn't received since the last *Mr. District Attorney* show on television. She routinely condemns as prevaricators those defense witnesses who do not answer with that "simple yes or no" because they insisted (probably on counsel's advice) on explaining background and context.

Adler is especially hard on the two high-ranking Army officers who provided key testimony supporting the thesis of CBS's documentary, that Westmoreland had deliberately deceived his superiors about the size of the enemy in Vietnam. She accuses them of changing their stories (in minor ways) and therefore lying.

The reality is quite likely that these officers were caught in the middle. They didn't want to hurt Westmoreland so their pretrial statements downplayed wrongdoing by him. When pinned down at trial and under oath, they were compelled to provide the damaging details and elaboration. Yet to Adler the changes in nuances and details of their testimony make them totally incredible.

There is nothing wrong with Adler's advocacy journalism, of course, so long as it is understood for what it is. But readers should be cautioned about the lessons Adler draws from her one-sided account of these two trials. Consider her views, supposedly derived from the Westmoreland and Sharon trials, about modern journalism. She regards the media (which she views as "unitary, powerful, and monolithic") as arrogant and unwilling to admit mistakes; self-protective and unwilling to criticize each other; and increasingly reckless or willing to fabricate in much of its investigative reporting.

Well, these are broad lessons to derive from two instances, especially two libel cases, which are clearly not typical of all of modern journalism. Moreover, each of Adler's conclusions is overdrawn or simply wrong.

She claims that CBS and *Time* acted defensively and were unwilling to admit mistakes. But this can be no surprise—one does not readily admit mistakes in the face of massive punitive libel suits seeking millions of dollars. This certainly does not show that the media are always unwilling to admit mistakes.

To her claim that there is little or no media self-criticism in this country, one must ask, where has she been? There is more media self-criticism than most readers can take. Indeed, media self-criticism (*TV Guide*'s "Anatomy of a Smear" cover story) was a major factor in the CBS broadcast at issue in the Westmoreland case, as well as countless other libel suits.

And she ignores history and writes recklessly herself in claiming that modern investigative reporters have newly acquired an itch to rush into print to expose wrongdoing and that they now often cut corners in doing so. Reporters like the muckraking Lincoln Steffens and young Turner Catledge (as a "picture-snatching" specialist in the 1920s in Memphis) would probably laugh at Adler's characterization of *Time* magazine, with its layers upon layers of writers and editors, as "reckless." For recklessness, the penny press reporters of the turn of the century who bribed or stole their way to city hall and police station scoops have it by a long shot over institutional journalists of today, who often work through volumes of documents and levels of bureaucrats to report and analyze global news.

Adler's conclusions about libel cases are similarly unwarranted by the Westmoreland and Sharon trials. She repeatedly suggests that the cards in the libel deck are unfairly stacked in the media's favor. But she overstates the media's advantages and shows little sense of respect for legal standards that promote fairness and constitutional values.

Perhaps her most outrageous claim is that *Time*'s use in its story of a confidential source "was entirely to *Time*'s advantage" in the litigation. Confidential sources make a libel case immeasurably more difficult to defend. The defendant cannot fully use a confidential source to help him without revealing its identity, and the defendant often must stand mute when plaintiff (often unfairly) attacks the source as unreliable or nonexistent. Adler later acknowledges *Time*'s "predicament," but only after repeatedly portraying the confidential source issue as a strategic advantage—the one thing it surely is not.

Adler also repeatedly claims that the media (which to her is "monolithic") uses its "enormous financial resources" to intimidate and overpower libel plaintiffs. This is unfair criticism. There is nothing in the book, except her own insinuations, to show that *Time* or CBS did anything unfair or overreaching in the two suits. And there is certainly nothing in her book to show that the media at large—mostly community newspapers, radio and television stations—have either the power or the inclination to abuse it that Adler ascribes to them.

Before she inveighs anew against the "enormous financial resources" and allegedly overreaching legal tactics of the "monolithic" press, Adler might want to read about the *Alton (Illinois) Telegraph*—a moderately sized newspaper that nearly went out of business as the result of a libel suit of questionable merit.

Finally, Adler unfairly portrays the landmark 1964 U.S. Supreme Court decision *New York Times Co. v. Sullivan* as illogical and encouraging media recklessness. Her flimsy analysis of *Sullivan* focuses on the word *malice*—although, as Judge Pierre Leval repeatedly cautioned in the Westmoreland case, "malice" is not a fair description for the *Sullivan* legal test that protects reporting on public officials. Her accusation that Sullivan encourages recklessness is totally unfounded, also; she merely surmises that reporters try to exploit what she acknowledges is a "simplistic" and incorrect interpretation of *Sullivan*.

More important, Adler does not explain and seems not to respect the constitutional origins of the *Sullivan* rule—the need to encourage and allow breathing space for reporting on public issues. Adler's own proposal for libel law is the simplistic solution, in her terms, of putting the Ninth Commandment (not bearing false witness) above the First Amendment. This position sounds very moralistic, but it leads precisely to the result that *Sullivan* properly protects against—the media self-censorship that would inevitably result if protection of public officials' reputations were elevated above press freedom to report on public issues.

Adler's book ultimately fails of its critical purpose. The book's various targets—*Time*, CBS, the libel law system, and modern investigative reporting—simply cannot be all that bad if an author must go to the extremes Adler does in order to criticize them. The last word on the merits of these two cases remains with the jurors in the *Sharon* case, who decided in favor of *Time*, and Westmoreland, who abandoned his case against CBS.

Coals of Fire and the *Alton Telegraph* Case

There is a roller-coaster ride in the law that has more dramatic ups and downs than you will ever find at any amusement park. It is called libel law.

Not too many years ago, after the Supreme Court's decision in *New York Times v. Sullivan* in 1964, some experts predicted that libel cases would vanish and the ride would end. This did not happen. Plaintiffs continued to file and prosecute libel cases—even the public figure plaintiffs who had the highest hurdles to surmount under *Sullivan*. But with a few rough spots, it was a bearable ride. The press usually won and never suffered life-threatening judgments.

Around the time of Watergate, the press was having a pretty smooth ride. There seemed to be an appreciation on the bench of the need and value of journalists as societal watchdogs. Controversial investigative reporting was popular, and the press was winning most suits, usually without trial, on purely legal grounds.

Things shifted sharply in the late 1970s. Watergate memories were waning, and the press, while still lulled by the relative calm, was being set up for some major falls. In sharp succession in the early 1980s, libel plaintiffs began scoring, and scoring big. Some of the hits were on fringe publications, like the *National Enquirer* and *Penthouse*. But mainstream journalism by pillars of the American press, including the *Washington Post*, was also hit hard. Textbook journalism—stories done the hard-hitting way they were supposed to be done—became take-out-your-checkbook journalism.

The rocketing downslide is continuing. More than a few million-dollar verdicts—unheard of in libel cases until the 1980s—have been rendered by juries, and some even affirmed by the appellate courts that were not so long ago considered the best friend of the press. Libel suits have become recognized as a major and potentially deadly threat to the press.

What is behind this new reality? How did it develop? And what can be done about it, to allow the press to go about its muckraking mission without losing its financial independence and editorial freedom? Any examination of these issues must begin with the analysis of the major libel cases of the 1980s. There is no case more appropriate for study than *Green v. Alton Telegraph*—a unique case initiated and brought to fruition in the Madison County, Illinois, courts.

The case arose out of a small-time builder's travails. The builder, James Green, became heavily indebted to a savings and loan association, which in turn suffered, and ultimately was shut down by federal regulators. The local newspaper, the *Alton (Illinois) Telegraph*, investigated both Green and the association and at one point pursued rumors that Green was connected to organized crime. The newspaper never published anything concerning these allegations—but an unpublished memo written by two of its reporters became the focus of a lengthy high-stakes libel suit.

The story of the *Green* case is told in a book published in 1988, *Coals of Fire: The Alton Telegraph Libel Case*, by Southern Illinois University Press. The author is Thomas A. Littlewood, professor of journalism at the University of Illinois and a former Washington correspondent for the *Chicago Sun-Times*. It is a short (199 pages), gracefully written book that was obviously researched with care. Littlewood, as might be expected, is a free press advocate who is greatly concerned with the result in the *Green* case—a $9.2 million verdict (the largest newspaper libel judgment in history at that time), never reviewed by an appellate court, based on a memo never published in the newspaper.

But the book is no whitewash of the *Telegraph* or hatchet job on the lawyers and litigants responsible for the verdict. It attempts to describe fairly the full factual, social, and legal background of the case. As a result, the book makes the important point that the verdict was not an unexplainable aberration. By the time the reader reaches chapter II, concerning the trial (titled "Give Him the Money," the theme of the brief jury deliberations), it is almost anticlimactic.

Readers will draw different conclusions from the book about libel law, the courts, and the future of the libel roller coaster. To this reader, two themes, concerning the newspaper and the community, stood out.

First, newspapers (and other news organizations) need to respond vigorously to the threat of libel, before and after publication, and before and after suit is filed.

The *Telegraph*, a small town paper attempting to break into investigative reporting in the late 1970s, never really had its act together. There seemed to be no unity of purpose or action among the family owner-managers, the crusading city editor, and the reporting staff. As a result, the paper embarked on the dangerous field of investigative reporting with too little resources, attention, and expertise. Journalists need to heed the advice sometimes given to trial lawyers: "Don't go bear-hunting bare-handed."

Hindsight is easy, of course, and even the most experienced journalists could make mistakes just as the *Telegraph* did. But these mistakes would more likely be caught and corrected within the newspaper organization if the paper had unified commitment and professional editors and managers determined to participate in and help decide important issues.

At the *Telegraph*, reporters took many crucial actions on their own, with little guidance or review. The crucial libelous memo, though it was addressed to federal investigators and should have been privileged, in retrospect was too important to have been left to two young reporters. Similarly, the action revealing the memo to a prospective plaintiff, a crucial link in the events leading to the verdict, was apparently taken by a reporter on his own.

In the legal proceeding, as in the journalistic efforts, the *Telegraph* did not treat the case with the seriousness it deserved. Management, somewhat like its young reporters, must have felt soothed by what Littlewood calls "an inchoate sense of immunity" from libel. But immunity from the sanctions of judges and juries is not a preexisting divine right; rather, it requires hard-fought efforts by the press, before and after suit.

The second key theme of the book concerns the importance of the community in which the suit arose. Littlewood's book attempts to portray the personal, institutional, and community setting that gave rise to the case and the result.

In this regard, the Madison County of the *Telegraph* case is an especially important study for those concerned with the trends in libel suits nationwide. As Littlewood portrays it, Madison County was a judicial forum known for lawyers and courts that would put a dollar figure (usually large) on any injury—a place where abstract issues like press freedom never would and never did interfere with the personal injury "hidden industry." In short, it was an ideal forum for a plaintiff in a libel suit.

The national significance of the *Green* libel case is that if the roller coaster's downward ride continues, what occurred in Madison County courthouses yesterday will occur in other courthouses across the country tommorow.

Littlewood offers much factual background to support his picture of the Madison County courts and clearly views the area's unique personal injury "hidden industry" as a major influence on the libel suit. But other parts of the Alton community are also portrayed as responsible for the climate that gave birth to the Green suit. For example, the *Telegraph* owners and editors come off in the book as well intentioned but weak—reluctant First Amendment champions who were unable and unwilling to make the total commitment that good journalism and press freedom both demand.

The business and social elites of Alton, Illinois, and the surrounding area are similarly portrayed by Littlewood as responsible by default for some of the circumstances that created the *Telegraph* suit and its sad consequences. Their priorities were safe, undisturbed business activity, and they treated the *Telegraph* not as a potentially beneficial check on abuses in local institutions but as a bother and a pest.

In short, Littlewood's theme is that community concerns and *mores*—in this case, the personal-injury-award orientation of Madison County lawyers and courts and the indifference of the community elite to issues of press freedom—are crucial influences in libel cases.

These conclusions are discouraging in some ways, because they dispel the notion that there are easy villains (plaintiffs, plaintiff's lawyers, press-hating judges, or runaway juries) to explain the libel setbacks that most bother the press. But although there are no simple villains, there are complex solutions—solutions involving more press vigilance before and after suit, and nurture of community understanding and sensitivity of the needs for and benefits of crusading journalism.

Littlewood is fond of paradoxes, and the *Green* case presents many. Alton, a city indelibly impressed in the history of freedom of the press as the place where abolitionist editor Elijah Lovejoy was murdered, became a test for press freedom again years later. But the press defender this time, the *Telegraph* (a newspaper that stood silent in Lovejoy's day) was unable to protect itself from another force just as powerful as an enraged mob.

The press, if it follows its duty "to present the news and raise hell," will often find itself on the defensive. News organizations in this era had better take heed of the Alton example and take seriously both their defense and the community support they need to survive.

Abuse of Libel Suits

Lawsuits can be abused. The all-American privilege of making a tort claim—that is, filing a civil lawsuit seeking compensation for damage caused by others—can also be a license to threaten and intimidate adversaries. Libel suits are particularly susceptible to abuse.

Ask any number of libel defendants—journalists, public interest groups, citizen activists, and others. Or review important historical libel cases, going back to Henry Ford's legal assault on the *Chicago Tribune*. Or, for a possible modern example, examine the Briggs and Stratton suit against the *National Catholic Reporter*.

The *Reporter*, a highly regarded independent journal headquartered in Kansas City, was sued in 1996 by Briggs and Stratton, the Wisconsin-based engine manufacturer. As the *Reporter*'s parent company, the National Catholic Reporter Publishing Company, has told it, the suit was no more than "an attempt by Briggs & Stratton to muzzle its critics and intimidate the press." The *Reporter* responded with a counterattack in the court of public opinion; it prepared and sent to many journalistic organizations a packet of information attacking the Briggs and Stratton suit and its motivation.

The Briggs and Stratton versus *National Catholic Reporter* dispute has its roots in the corporate restructurings of the nineties. In its December 2, 1994, issue, the *Reporter* published a cover article concerning the disruption to workers and their communities caused by corporate layoffs, using Briggs and Stratton as a case study. Headlined "*Adios*, American Dream," on the cover and "Briggs and Stratton Layoffs Tear Family Hopes" on the inside, the article focused both on a May 1994 Briggs and Stratton announcement that the company would eliminate 2,000 jobs from Milwaukee to Mexico and the broader context of such job shifts.

The chief article written by Leslie Wirpsa traced the Briggs and Stratton labor changes to the late 1980s, when the company began to shift jobs from Milwaukee to lower-wage locations including Poplar Bluff, Missouri. She noted that after job-shifting and worker concessions, the company more than halved its Milwaukee job force but saw "profits zip to a record $102 million in 1993" and "watched stock values multiply fourfold."

Most of the article centered on some longtime Briggs and Stratton employees in Milwaukee, several of whom would lose their jobs in connection with 2,000 layoffs announced in 1994. In some cases, the employees feared losing homes, marriages, and health insurance that was vital for children with special medical needs. The article also cited experts and studies that suggested the Briggs and Stratton layoffs were part of a national trend that was "prompting a radical decline in the quality of middle-class life in the United States."

With particular reference to Briggs and Stratton, the article pointed out that the company refused to discuss its strategy or even make a telephone statement. And it quoted a Briggs and Stratton worker and union activist as claiming it was "contradictory" that many Briggs and Stratton executives were prominent Milwaukee Catholics. The article noted that the company's president was a Catholic and graduate of three Catholic institutions and the company's public spokesman and outside labor lawyer were both Marquette University graduates.

An editorial accompanying the article characterized the article as revealing "how corporate decisions hurt ordinary people and what they reveal about decision makers who live in either denial or moral blindness." The editorial signed by *Reporter* editor Tom Fox faulted Briggs and Stratton's executives (which it noted included "Catholics educated in Catholic institutions") and contrasted their decisions with the principles outlined by U.S. Catholic bishops in a pastoral letter on economic justice.

Briggs and Stratton responded to the article and series with an immediate lengthy rebuttal, in the form of a seven-page letter to the editor of the *Reporter*. The letter defended Briggs and Stratton's refusal to talk to the *Reporter* ("We refused to participate in our own lynching"), attacked the *Reporter* ("mean-spirited," "fundamental lack of fairness"), and gave its side of the story. Among other things, the letter criticized the articles because the reporters it quoted were union activists and pointed out that worker wages and profit-sharing payments had in many cases increased because of the company's restructuring.

The letter explained at length the ethical principles that it stated Briggs and Stratton follows, and it sharply took issue with the suggestion that Briggs and Stratton officials had acted unethically. "We do not believe that any ethical or moral construct (including the Bishops' Pastoral Letter) requires that Briggs and Stratton resign itself to the scrap heap of failed American corporations," it noted.

Fox, the *Reporter* editor, refused to publish the rebuttal unedited but offered to print either a shorter letter or an interview. At that point, both sides deadlocked, and despite further negotiations, they were unable to reach agreement on a published rebuttal or other issues.

In June 1996, Briggs and Stratton took the dispute to another level, with its federal court suit alleging libel and invasion of privacy. The suit, filed against the National Catholic Reporter Company, Fox, Wirpsa, and a graphic artist for the *Reporter*, complained of nine passages from the article and three from the editorial. It alleged both libel and invasion of privacy; the privacy claim is based on the unique theory that the publicity given to the religious affiliation of the individual plaintiffs constitutes an invasion of privacy. The suit sought $10 million in compensatory damages and $20 million in punitive damages.

Is the Briggs and Stratton suit a classic misuse of a lawsuit to "muzzle critics" and "intimidate the press" as Fox and the *Reporter* claim? The answer in this situation will depend upon the facts as they emerge in the lawsuit in Milwaukee.

But unquestionably many defamation suits nowadays are used for abusive purposes, as Fox and the *Reporter* claim occurred in this instance. For many reasons, libel and slander suits can readily be abused. The concepts of reputation and damage to reputation are so vague and pliable that plaintiffs can plausibly claim that almost any negative statements made about them—even statements warranted and needed in public discussion—have libeled them. That leaves the common law and constitutional elements and defenses of defamation law as the only barriers to abusive suits—and experience has shown that many an unwarranted suit can overcome these barriers long enough to engage in quite a bit of muzzling of critics, intimidation of the press, and all-around creation of a "chilling effect."

For these reasons, in several states efforts have been made to create a new screening device for libel suits in order to prevent abusive suits that are primarily designed to muzzle and intimidate. A name has even been given the abusive suits: SLAPP, meaning Strategic Lawsuits Against Public Participation.

The granddaddy of anti-SLAPP legislation is the California Anti-SLAPP act, a statute enacted in 1993 specifically to weed out and prevent "lawsuits brought primarily to chill the valid exercise of the constitutional rights of freedom of speech and petition for the redress of grievances." The statute singles out cases "arising from any act . . . in furtherance of [the defendant's] right of petition or free speech . . . in connection with a public issue" and provides in those cases for a possible early cutoff of such suits. Essentially, when a defendant challenges a libel or slander case as a SLAPP suit, the court must examine the suit critically, and, if it finds that the plaintiff is not likely to succeed, the court must dismiss the action.

The California statute has been used successfully by defendants in a number of cases. An individual who criticized a charity's plan to build a shelter for battered women in her neighborhood got the charity's lawsuit against her, based on her critical comments, dismissed. A political candidate who criticized an opponent was able to get the opponent's suit against him dismissed. A critic of the Church of Scientology was able to get the church's libel suit against him dismissed. A university that offered unusual courses was prohibited from suing a newspaper that wrote a series of critical articles about them. These are a few of the more than a dozen reported anti-SLAPP decisions in California in the last few years.

Several other states have followed California in enacting anti-SLAPP statutes, Colorado courts have adopted similar procedures on their own, and the leaders of the anti-SLAPP movement have campaigned for a federal act.

Under existing law in most states, a defendant that is confronted with a SLAPP suit realistically faces a serious problem. Given the significant cost of defending a lawsuit, particularly one brought by a well-heeled corporation, and the time and uncertainty also involved, most defendants cannot help being somewhat intimidated.

Of course, defendants usually say they won't be intimidated. Commenting on similar cases in the 1980s, Dan Rather of CBS asserted that while CBS is never chilled by these suits, he knows that smaller publishers are chilled. Similarly, Fox has issued a strongly worded press release stating that he and the *Reporter*—though they do not have the resources of large media companies—have "sufficient resources" to fight and will defend to the hilt their freedom to criticize Briggs and Stratton.

Initial statements like that are typical, but often they represent brag-gadocio and wishful thinking intermingled with real courage. Unless in-surance, *pro bono* legal help, or special contributions are available to defray legal costs, many small-budget individuals and public interest groups con-front practical and financial limits in fighting the suits—and hence real temptations to change or moderate their message—when suits of this na-ture are filed against them.

As many journalists, public interest groups, and citizen activists have learned, under existing law there is little built-in protection from abusive libel suits. Until and unless anti-SLAPP legislation becomes more preva-lent, libel and slander lawsuits will continue to be misused, to muzzle, to intimidate, and to chill.

Libel Reform Efforts

For perhaps twenty years after the Supreme Court's libel landmark *New York Times v. Sullivan*, the Court regularly accepted libel cases and considered unresolved or difficult issues in the application of *Sullivan*, and these issues were often widely debated in the press and other public forums.

By the late 1980s, the regular development of libel law at the Supreme Court slowed down. Constitutional libel law had become established. But did this mean that the purposes of *Sullivan*—greater freedom of speech and protection from the chilling effect of defamation suits, particularly by public officials—had been satisfied?

Possibly not. The calm on the op-ed pages in the period of the ma-turity of constitutional libel law may belie the carnage in the courtrooms. Though the Supreme Court may not have been making much new law in the late 1980s and early 1990s, plaintiffs across the country are finding the existing law, and attitudes, just fine.

If anything, the prevailing quiet may signify that we have crossed a significant barrier in society's attitude toward libel suits. We now *expect* lengthy suits and multimillion-dollar verdicts and aren't surprised or even alarmed by them anymore. Either that, or we haven't noticed what has been happening. Consider the verdicts in some early 1990s media libel cases:

- A $58 million libel award, to a former county prosecutor who sued Dallas television station WFAA-TV, made a list of the twenty-five biggest verdicts in the nation in 1991.

- The $34 million libel judgment against the *Philadelphia Inquirer*, in the suit brought by former prosecutor Richard Sprague, made a list of the ten largest personal injury suit awards of 1990.
- A Chicago jury returned a $2.2 million verdict against the publisher of the *Wall Street Journal* for a story that the *Journal* retracted shortly after publication. (This verdict was later set aside.)
- The former owner of Buffalo television station WKBW was hit with an $18.5 million judgment for a broadcast that mistakenly identified a crime victim—a mistake that the station corrected (although not fully or forthrightly) as soon as it became known.
- A Pennsylvania state supreme court justice won a $6 million verdict against the *Philadelphia Inquirer*. The jury inexplicably cleared the paper's original series but imposed this heavy penalty on distribution of a *reprint* of the series.
- Several auto racing promoters won a $13.5 million verdict against the *Cleveland Plain Dealer* in late 1990, based largely on a claim of a misleading headline.
- A Texas heart surgeon won a $31.5 million judgment against station KENS-TV in mid-1990 even though his hospital privileges had been revoked long before the broadcast.

As a result of those and other large verdicts, a 1991 study concluded that "the market value of the garden variety libel case has gone up, and verdicts in the $500,000 to $3,000,00 range seem to be . . . expected by most evaluating counsel."

The story is not just big verdicts against big media companies. It also involves heavy burdens being imposed on individuals, non-media businesses, and small publishers. Some of the examples:

- A small trade newsletter, *Food Chemical News*, was hit with an $875,000 judgment for publishing a letter in which a company in the food chemical industry reprimanded the plaintiff, a self-styled employee-whistleblower. An appeals court reversed the judgment, noting that the heavy damages award imposed "exorbitant costs on public debate."
- A medical-products firm's libel suit against a scientific journal, based on a letter to the editor, imposed heavy litigation costs on the *Journal of Medical Primatology*, its editor, and the letter writer. And after the U.S. Supreme Court narrowed the protection for statements of

opinion in 1990, the defendants faced the serious threat of a crippling judgment. The case commanded considerable (and nervous) attention in the scientific publishing community. The defendants ultimately won when New York State's highest court used it as the vehicle for expanding *state* constitutional protection for statements of opinion, thereby avoiding the new limits in federal law on protections for opinion.

- Libel suits against publishers of other trade newsletters have imposed enormous litigation costs on those small publishers. An insurance newsletter, for example, was sued for highlighting the risks of policies issued by low-rated insurance companies.
- A Duluth, Minnesota, jury brought in a $785,000 verdict in 1988 against the local newspaper over articles that the plaintiff admitted were factually correct. (He claimed they left a false impression.) The Minnesota Supreme Court reversed the judgment in 1990.
- Non-media libel cases have also been swept up in the high-verdict trend. A St. Louis City circuit court jury awarded a downstate Missouri woman $86 million in a libel case against a company that defamed her, and a Florida jury in late 1989 awarded GTE Corporation $100 million in libel damages in a dispute with Home Shopping Network. Such verdicts, while they do not affect the media directly, tend to encourage the use of libel suits as a means of addressing grievances.
- Individuals and businesses are also finding themselves enmeshed in protracted libel litigation. For example, the Church of Scientology sued a Paine Webber analyst over a stock report that claimed the church had a "vendetta" against Eli Lilly and Company.

So the overall trends are unmistakable—increasing resort to libel suits as a weapon of intimidation and means of redress of wrongs, and increasingly large verdicts in those cases in which plaintiffs prevail.

Meanwhile, alternatives to libel law seem to be going nowhere. The Iowa Libel Research Project, an ambitious experimental project designed to promote non-litigation alternatives to libel suits, disbanded after a trial period, with little encouragement for new reformers.

Founded on research showing that the current libel law system failed at almost all of its legitimate objectives, the Iowa project attempted to provide potential plaintiffs with a realistic alternative to suing the media: the chance to clear their names promptly and publicly. In hardly any cases, however, would both the plaintiff and the media company agree to this alternative dispute resolution procedure.

There is some real irony that this increasing allowance of libel suits and size of libel verdicts is occurring now. American journalists, lawyers, and jurists have debated for decades whether libel suits cause an unacceptable "chilling effect."

But the collapse of the Robert Maxwell media empire in late 1991 should settle any doubts. Maxwell was one of the world's premier libel plaintiffs. He played the intimidation game to the hilt, as British laws allow. As a result, he silenced almost all his critics and shielded from public scrutiny his multimillion dollar plundering and misuse of his privately held firms.

Maxwell's misconduct caused hundreds of millions of dollars of losses, here and in Europe, and affected thousands of persons. Almost undoubtedly Maxwell would have been caught earlier, and some of this harm prevented, were it not for his libel suits. Maxwell's example shows that libel suits *do* chill important speech. It demonstrates that the trends in this country are chilling indeed.

Defending a Libel Case

A few days ago a man in a trench coat knocked on your door and politely asked, "Mr. Reporter?" When you acknowledged it, he thrust some papers into your hand and quickly walked away. It took a bit of fumbling through the papers and translating the legal mumbo jumbo into plain English, but the reality was soon plain: You have been sued for libel.

It seems ironic. That big investigative piece two months ago was the one that everyone worried about. It mentioned businessmen, professionals, and several status-conscious rising young politicians. Your sources, though reliable, had less than savory backgrounds. Your editor asked you to keep libel in mind as you wrote it and even consulted the newspaper's lawyer before publication. But that piece passed without the hint of a libel suit. Instead, a fairly routine story from the city hall beat has set you on a journey through the libel law system.

You know how the civil courts work, and you understand generally the substantive issues in a libel case. But being the key defendant in a libel suit is a new experience. You wonder what you should have done, before suit, to best prepare for suit—and what you should do now, after the suit has been filed, to help resolve it favorably.

Your pre-suit conduct should be directed at laying the groundwork for resolving any complaints, or defending any suits, if they arise. It should include the following steps:

Write with a View to Libel. This is second nature to most journalists, especially investigative reporters. But every journalist ought to do this. While some important stories may undergo prepublication libel review by editors or lawyers, a surprising number of libel suits result from routine, seemingly noncontroversial stories.

Every reporter ought to write as if any one of his or her pieces could develop into a suit. Ideally, this means you should be able to prove every fact you publish.

Maintain Clear Understandings and Good Relations with Your Sources. Confidential source relationships, though often necessary in reporting, are troublesome in litigation. Try to minimize reliance on confidential sources, and where they are needed, make explicit arrangements as to the nature and extent of your confidentiality agreement. This will help you demonstrate later that your source relationships were necessary and deserve to be respected by the court.

Also, keep up with your sources. Their role does not always end upon publication. Whether they are named or unnamed, high-level or low-level, they cannot only help you get the story; they can help you defend it.

Have a Consistent Policy (and Follow It) on Notes—How You Keep Them, and How (or Whether) You Save Them. It doesn't matter whether you take notes on the back of envelopes or interview only with cameras rolling. The focus in a libel suit is often on consistency with usual practices, so you should be able to explain either that you follow a workable, standard procedure as to notes or that you departed from it for good reasons.

Some reporters routinely discard their notes, but those who save notes often find them helpful as evidence and as an aid to refreshing memories.

Try to Resolve Complaints Promptly and Courteously. Libel suits sometimes result as much from poor postpublication handling of complaints as from the publication itself. Studies have found that reporters often respond to complaints with defensiveness and hostility.

If you handle complaints with skill, sensitivity, and an open mind, you may be able to encourage the complainer to accept some non-litigation remedy, such as a clarification, a follow-up story, or simply an understanding response to any hurt feelings involved.

Your post-suit conduct, just like what you did before suit, can be important. Your role as a defendant need not be purely passive; you can and should actively help to resolve the case. Among other things, you should:

Keep Yourself Involved in the Fact-Finding Efforts. As the reporter, you know more than anyone about the facts of the case and can contribute much to the legal defense effort. You can direct your lawyer to helpful areas of inquiry by suggesting witnesses to interview, documents to subpoena, and experts to consult. You may also be able to do follow-up research at the newspaper office, courthouse, or elsewhere better than the law firm's investigators.

Explain Your News Reporting Work and Its Social Importance. In today's world of specialization, each worker tends to become lost in his own specialty. Journalists must avoid this trap. In lawsuits, reporters should explain fully (even to their own lawyer, if he or she is not knowledgeable in journalism) not only what they did but why they did it and how their daily journalistic work is beneficial to the community.

The force of the First Amendment does not come from out of the sky. Rather, it is built up from the accumulated convictions of individual citizens, jurors, and judges, based on the facts they have learned, that news reporting serves important social functions.

You can help give them the facts that will demonstrate that your reporting is deserving of special protection. This will enhance public understanding and refute the simplistic plaintiffs' lawyer's argument that an alleged libel is "just another injury."

Keep Abreast of the Suit and Give Your Input to Its Direction. Pester your lawyer. Make sure he or she is aware of all relevant facts and is following a strategy that appears sound and compatible with your work and objectives.

As a client you have the right and responsibility to ensure that the case is being handled to your satisfaction. Your superiors and your lawyer should not be bothered by your scrutiny. The stakes are high enough so that the only legitimate concern is whether you are providing *enough* scrutiny.

Treat the Case with Proper Seriousness. Unlike many events and activities that journalists attend, libel suits (and especially reporters' depositions under oath taken in the course of discovery) are not good places for jokes, facetious comments, or generally lighthearted attitudes.

Most likely, if you are a typical reporter, beneath your glib exterior is a serious, hardworking journalist dedicated to the truth. A libel suit is the time to reveal that hidden reality.

Following the guidance described above may not ensure victory, since that depends on many factors. But it will help develop and advance your best defenses. It will ensure that your legal strategy is consistent with your journalistic work and objectives. Most important, it will make your conduct in the course of the libel suit a reaffirmation of the quality and professionalism of your work as a journalist.

Privacy

The "Right of Privacy"

LEGAL THEORIES, LIKE PEOPLE, SOMETIMES AC-
quire larger-than-life images. They seem pure, invincible,
and all-important. One such theory has been the *right of
privacy*, a theory that sounds at first blush as laudatory and noncontroversial as motherhood and the American flag. Larger-than-life theories,
however, like larger-than-life people, sometimes must be cut down to
size. In the case of deflating an overblown right of privacy, Missouri
courts have taken the lead.

There are actually several different legal rights of privacy, ranging
from statutes dealing with credit reporting to the theory supporting the
Supreme Court's decisions on abortion. Journalists are most concerned
with the right of privacy concerning personal information.

The general theory or right of privacy relating to personal information developed out of a famous *Harvard Law Review* article published in
1890, written by Charles Warren, a law professor, and Louis Brandeis,
the future Supreme Court justice. Warren and Brandeis—spurred partly
by press reports about Warren's wife, a wealthy Boston socialite—attempted to spin various long-standing legal doctrines, ranging from tres-

passing to copyright, into a new unified theory of privacy. Their efforts were refined by William Prosser, a leading legal scholar, who later defined a four-pronged right of privacy.

One aspect of this right is known as the tort of *false light*. Under the prevailing theory, false light invasion of privacy occurs when someone publishes a statement about the plaintiff that places him in a false light in a manner that would be highly offensive to a person of ordinary sensibilities.

The other three prongs of Prosser's right of privacy concern intrusion into one's personal privacy (for example, by trespassing or eavesdropping); public disclosure of a person's intimate embarrassing facts; and unauthorized exploitation of a celebrity's name or personality.

Prosser's privacy theory, including the false light tort, has gained wide—but not total—acceptance in state courts. This has meant that even without legislative action, these legal theories have entered into the court-made laws of most states, and persons who feel aggrieved by privacy invasions can sue for violations.

Journalists have been largely alone in cautioning against expansion of privacy law. Their professional concern and recognition are that greater information privacy will mean greater restrictions on news gathering and reporting. In particular, false light invasion of privacy is a broad and ill-defined theory that, if it became widely accepted or expansively applied, could chill and restrict many publications.

The definition of false light is so broad and open-ended that almost every unfavorable statement about someone could be construed a false light invasion of privacy. Indeed, many plaintiffs' lawyers regularly employ such a broad construction. It is almost commonplace for a plaintiff in a libel or slander action to also claim false light—thus turning many defamation cases into defamation *and privacy* cases. Many courts have simply accepted this overlap between privacy and defamation.

But in a 1986 decision, the Missouri Supreme Court scrutinized the basis and validity of false light theory where it overlaps with defamation—and concluded that there was no justification for such a broad theory. The case was *Sullivan v. Pulitzer Broadcasting Co.*, a privacy suit brought in 1983 against KSD-TV. Sullivan claimed that a 1978 KSD-TV broadcast created a false impression that he had engaged in certain wrongdoing and thus portrayed him in a false light.

The trial court, on KSD's motion, dismissed Sullivan's false light claims on the theory that they were really defamation claims and hence barred by the statute of limitations applicable to defamation. The case was taken up by the state supreme court, which upheld KSD's position in 1986.

The court in its decision undertook an exhaustive study of the origins and rationale for the false light tort and, as a result, found several major concerns with false light theory. Most important, the court noted that because the false light tort resembles defamation, it is either unnecessary (if it merely duplicates defamation) or it creates serious constitutional concern (if it would allow circumvention of the delicate constitutional defenses and privileges applicable to defamation).

Thus, the court ruled that in Missouri false light tort will *not* be recognized for claims that appear to be "classic defamation." This is a most significant ruling, since most false light claims to date, like Sullivan's, have been asserted in classic defamation contexts.

The court left open the possibility that false light might be recognized in some other more limited context. For example, the false light tort might make sense when a plaintiff complains of a false impression left by a nondefamatory communication, "such as claiming that the plaintiff wrote a poem, article or book which plaintiff did not in fact write."

Because *Sullivan* concerned state law and was decided by Missouri's highest court, all state and federal courts in Missouri must follow it. Two federal courts did so in a case from Independence, causing the reversal of a $70,000 verdict for the plaintiff, which had been rendered only weeks before the announcement of the *Sullivan* decision.

The *Sullivan* decision put Missouri in the forefront of critical analysis of false light theory. One other state, North Carolina, has rejected the tort even more soundly than Missouri. Few other states have seriously analyzed it.

Other states should find the *Sullivan* decision persuasive and noteworthy in several ways. First, as the Missouri Supreme Court noted in *Sullivan*, any liability imposed on expression implicates constitutional concerns. Yet those who fashioned false light theory notably neglected these concerns. They accepted broad formulations that if literally applied would eviscerate many constitutional limits on defamation law.

Moreover, even apart from its overlap with defamation, false light may constitute an unconstitutional abridgment of free speech if applied to restrict publications of truthful facts or comment on matters of public concern. Additionally, the privacy rationale that has been wrapped around false light theory is misleading. It is primarily a theory concerning publication, not privacy, and the legitimate needs of personal privacy as to publications have already been factored into the law of defamation.

Finally, false light theory carries real dangers, particularly because it constitutes a drastic, unannounced, and untested liability expansion. Unlike the law of libel and slander, which evolved over centuries, the law of false light was developed by theorists and plopped down ready-formed into the sensitive arena of social communication.

Legal theories of this nature demand critical attention, not blind acceptance. Indeed, similar judge-made expansions of the law, such as have occurred with medical malpractice and product liability theories, usually prompt intense debate. Only the comfortable glow that has surrounded the concept of privacy has—until recently—exempted privacy theory from similar scrutiny.

Journalists' Right of Privacy Primer

The law of invasion of privacy is a little bit like a new computer system introduced into a workplace—some people love it, some people fear it, and few people really understand it.

The public, on the whole, loves the idea that legal remedies are available for invasions of personal privacy. Working journalists, for that reason, fear the implications for their work of a broad privacy concept. And often neither side fully understands privacy law, as it has evolved over the years. Just what are the general principles of the right of privacy as it relates to journalists and writers?

The Different Laws of Privacy. Privacy is not a separate, distinct, established area of law like contracts, property or securities law. It is more of a name in search of a principle or, more accurately, several different principles, each utilizing the same attractive name.

The right of privacy, for example, is often used in political debate as shorthand for the rights of personal reproductive freedom underlying *Roe v. Wade* and related decisions relating to abortion, contraception, and other sexual and child-bearing-related issues. The terminology comes from Justice William O. Douglas's opinion in a forerunner to *Roe v. Wade*, in which he observed that from many enumerated constitutional rights he detected a "penumbra" of a right of personal integrity and privacy.

The phrase *right to privacy* is used almost as often in the context of consumer affairs, particularly relating to the desire of consumers to limit or control personal information that is recorded on mailing lists, credit reports, and business data banks. Although some statutes create rights for consumers in this area, these privacy issues are quite removed from most media privacy issues.

Finally, even the media-related right of privacy contains disparate concepts. Journalists are usually taught that there are four prongs to the right of privacy, as it affects them—even though one of those four branches (sometimes known as "appropriation" or the "right of publicity") relates to matters that are usually *not* desired to be kept private by anyone. And other important laws relating to privacy as it affects the media are not included in the standard four branches.

The difficulty in understanding the media privacy torts can be overcome, somewhat, by focusing on two of the primary things journalists do: gather and report the news. The right of privacy relating to media activities really has two entirely separate branches: one for intrusions that occur during the *news-gathering* process, and one for privacy violations caused by *publications* themselves.

News-Gathering-Related Legal Issues

News-gathering activities may violate a person's right of privacy if the journalist unreasonably intrudes (physically, electronically, or otherwise) upon an area in which that person has a reasonable expectation of privacy.

Trespass. An obvious example would be trespassing. Entering into another person's home, without permission, is an unlawful trespass. The owner presumptively has a reasonable expectation of privacy in his own home. Criminal or civil sanctions can be brought against trespassers, even if no specific damage can be attributed to the trespass.

The alleged trespasser may defend himself by demonstrating consent, either explicit or implicit. If, for example, a reporter accompanies police to a crime scene on private property, the consent of the police to the reporter's presence may constitute implied consent or official authorization to what would otherwise be a trespass.

Similarly, consent (or absence of a reasonable expectation of privacy) may be implied under the circumstances, such as property that has traditionally been open to the public. For example, in a so-called ambush interview occurring on business property open to the public, the danger of a trespass violation begins only if the owner overcomes his surprise from the ambush and utters the magic words, "Get off my property!"

Intrusion. Trespassing has been against the law for ages and generally is not classified as part of the law of privacy. But the modern tort of intrusion, usually recognized as the first of the four branches of the law of privacy as it relates to the media, is nothing but trespass law updated to the age of potentially intrusive devices.

The techniques of intrusion include hidden cameras, hidden tape recorders, parabolic microphones, and simple human deception. Whatever the means, an intrusion occurs when a journalist breaches a news subject's (or bystander's) reasonable expectation of privacy.

Practicalities override technicalities in this area. To determine if an intrusion violation has occurred, it is often necessary to examine the totality of a situation and what is practically understood among the parties. For example:

- Even if a news subject invites a reporter into his house or business, an intrusion may nonetheless occur if the reporter uses a concealed camera or recording device during the consented-to interview. In one such case, a court held that the subject's consent extended only to the face-to-face interview, not the concealed taping and filming, which the court considered unlawful intrusions.
- Even if a journalist never trespasses on a subject's property, an intrusion might occur if he or she obtains a story by intrusive prying with telephoto lenses or parabolic microphones. The issue in such cases is whether, in the circumstances, the devices breached the subject's reasonable expectation of privacy.
- Even in a public place, intrusion can occur if inappropriate cameras, lights, or techniques are used. A court found a violation, for example, when a television crew, with film rolling and lights glaring, barged uninvited into a dark restaurant, prompting many customers to leave.
- But a concealed filming even in a private place may not constitute an intrusion, depending on the circumstances. In an unusual Illinois case, an undercover police officer was surreptitiously filmed in a massage parlor. Because he was on duty and because of a warning he received but did not believe, the court found he had no reasonable expectation of privacy.

Some journalists have argued that their intrusions should not be considered unlawful because of their news-gathering purpose. But arguments like this, based either on the First Amendment's provision for freedom of the press or the "necessity" for reporters to record or film interviews in order to protect themselves, have so far been rejected by the courts.

Surveillance. Extended surveillance of a news subject—a technique seen more in movies than in real life but occasionally used by investigators and journalists—is usually not considered an invasion of privacy.

The test here is simply whether the surveillance is conducted in a reasonable and unobtrusive manner. For example, if the surveillance was conducted in such a way as to be deliberately bothersome to the subject and apparent to others with whom he or she associated, it might be considered an unlawful intrusion.

Recording of Conversations. Both federal and state statutes regulate electronic eavesdropping, including tape-recording of conversations. Although these laws are not taught as part of the traditional four-part media privacy tort, they are among the most important privacy laws affecting journalists.

The federal eavesdropping statute is generally considered a "one-party-consent" statute. That is, if one party to a conversation (e.g., the reporter) consents to recording it, it is lawful to record it even without the other party's consent.

However, the federal statute and some state statutes also ban concealed recording if the person doing the recording had a criminal or tortious purpose. Some creative plaintiffs have claimed that journalists who recorded their conversations did so as part of a tortious scheme—a scheme to libel them. So far, courts have rejected this argument and allowed journalistic recordings under the federal law.

State laws present a more serious problem, because eleven states, including some large and important states such as California, Illinois, and Florida, have two-party-consent eavesdropping statutes. All parties to a conversation must consent, or the conversation cannot be recorded.

The Illinois eavesdropping statute is part of the state criminal code, and violations may subject violators to both criminal penalties and civil lawsuits. It effectively prohibits recording of telephone conversations or other concealed tape-recording in the state. Missouri's eavesdropping statue allows recording with the consent of only one party, although there may be a special two-party consent requirement when a wireless microphone is used.

All of the news-gathering-based privacy claims—trespass, intrusion, and eavesdropping—require serious attention by the media. In each case, the law allows imposition of damages and penalties even where the claimant may not be able to prove any out-of-pocket loss or damage.

Publication-Related Violations

Some facts about people are so intimate, embarrassing, and private or so misleading and offensive that they should not be published. That proposition, at any rate, is the foundation of the law relating to publication-based right of privacy claims.

Publication-related privacy violations are of broader concern than the news-gathering-related privacy claims, which generally apply only to journalists. They affect all writers who write truthful accounts about real people. The two key publication-related privacy torts are public disclosure of private facts and false light.

Public Disclosure of Private Facts. This tort is designed to protect individuals from the embarrassment that would result from public disclosure of intimate and offensive—but true—facts about themselves. It is unusual, if not unique, in publications law in that it imposes sanctions on truthful and non-misleading publications.

The private facts tort comes closest of all the privacy-based legal claims to most people's ordinary understanding of privacy. It is based on the premise that certain information about a person is so intimate or offensive, and of so little legitimate public interest and concern, that it can and should be removed totally from public discourse.

The danger in this tort, however, stems from this very subjectivity. It requires courts (and juries) to make difficult judgments as to the offensiveness of the publication and the *legitimacy* of the public's interest in it. Although courts and juries are instructed to follow the standard of the sensibilities of *a reasonable person*, this standard merely emphasizes the inherent subjectivity.

One of the leading private facts cases—and still one of the best illustrations of the concept—is a Missouri case, *Barber v. Time.* It arose when a wire service learned that Dorothy Barber, a compulsive overeater, had been admitted to General Hospital in Kansas City. A reporter and photographer visited Mrs. Barber in her hospital room, interviewed her, and took her photograph—against her consent.

Time magazine picked up the story and published it. *Time*'s story, headlined "Starving Glutton," treated Mrs. Barber's affliction humorously, referring to the candy bars she ate as she described her hunger and inability to stop eating. A photo ran with the story, above the cutline, "Insatiable-Eater Barber: She Eats for Ten."

Mrs. Barber sued *Time* and won. The judgment was appealed to the Missouri Supreme Court, which, in 1942, grappled with the relatively new concept of the private facts tort.

The court upheld the jury verdict, reasoning that facts and information about a person's medical treatment lay at the core of the right to privacy. And the court had little difficulty in determining that the photographs of Mrs. Barber, taken without her consent while she was ill and in bed for medical treatment, were also well within her right of privacy.

Later cases have applied the private facts tort in many other fact situations, but disclosures about a person's medical condition and treatment continue to be one of its prime applications. Plaintiffs have successfully sued over disclosures about such things as their mental retardation, use of plastic surgery, and participation in in vitro fertilization.

Similarly, photographs of a person in an embarrassing state of undress, disclosures of a person's homosexuality, and reports of personal failures of private persons may all be recognized as private facts violations.

Courts are given broad discretion in making the two key determinations in a private facts case: whether the publication is highly offensive to a reasonable person and whether it is a matter of legitimate concern to the public. Even defenses, like consent, are susceptible to different interpretations. Consequently, few, if any, generalizations can be made, and it is often difficult to predict whether a publication will cause a private facts violation.

For example, in a case from St. Louis, a court recognized a private facts case brought by a couple who were filmed at a reunion for participants in a hospital's in vitro fertilization program, even though the reunion was held in public and a television station was invited. Yet the disclosure of the homosexuality of Oliver Sipple, who saved President Ford's life during an assassination attempt, was held to be a matter of legitimate public concern, even though he kept his sexual preference private and it had nothing to do with the actions that brought him into the limelight.

False Light. This tort is designed to cover published statements that give an inaccurate and offensive picture of a person. As with private facts, false light is measured by what is highly offensive to an ordinary person. Private facts claims are based on *truthful* publications that are so offensive; false light deals with *false* publications that are so offensive.

One problem with false light is that it is often used as a privacy-law analog to libel. Sometimes courts permit this, not only confusing two much different concepts but also disregarding the constitutional safeguards and defenses that have been imposed in libel cases. This has not been a problem in Missouri since 1986, however, when the Missouri Supreme Court expressly prohibited use of false light claims in situations of classic defamation.

The legitimate areas of false light that remain after the Missouri Supreme Court decision in *Sullivan v. Pulitzer Broadcasting Co.* are quite limited. The situations most likely to lead to false light include publications placed in an offensive context and publications making a false but favorable attribution.

- *Offensive context.* Placement of a truthful publication in a highly offensive context may constitute false light. The classic case involved a cute story about a trained pig. Nothing was wrong or inaccurate about the story—but the woman involved found it highly offensive for the story to be placed in *Chic* magazine, a sex publication, amid stories of bizarre sexual exploits.
- *False but favorable attribution.* The kind of case of that is best suited for the false light tort involved statements that are praiseworthy but false. Perhaps not surprisingly, these cases arise infrequently. In one case, Warren Spahn sued over an article that incorrectly credited him for many good works. Claims like this are most likely when the credit and the person credited just don't fit—for example, a statement praising a liberal *Mother Jones* editorial writer for supporting the Reagan-Bush economic plan.

Other Publication-Related Claims. One other kind of publication-related claim is sometimes classified as a "privacy" claim, although it really has little to do with privacy. These cases involve use of a person's name, photographs, or other personal attributes for commercial purposes and are known variously as "appropriation," "commercialization," or "right of publicity" claims.

The essence of these claims is really the right of the person whose name, photograph, or other attribute is used to control and profit from those attributes, which are not private, embarrassing, or offensive. Hence, these claims are more analogous to claims of intellectual property rights than to the right of personal privacy.

Right of Privacy and Gary Hart

As a result of a *Miami Herald* investigation in 1987, former Colorado senator Gary Hart, disheartened, found his presidential aspirations cut short. Within a few days of the *Herald*'s disclosure of Hart's affair with Donna Rice (including a politically costly pleasure trip on the yacht *Monkey Business*), Hart quit the 1988 presidential race.

The Gary Hart sex scandal of campaign 1988 was over. But could Hart have made something of it? Could Hart have sued the *Herald*? Think again before you dismiss it as impossible.

The conventional wisdom says that public figures should not sue the press—and cannot possibly win if they do. But General William Westmoreland, Senator Barry Goldwater, columnist William F. Buckley Jr., former St. Louis mayor Alfonso J. Cervantes, and many other notables have all sued the national press.

Many of these suits followed debates within the journalistic community as to the propriety of the journalistic techniques and judgments involved in major stories—just as the public saw in connection with the *Herald*'s stories on Hart.

To an involuntarily retired politician, moreover, a suit against the press may seem like an ideal form of recreation. One is reminded of the *New Yorker* cartoon showing a physician telling his patient, "Perhaps you should sue me. Litigation can be very therapeutic."

Of course, Hart never sued and was unlikely to have even considered legal action. But it is interesting to consider the issues that would be raised if Hart had sued the *Herald*.

- Can someone as prominent as Hart really sue, or would his suit automatically be thrown out of court?

- Would the *Herald*'s "keyhole journalism" stand up under judicial examination?
- Does a national politician have any real right to privacy and, if so, where does it begin and end?
- By suing, would Hart actually open the door to greater prying into his private life?
- Is there any legal remedy for the emotional harm to Hart, or his family, or the woman implicated with him by the story?
- Could a suit affect the news judgment of reporters and editors concerning coverage of presidential politics?

Of course, Hart could have sued. Under existing law, no public official or candidate, no matter how prominent, is barred from suing the press for libel, invasion of privacy, or any other tort.

This means that even disputes between politicians and the press that really turn on political and judgmental matters can get into court. In libel cases, at least the politician has a heavy burden to show serious errors in the stories published and serious fault in how the stories were put together. For public figures, libel suits are somewhat like the carnival games that are designed to attract players but are rigged so that the players hardly ever win.

In a suit, could Hart make an issue of the *Herald*'s unusual reporting techniques? Possibly. Many libel suits have been built on journalistic disputes and controversial reporting methods. Many journalists are offended by surveillance journalism and reporting of the private lives of public persons. The dispute about these issues could fuel and shape discovery in the case, as Hart's lawyers attempted to develop any conceivable evidence of reportorial recklessness.

But surveillance journalism is perfectly defensible if done within legal bounds. Assuming the *Herald*'s reporters did not trespass on Hart's property, use illegal eavesdropping devices, or otherwise illegally intrude upon or harass him, the surveillance cannot be legally actionable. Watching someone on a public street, and reporting what you saw, is perfectly legal.

Isn't there a limit to reporting, however, when it intrudes into someone's personal private life—even if that person is a presidential candidate? Probably not. Courts in deciding legal claims for rights of privacy are guided by contemporary mores. In the era of *People* magazine, the *National Enquirer*, *Penthouse*, and *Lifestyles of the Rich and Famous*, it would be difficult to condemn the *Herald*'s reporting as totally beyond current social conventions.

Moreover, voters may be legitimately concerned with the private lives and character of political candidates. Indeed, the U.S. Supreme Court commented on this very issue many years ago, noting, "A candidate who, for example, seeks to further his cause through the prominent display of his wife and children can hardly argue that his qualities as a husband or father remain 'purely private.'"

Voters and the press, in short, are entitled to inquire into a candidate's private life. (Of course, Hart would have even weaker ground to stand on than most candidates, since he *invited* the press to follow him and check out his personal life.)

A libel suit inevitably puts the spotlight on two issues: the plaintiff's character and the truth of the allegedly libelous statements. That spotlight can cause more damage to the plaintiff than the initial publication. It is one reason why libel suits are more often threatened than filed. If Hart had other things to hide, for example, evidence of those incidents would likely be discovered and revealed in the course of a libel suit. And the *Herald* would likely marshal all available evidence to support the truth of its news account. Either side could try to keep the evidence confidential until trial, but the news would almost surely get out.

Hart might hope for ultimate vindication at trial. But even that opportunity could be denied Hart. Media defendants like the *Herald* frequently get libel cases dismissed before trial, on motions to dismiss for summary judgment, because of various constitutional, common law, and procedural protections.

Could Hart overcome these formidable barriers to libel suits by suing on a different theory altogether, such as invasion of privacy or intentional infliction of emotional distress? That is a possibility, and Hart could take some encouragement from a suit brought by a Republican, the Reverend Jerry Falwell, which was pending at the time of the Hart-*Herald* incident. Falwell sued *Hustler* magazine, and the jury awarded him $200,000, on a unique "emotional distress" theory. However, *Hustler* appealed, and the U.S. Supreme Court later overturned the award as inconsistent with the Constitution's free speech guarantees.

The emotional distress or privacy theories, moreover, could conceivably also be used by Hart's family or by Donna Rice, the woman mentioned in the *Herald* stories as staying overnight with him. Until Falwell's victory in his trial, most courts prohibited end runs around the legal barriers in public figure libel cases. The Supreme Court's reversal in the *Falwell* case made it tougher for plaintiffs to fall back on other legal theories like privacy and emotional distress as a way around the barriers imposed on public figure libel claims.

Of course, even these "creative" theories, where permitted, are no panacea. They have their own proof requirements, and costs, including legal expense.

Would there also be an effect on the press or on the way other presidential campaigns are covered? It seems unlikely. Ironically, although many editors perceive that legal actions against the press have caused a "chilling effect" somewhere in their profession, those very same editors take personal pride in avoiding any such "chill" in their own practice. A Hart suit, far from chilling the *Herald* and other newspapers from future "keyhole journalism," could simply cause them to redouble their efforts and, in such cases, quadruple their proof.

In retrospect, suits by public figures against the press usually fail either to vindicate the plaintiff's reputation or to change journalistic practices. If Hart had filed a lawsuit, most likely he would have found it a frustrating experience, punctuated by a few titillating moments, culminating in a disappointing outcome—in short, an experience much like the last days of his campaign.

Scandal, Victims' Names, and Ethical Limits

April 1991 may go down as the month that gossip became respectable—or tried to.

First, Kitty Kelley's loosely documented scandal-laden celebrity biography of Nancy Reagan was published by the esteemed publishing house of Simon and Schuster. Then, the Palm Beach rape case involving the Kennedy family broke, leading to intense coverage and even publication of the victim's name and details about her life—not just by scandal sheets but also by NBC Television and the *New York Times*.

These incidents seem to point to a breakdown or blurring of the sharp ethical and legal limits that used to be accepted in mainstream journalism. More important, however, they demonstrate that our legal system, at least in recent years, has left difficult journalistic ethical decision making to editors and publishers.

Not too long ago, decisions of the kind involved here were effectively predetermined by the law. For example, under present law, NBC and the *Times*, and other papers that decided to print the name of the alleged victim of the Palm Beach rape, could do so with relatively little risk that this would be illegal.

In the past, state statutes have attempted to prevent or punish publication of certain names and information that legislators believed improper—most notably, the names of rape victims and of accused juvenile offenders. But the U.S. Supreme Court has so far struck down prosecution under statutes of that nature.

In one such case, in 1989, the Court held that a newspaper could not be prosecuted for violating Florida's rape-victim-confidentiality statute when the paper obtained the victim's name from official police records. So although the Florida statute is still on the books, NBC, the *Times*, and other publishers obviously felt free to publish the Palm Beach victim's name without undue worry about it.

In the same way, Simon and Schuster's decision to publish Kelley's Nancy Reagan biography was undoubtedly based in part on a determination that the book fell within the permissible boundaries of libel and privacy law.

This is important because celebrity biographies can easily lead to litigation. Celebrities are by nature image conscious and usually employ skillful and aggressive attorneys. Indeed, Kelley had to fight a short but bitter prepublication legal battle with Frank Sinatra before coming out with her biography of him several years before the Reagan book.

In clearing the Nancy Reagan biography for publication, Simon and Schuster was undoubtedly guided by the "public figure" standard of *New York Times v. Sullivan*, which frees authors and publishers from proving the truth of their writings about public figures so long as they do not publish intentional or reckless falsehoods.

This standard makes all the difference in a book like Kelley's. Prior to the *Sullivan* decision in 1964, publishers would probably have greatly edited or refused to publish biographies that relied so heavily on defamatory accusations made by unnamed sources. So both publication of the Kelley biography of Nancy Reagan and reporting of the name and background of the rape victim in the Palm Beach case can be attributed in part to liberalization of press law in the last few decades.

Critics of expanded legal protection for the press may, and probably will, point to this as a reason for cutting back on press freedoms and resuming statutory and other legal controls over the content of books and journals.

But there is another side to this issue, which the controversy at hand also illustrates. For those who focus on responsibility, the episodes of April 1991 also demonstrate that even in the absence of direct legal controls, the press as a whole *is* responsible and mindful of ethical considerations.

Kelley's biography, after all, engendered scores of critical reviews, analyses, and commentaries, led by the *Washington Post*'s reports of Kelley's exaggerations about her own background and investigative work. This broad media critique of the work probably countered its believability and effectiveness far more than any libel suit by Nancy Reagan ever could have.

And the NBC–*New York Times* reports on the alleged Palm Beach rape victim, far from taking mainstream journalism standards down to the supermarket tabloid level, actually rekindled the ethical debate on this issue. Although the debate revealed serious reasons why alleged victims' names should sometimes be revealed, the overall discussion seems to have reinforced the ethical policies of most newspapers not to print such information. Again, this debate is likely to do more to ensure that the proper approach is followed on this issue than any statute ever could.

So the lessening of legal controls on the press has not diminished the pressures for responsible journalism. It has simply shifted the burden of making correct ethical decisions and drawing the lines correctly to the press itself. As former Chief Justice Warren Burger noted some years ago, the choice of material to go into a newspaper is the classic "exercise of editorial control and judgment" and cannot be controlled by government regulation consistent with the First Amendment.

Cases of line-testing, such as Kitty Kelley and Palm Beach, may bother some. But the result of self-regulation within a system of press freedom is ultimately far better than the alternative of having legislators and judges decide what is ethical and proper journalism.

7

Lawbreaking, Negligence, and Unusual Claims

Reporter Deception and Lawbreaking

C AN REPORTERS VIOLATE THE LAW? NOT WITH-out incurring some risks.

While journalists enjoy some special privileges in society, immunity from basic criminal and tort laws isn't one of them. Courts have repeatedly refused to construe the First Amendment to grant reporters any privilege to break the law.

Hence, most cases of alleged journalistic illegality depend upon factors such as whether the reporter really broke the law—considering not only the letter of the law but also the intent and context of the actions taken—and whether prosecution is likely or appropriate in the situation presented. Most of these issues arise in connection with *news-gathering* activities, whether or not they result in publication of stories.

Let's follow eager young reporter Janet Woodstein as she conducts an investigation of Murray Bigshot, a St. Louis businessman who Woodstein believes is embezzling funds in order to maintain some expensive illegal habits.

Identity Deceptions. Woodstein applies for a job with Bigshot's company. Since her name might be recognized from her byline, she uses her mother's maiden name on the application and omits mention of her current employment.

Deceptive? Yes. Illegal? Probably not. Unless the potential employer is a government agency or otherwise involved in sensitive government work, there's probably nothing criminal about making out a misleading employment application. Woodstein gets the job and begins working as a clerk at Bigshot Corporation.

Trespass. Since she now possesses a key to Bigshot's office, Woodstein returns after midnight one night, using the key to gain admission. She justifies it to herself because she had legal possession of the key—after all, her new employer gave it to her on her first day of work. Clever but probably wrong, Woodstein. If the circumstances indicate that she wasn't authorized to use it at night, she may well be trespassing—both a tort (a civil wrong) and a crime in most jurisdictions.

The trespass in these circumstances is a bit unclear. It's often ambiguous whether someone has a right to enter a certain place, even if the place is private property. (The clearest situation of trespass is when the property owner tells the unwelcome guest those magic words, "Get off my property!")

Eavesdropping. The next day at work, Woodstein places her tape recorder and microphone in her desk drawer and turns on the recorder, hoping to record conversations with coworkers, which might include incriminating facts about Bigshot. If she's in Illinois, she's probably violating the Illinois Eavesdropping Act, a criminal law, by recording people without their consent. If she's in Missouri, she's safe because Missouri law requires only the consent of one party to the conversation—and in this case, she of course is consenting.

Woodstein may think that restrictive eavesdropping laws like Illinois's weren't meant for reporters like her, and there should be a First Amendment exception for eavesdropping. But the Florida Supreme Court, construing an eavesdropping statute essentially the same as the Illinois one, turned down such a First Amendment challenge years ago, and most courts would agree.

More Eavesdropping. Having obtained nothing from her desk recorder, Woodstein opens up her investigative team's closet full of spy equipment.

First, she wires herself for sound, using the ultraminiature "SN" tape recorder favored by CIA types, and begins recording conversations with coworkers and others in the hallways, around the water cooler, and while sharing rides. For this recording, the same rules apply as with the desk recorder; she'd better turn off the recorder every time she crosses the Mississippi going east.

Next she finds a parabolic microphone—the kind that is advertised in catalogs as ideal for nature lovers because they magnify otherwise inaudible distant sounds. She sets it up in a warehouse across the street from Bigshot headquarters, aims it at Bigshot's personal office, and tapes Bigshot's conversations. This eavesdropping from far away presents few ambiguities; it's a tortious invasion of privacy in most states, and a crime as well in many, since no party to the conversation is consenting to the recording, and under the circumstances the parties overheard had a reasonable expectation of privacy.

Photographic Intrusion. Not yet through with fancy electronics, Woodstein takes her subminiature Minox camera to the office and uses it to take photographs surreptitiously.

It depends on the circumstances whether this is a tortious intrusion. Most everything that can be photographed with a subminiature camera is in plain view of the photographer anyway and hence unlikely to be an intimate matter.

If Woodstein uses her Minox to photograph areas of the Bigshot business premises (or documents) that are maintained under some secrecy or confidentiality controls, however, her photography may violate some express or implied confidentiality obligations. How she *uses* the photographs could be critical on this point.

More Photographic Intrusion. Woodstein doesn't give up easily, and she *loves* electronics. She next sets up a camera with a 1,000 mm telephoto lens and polarizing filters at the warehouse, next to the parabolic microphone, and focuses the camera on Bigshot and others inside Bigshot's private office.

If the camera records events not ordinarily visible from outside, it probably constitutes an intrusion into an area within Bigshot's reasonable expectation of privacy, which could give rise to a suit by Bigshot.

Woodstein may think that this intrusion is relatively insignificant and shouldn't apply to journalists. But courts have turned down First Amendment and journalistic "necessity" defenses to intrusions of this nature; journalists, they say, must gather news without infringing anyone's reasonable expectations of privacy.

Theft of Documents. As her spy equipment fails to deliver her the goods on Bigshot, Woodstein gets desperate. She suppresses all the lessons she learned as a child about obeying the law and begins rifling through files at Bigshot's firm. She finds a few folders of Bigshot's personal expenses and takes them home. This, of course, appears to be plain old-fashioned theft.

But even Woodstein has pangs of conscience. She takes the files back the next day. That's nice, and it might keep her from being caught, but she may well still be guilty of stealing based on the period of time when she had the documents in her possession.

Woodstein remains incorrigible. It turns out that she kept *photocopies* of the documents that she took and later returned. That gets her back in hot water because she has arguably still taken and retained the *information* contained in the documents, which may be considered the valuable property of Bigshot Corporation. And, strictly speaking, Bigshot's firm also owns the copyright on the content of the documents, and the copying and use of that content may infringe the copyright—another potential dual criminal/civil law violation.

Aiding and Abetting. Woodstein is impatient. She just *knows* Bigshot is guilty, and time is running out to prove it. She calls an old high school chum, Billy Badguy, and suggests that Badguy set up Bigshot in a cocaine sale. Badguy, who deals in illegal drugs, agrees. He calls Bigshot, sets up the deal, and arranges a time and place for the exchange of money and drugs.

Woodstein is overjoyed, and she sets up all of her electronics to record the deal. She feels a slight pang of ethics, however, so she explains to Badguy that she doesn't want the deal to go through—Badguy should hold onto Bigshot's money just long enough for the cameras and microphones to record it and then give it back and refuse to go through with the deal.

This deal will create more serious complications. Woodstein has effectively aided and abetted an illegal drug deal. She may not be able to stop the deal from going through, and, even if she can, she still participated in proposing an illegal transaction and in enticing Bigshot into it.

In addition, she may be open to civil liability—in an extreme case, for example, to Bigshot or his heirs for wrongful death in case the drugs harmed or killed Bigshot.

Obstruction of Justice. The drug deal does not go off as expected. Bigshot arrives, but instead of buying drugs, he attempts to convert Badguy to religion, morality, and clean living. And after that effort gets nowhere, Bigshot's security chief attempts a citizen's arrest of Badguy.

Badguy gets away and flees to Woodstein's apartment, where he stays for several days. As he and Woodstein watch the television news one night, they learn that the county district attorney has a warrant out for Badguy. Woodstein concludes that Badguy needs some R and R, and she buys him a ticket to Cancún. In parting, she renews her reporter's promise to keep his identity and location confidential.

Woodstein's ticket purchase and her sharing of her apartment with Badguy present serious problems of obstruction of justice and harboring of a fugitive from justice. She will only compound her problems if, when questioned by authorities, she refuses to reveal Badguy's location. In the circumstances, courts are highly unlikely to uphold her argument that the reporter's privilege should allow her to keep Badguy's identity and whereabouts confidential.

Other Tactics. Finally, tired of the story and its disappointments, Woodstein resigns from Bigshot Corporation, citing the inability to perform her job in a capable manner. Although she viewed this excuse as another minor deception, this is not a problem. This time Woodstein is telling the truth.

"Negligent" Publications

- Hired hit men murder their patrons' spouses.
- A teenager suffocates in the course of a bizarre sexual experiment.
- A kidnapper on the loose haunts his victim even after she escapes from him.
- Fireworks explode in the hands of an Independence Day celebrant.
- A cook, while preparing a new dish, samples it and suffers food poisoning.
- An investor purchases corporate bonds and quickly realizes a major loss.

These situations all may seem appropriate for some kind of court action. In fact, all these cases went to court—but with an unusual twist.

The defendant in each case was not the primary wrongdoer but rather a *publisher*—respectively, a magazine that published classified ads for mercenaries for hire; a magazine that published an article about a dangerous sex act; a newspaper that published a kidnap victim's name before her captor was caught; a magazine that advertised untested fireworks; a cookbook publisher; and a financial newspaper publisher. The theory in each case was that the publisher was somehow responsible for the plaintiff's injury.

These cases are examples of a legal theory that is being asserted against publishers with increasing frequency, a theory known as *negligent publication*.

Negligence is the legal theory in most personal injury actions. The underlying concept is that in most aspects of ordinary life, such as driving an automobile, one is charged with the responsibility not to act negligently. In these cases, courts award damages to persons harmed by another's negligence.

Negligent publication suits are attempts to extend this theory to hold publishers responsible for injuries that come about through some chain of events that can be traced back to a publication, such as an article, advertisement, or recipe.

These theories have usually been rejected—for example, in five of the six cases described above, courts refused to let the negligent publication claims go to trial. But in the late 1980s and early 1990s, several courts approved the theory and gave it new life.

Three key cases involved *Soldier of Fortune* magazine, a publication that views itself as a kind of trade publication for mercenary soldiers. The classified advertising section in *Soldier of Fortune* has offered some unusual personal services. One brief ad, published in 1984, offered the services of an ex-Marine who boasted that he was a "specialist–jungle warfare" and would accept "high risk assignments."

Three other litigated classified ads began with the phrase "GUN FOR HIRE." One went on to offer to provide "bodyguard, courier, and other special skills." Another boasted of a "NAM sniper instructor" who would consider all jobs and guarantee privacy.

Each of these ads in fact offered the services of hired killers. The ex-Marine of the first ad (John Wayne Hearn) carried out the contract murder of a woman for her husband. The hired guns of the other three ads (one of them named Richard Michael Savage) were hired for similar contract murders. The victims and survivors in the cases sued *Soldier of For-*

tune magazine and claimed that *Soldier of Fortune* was responsible for the harm they suffered because it published the ads.

Those four advertisements, and three crimes, led to three reported cases, all focusing on the key issue of whether *Soldier of Fortune* could be held responsible to the victims and survivors solely because it published the advertisements for contract killers. Juries were not sympathetic to *Soldier of Fortune*. And appeals courts split in their rulings on the negligent publication theory.

In all of the cases, federal trial judges denied the magazine's motions to dismiss—thus ruling, in effect, that negligent publication was a viable legal theory. The magazine settled one case before trial. The John Wayne Hearn case went to trial in Houston and resulted in an award of $1.9 million actual damages and $7.5 million punitive damages against *Soldier of Fortune*. The third case, tried in Alabama, resulted in a $12.37 million verdict against *Soldier of Fortune*, reduced to $3.37 million by the trial court. Both verdicts against *Soldier of Fortune* were appealed, and the two appeals reached significantly different results.

In the first case, *Eimann v. Soldier of Fortune*, the U.S. Court of Appeals for the Fifth Circuit in 1989 applied standard tort liability principles and found that the advertisement in question—Hearn's "specialist jungle warfare" advertisement, which stated that he would take on "high risk assignments"—was "facially innocuous" and not "a readily identifiable criminal solicitation."

Moreover, although it did not reach *Soldier of Fortune*'s First Amendment arguments, the appeals court in *Eimann* held that the jury's verdict imposed too high a standard of conduct on the magazine. Permitting such verdicts, it held, "allows a jury to visit liability on a publisher for untoward consequences that flow from his decision to publish any suspicious, ambiguous ad that might cause serious harm. This burden on a publisher to avoid liability from suits of this type is too great; he must reject *all* such advertisements."

In the other appeal, however, the federal Court of Appeals for the Eleventh Circuit, in Atlanta, in 1992 upheld liability against *Soldier of Fortune*. In that case, *Braun v. Soldier of Fortune*, the court specifically distinguished *Eimann* and rejected *Soldier of Fortune*'s First Amendment defenses.

At issue in *Braun* was one of Richard Michael Savage's ads: "GUN

FOR HIRE: 37 year old professional mercenary desires jobs. Vietnam Veteran. Discrete [*sic*] and very private. Body guard, courier, and other special skills. All jobs considered. Phone (615) 436-9785 (days) or (615) 436-4335 (nights), or write: Rt. 2, Box 682, Village Loop Road, Gatlinburg, TN 37738."

The two-judge majority of the court of appeals in *Braun* found that this ad was *not* ambiguous. Rather, after closely analyzing the ad with its "combination of sinister terms" and "implication . . . that the advertiser would consider illegal jobs," the majority held that its publication presented "a clearly identifiable unreasonable risk." In such cases, where the risk is high, and apparent on the face of the advertisement and requires no further investigation, the court held that tort liability—like the $4.37 million damages award—was permissible. One of the three judges on the appellate panel dissented in *Braun*, stating that the language of Savage's ad was "ambiguous, rather than patently criminal" and the "crushing liability" on *Soldier of Fortune* was inappropriate.

Based on the *Braun* decision, the negligent publication theory now has a foothold in the law, and it is likely that plaintiffs will further test and attempt to utilize this theory. This doctrine, however, is flawed and poorly thought out, and future cases brought on this theory could significantly chill legitimate publishers' free expression.

Soldier of Fortune magazine may seem like an unsavory and unsympathetic victim, but if this theory ever takes off, the targets next in line could well include Betty Crocker (negligent publication of recipes), Dow Jones (negligent publication of financial advice), and Mickey Mouse (negligent production of the *Mickey Mouse Club*).

Don't laugh. Suits like these have actually been filed, including one against Walt Disney Productions alleging negligent production on the *Mickey Mouse Club* television show of a stunt that a viewer later imitated in a way that caused him to injure himself.

Until the *Soldier of Fortune* lawsuits, these cases were usually dismissed before trial for two sound reasons. First, the negligent publication theory violates a settled rule of injury cases that one person should generally not be responsible for injury that is not directly foreseeable or that occurs because of the intervening act of another.

Second, the theory allows punishing blows to be inflicted against legal speech—speech (like cookbooks, financial advice articles, entertainment shows, and even a mercenary magazine) that has real value to society and enjoys explicit protection in the First Amendment to the Constitution.

Publishers and producers of magazines, newspapers, books, movies, and television programs would become greatly inhibited in the exercise of their free speech rights if they faced liability for all injuries that can be circuitously attributed to their publications. Many would quit the field or steer the content of their publications into noncontroversial pabulum.

Courts, moreover, have recognized the real dangers unlimited damage awards pose to First Amendment freedoms. That is the reason the Supreme Court has imposed difficult and demanding barriers to recovery in libel cases—even though libels are presumed to cause *direct* injury, not merely the *indirect* injury claimed in negligent publication cases.

The majority in *Braun v. Soldier of Fortune* may have felt that the negligent publication theory as applied in *Braun* avoids these problems, by requiring a clearly identifiable and nonambiguous risk. But as the *Soldier of Fortune* cases show, and as common experience confirms, juries may well apply hindsight standards and act on their sympathy for victims in applying the fuzzy legal standard of "clearly identifiable" and "unreasonable" risk. The threat of damages verdicts rendered under such circumstances cannot help but chill and inhibit many valuable publishing efforts.

Failure to Publish

Newspapers are often enough challenged in court for what they publish. But sometimes they are also challenged for what they do not publish.

In one case, the *New York Times* almost had to go to trial to defend what it did not publish. The issue was a book that did not make the *Times'* bestseller list. The author, William Peter Blatty, sued the *Times* for damages of more than $3 million. He claimed his book *Legion* would have earned that much more, if only it had been a regular entry on the *Times* fiction bestseller list.

Although such suits often seem frivolous, they are not always dismissed out of hand. Blatty's suit against the *Times* traveled through three levels of California courts. One of those courts would have allowed him to proceed to trial.

Blatty, author of the bestseller *The Exorcist*, claimed that by his and his publishers' calculations, his second novel *Legion* was selling enough copies in mid-1983 to be on the *Times* fiction bestseller list. He alleged that his publisher gave its sales figures to the *Times*, but the *Times* refused to examine them. The book finally made the list in September 1983, but only for one week, and as the last book on the list.

Blatty sued the *Times* in Los Angeles, on four different theories. The trial judge dismissed the case. Blatty then appealed, and the California Court of Appeal gave him a minor victory. The appeals court held against Blatty on three claims but ruled that he had a potential claim against the *Times* for "intentional interference with prospective economic advantage." Under this theory, Blatty would have had to prove, essentially, that the *Times* was out to get him—that the *Times* manipulated its bestseller list with the intention of discouraging bookstores from ordering Blatty's book.

As implausible as this theory seems, the appeals court ruling probably would have forced the *Times* to trial, where the key issues would have been how and why the *Times* editors published the bestseller list as they did. In 1987, however, the California Supreme Court unanimously reversed the appeals court decision and upheld the trial court's complete dismissal of Blatty's suit.

The California Supreme Court initially recognized that there is a "broad zone of protection" for the press under the First Amendment. This zone of protection was originally established in defamation (libel and slander) actions. However, the court stated, it applies to all legal claims based on "the alleged injurious falsehood of a statement," regardless of the particular legal theory asserted.

Without such a broad view of First Amendment protections, the court stated, "plaintiffs suing press defendants might simply affix a label other than 'defamation' to their injurious falsehood claims." Since the essence of Blatty's claim against the *Times* was that he was harmed by a false publication, the California Supreme Court said, his claim must be subject to the limitations imposed on libel suits.

Measured against these limitations, Blatty's suit clearly failed. The *Times* bestseller list did not mention him so it could not defame him. Nor did the *Times* bestseller list purport to be anything other than a *sample*, not necessarily an infallible compilation, of book sales so it could not be proven false.

Therefore, the court held that all of Blatty's claims, regardless of the narrow legal labels applied, had to be dismissed outright. As a result, the

Times no longer faced the peculiar prospect of a trial over what it did not publish.

Blatty is not the first—or last—litigant to go to court complaining of what a newspaper did not print. Most of the suits seek compelled publication, but damages claims (like Blatty's) are increasingly popular.

Consider several cases:

- A political gadfly in the U.S. Virgin Islands sued to compel a newspaper there to publish his "news releases" claiming that the governor was corrupt. And when the local television stations didn't report on his suit, he sued them, too.
- A contractor sued the *Chicago Tribune* for $250,000 when the paper supposedly "lost" and did not publish a legal notice he submitted.
- An Arab activist in Philadelphia sued to compel newspapers, wire services, and press organizations to publicize what he claimed was the illegality of U.S. foreign policy toward Israel. He claimed the press "discriminated" against him by refusing to print this "news."
- Numerous advertisers have sued newspapers that rejected proposed advertisements because of matters of taste, standards, and perceived libel problems.
- A restaurant owner sued KMOX radio in St. Louis on contract, tort, and antitrust theories when the station refused to have one of its popular announcers give testimonials for the restaurant.

The plaintiffs lost in all these cases. In deciding these cases, courts have developed a growing body of *nonpublication* law.

In advertising cases, courts have upheld newspapers' discretion to set their own advertising standards, so long as the newspaper does not violate antitrust laws in choosing advertisers or discrimination laws in classifying advertisements.

As to editorial content, publishers' discretion not to print is even stronger. The United States Supreme Court in 1974 held unconstitutional a Florida law that sought to create, in essence, state-compelled opened pages for political candidates. In that case, the Supreme Court set forth the guiding principle that "the choice of material to go into a newspaper"—including decisions on what not to print—cannot be regulated by the government, "consistent with First Amendment guarantees of a free press as they have evolved to this time."

The "failure to publish" cases indicate that many people see news media publicity as a valuable legal entitlement—something that a court should give them if an editor or publisher does not. The legal rule remains, however, that publishers do not have to answer in court for what they do not publish.

Threats to Publishing

Book publishing used to be considered a quiet and dignified trade, a business carried out among literary types in ivory towers remote from the angry conflicts of everyday life.

Things have changed. Just ask the publishers of Salman Rushdie's *Satanic Verses*, the novel that so offended Islamic fundamentalists that in early 1989 they put a $5 million bounty on the author's life. Or ask writers and editors who have felt the waves of legal and social changes that have increased the legal risks of book publishing.

Not too long ago, the legal concerns of the publishing industry were few. A working knowledge of defamation and copyright was sufficient for an editor, and most writers didn't have to concern themselves much about either area. But the continuing expansion of tort and contractual liabilities, and the litigation explosion, have greatly changed the legal playing field for publishing in many different ways.

These new liabilities, moreover, extend beyond what might be considered the riskiest part of the business—nonfiction investigative exposés. The changes affect even fiction, biography, history, and "safe" current nonfiction works that are based on reliable official records.

One new liability of the 1980s, for example, was the so-called Son of Sam law, which had been enacted by Congress and the legislators of several key states (including New York and California). Sparked by the case of David Berkowitz, the "Son of Sam" killer in New York City, and designed to preclude criminals from profiting from their misconduct, the Son of Sam statutes essentially prohibited publishers from paying criminals for books based on the stories of their criminal activities.

Several of the statutes, moreover, were "self-enforcing" in that they required publishers on their own initiative to withhold royalty payments from a so-called author-criminal. This put a difficult burden on publishers, given the vagueness of the Son of Sam law and the many indirect means by which royalty payments could reach persons deemed to be criminals.

The United States Supreme Court ultimately held the New York Son of Sam law unconstitutional because it singled out for forfeiture only income derived from expressive activities. The Court recognized that the state has an important interest in ensuring that victims of crimes are compensated by the criminal perpetrators. But the court held that withholding income only from the criminals' books was the wrong way to compensate victims.

The Son of Sam laws essentially amounted to viewpoint censorship in that they burdened only speech with a certain content: writings by criminals about their crimes. And perhaps even more dangerously, the statutes were so broad that they penalized works on *any* subject, so long as it in some way expressed the author's thoughts or recollections about a crime. As the Supreme Court noted:

> Had the Son of Sam law been in effect at the time and place of publication, it would have escrowed payment for such works as The Autobiography of Malcolm X, which describes crimes committed by the civil rights leader before he became a public figure; Civil Disobedience, in which Thoreau acknowledges his refusal to pay taxes and recalls his experience in jail; and even the Confessions of Saint Augustine, in which the author laments "my past foulness and the carnal corruptions of my soul," one instance of which involved the theft of pears from a neighboring vineyard.

Of course, the Supreme Court's decision has not totally ended the threat to publishers from Son of Sam laws; the decision intimated that such laws may be permissible if they reach all income of convicted criminals, not just income from expressive activities. Such revised victim-compensation laws, if upheld, may still impact on publishers.

Another relatively new liability for publishers is the tort liability that has been applied to fictionalized accounts that are alleged to be takeoffs on real persons. Under the fictionalization theory, a story that is told as fiction may nonetheless create liabilities as if it were an assertion of fact. The theory is that a damaging barb at a person contained in thinly veiled fiction can be as harmful as if it were made as an outright factual claim.

But while fictionalization may be simple in theory, in practice it imposes difficult burdens on writers and publishers. It is easy for a prospective plaintiff to take offense at a literary character with whom he or she shares a few characteristics and difficult for writers and publishers to protect themselves from hypersensitive readers. One can well wonder, for example, how many fictionalization claims might be filed in Hannibal, Missouri, if Mark Twain were writing today.

Another relatively new legal theory affecting book publishing is the growing recognition of celebrities' rights connected with use of their names, personal characteristics, and reputations. Especially in California, the law gives special deference to a celebrity's "right of publicity." Although the right of publicity was designed to protect the celebrity's expression rather than to inhibit authors' expression, it is often used offensively—against critical writers.

Thus, a writer who writes an unfavorable biography of an entertainer may find himself sued by the entertainer, alleging that the unauthorized biography illegally "appropriates" elements of the subject's protected right of personal publicity. Frank Sinatra asserted claims like this when he attempted to stop Kitty Kelley's critical biography.

Copyright law can similarly be used offensively to seek to restrain critical books. Since J. D. Salinger used a belated copyright on his unpublished letters as a device to restrain a critical biography in 1986, several other copyright holders similarly attempted to use their copyrights to prevent publication of critical books.

Many other new legal theories create potential liabilities for book publishers. One of the most ominous threats is the federal "RICO" (Racketeer Influenced Corrupt Organizations) Act, which provides for forfeiture of profits from enterprises found to be "racketeer influenced."

RICO is illustrative of an increasingly popular type of statute—one so single-mindedly directed against some unpopular vice (such as racketeering, fraud, eavesdropping, pornography, and child abuse) that it ignores constitutional concerns regarding its effect on First Amendment activities such as publishing.

The RICO forfeiture remedy has been threatened against publishers of allegedly obscene books and could be extended under some liberal theories to allow confiscation of profits of books found to further certain kinds of criminal or fraudulent activities. The Supreme Court has recognized First Amendment limits on some of the broad remedies of the RICO law, but many similar issues remain.

The legal risks and liabilities represented by all these theories—Son of Sam laws, fictionalization, right of publicity, offensive use of copyright, and RICO and other statutes—have necessarily threatened publishers and affected their publishing decisions. And as the dramatic death threats to Salman Rushdie have brought home, no reader can be indifferent to any serious threat to free expression.

Silly Media Lawsuits: Aberrations or Barometer?

(One always wonders if archaeologists and historians reach the right conclusions from the fragmentary evidence they study. The following proposal gives us a glimpse of how modern American media law could be misunderstood if scholars of the future could study only a few of the most unusual—and even silly—cases of the 1990s.)

To: Editor, *Journal of Ancient History*
From: Legal Archaeology Team, Oceana University
Date: Sometime in the Fourth Millennium
Re: Proposal for an article, "American Media Law in the 1990s: Sex, Hyperbole, and Entertainers' Rights"

We propose an article describing media law in the United States in ancient times (the late twentieth century), based on our analysis of a number of court decisions that we recently uncovered. The decisions, by various state and federal courts in the early 1990s, had been miraculously preserved in a mudslide caused by a great flood in 1993.

Scholars have long sought an insight into the law of this period, especially after so many records were lost after the Kill-All-the-Lawyers Act of the twenty-second century, and, of course, the World Computer Outage of the twenty-fourth century.

The unquestionably authentic decisions we found appear to shed considerable light on American media law of that period. A brief summary of the cases follows:

Damage Claims Based on Publications. Several of the court decisions we found described libel and invasion of privacy cases, in which the plaintiffs sought damages for statements published or broadcast about them:

- A radio announcer was sued for calling the manager of a competing station a "sleazy whore." The trial judge, in state court in St. Louis, Missouri, dismissed the suit, while noting that the broadcaster's work represented "modern broadcast journalism at its best."

- A court in Illinois permitted a case to proceed against radio announcers who made fun of a man who had organized a benefit for a charity devoted to helping persons afflicted with the so-called Elephant Man's disease. The announcers implied that the man's wife and son had deformed heads and that his wife was so physically unattractive that he would not have married her except in a shotgun wedding.
- A ninety-seven-year-old woman sued and won more than $850,000 in damages from a newspaper that used her photograph to illustrate a fictitious article in a national scandal sheet. The article stated that an elderly woman in another city had become pregnant on her paper route. (The courts that affirmed this judgment, including the federal court of appeals in St. Louis, noted that no one actually believed the centenarian had become pregnant—but the article imputed unchastity to her nonetheless.)
- The highest state court in Missouri, in allowing a libel case to proceed, noted that under existing law, the more "vituperative and abusive" a statement is, the more likely it is to be protected.

Conclusions: Assuming that these cases are typical, we conclude that late twentieth-century Americans often used hyperbole and reckless charges and accusations as their primary means of public communication. It also appears that in cases like this libel and privacy laws led to almost random, haphazard results.

Business Rights and Sexual Themes. A number of cases dealt with business rights, often involving the use of sexual themes and parodies:

- A manufacturer of condoms sought to market its product under the name "Old Glory Condoms," using the symbol of a condom painted like an American flag waving in the breeze. Federal authorities held the symbol was not scandalous and could be protected as a trademark.
- Two manufacturers of T-shirts fought in federal court over their rights to drawings of skeletons engaged in various sexual acts. The court ruled that the concept of "skeleton sex" T-shirts was not protectable under the federal copyright law—although particular drawings of skeleton sexual acts were. (In one footnote, the court discussed the number of sexual positions one might expect of skeletons.)
- Two of the coauthors of the song "Why Do Fools Fall in Love?" sued another coauthor for publishing the song without crediting them as

authors. They claimed, among other things, that they were deprived of the opportunity to develop reputations as songwriters. The court found that they had not proved their case.

Conclusion: Courts decided business and advertising issues, even involving the ever-popular sexual themes and imagery, based on laws of general application, giving considerable deference to the needs of businesses.

Celebrity Rights. In a number of the cases, celebrities asserted (and usually won) some unusual claims:

- Vanna White, a television entertainer known for the stylish turning of letters on a game show set, sued Samsung Electronics over an advertisement that suggested that eventually she might be replaced by a robot. Courts, apparently feeling protective of her right to corner the market on game-show letter-turning, ruled that she could take her claim to trial. (She was eventually awarded $403,000.)
- A well-known chef and writer, Paul Prudhomme, was permitted to sue Folgers Coffee Company over a television commercial that, among other things, portrayed a chef who, like Prudhomme, had a portly build, dark hair, and full beard.
- Tom Waits, a singer known for his raspy voice and skat-singing style, sued Frito-Lay over a Doritos corn chip television commercial that employed a similar singing style. Ironically, one of Waits's own songs borrowed from and mimicked hard-sell advertising sales pitches of others.
- Mickey Dora, a pioneer surfer, sued the makers of the video documentary *Legends of Malibu*, claiming that he did not authorize them to use film footage taken of him in the early days of surfing. This time, the courts drew the line and held that Dora's rights to control exploitation of his likeness were subservient to the public interest and he could not prohibit use of his image in a documentary.

Conclusion: Courts of that time period were strongly protective of celebrity rights—even mannerisms, general appearances, and associations with a particular menial role.

Overall Conclusions: The decisions of that period relating to libel and privacy claims appear to vindicate neither the freedom to publish nor the dignity of individuals. Indeed, the rulings appear almost haphazard, and to that extent, neither individuals nor publishers could have much confidence in this law. By contrast, claims of businesses and celebrities, even involving frivolous subject matters, appear to be more carefully and consistently protected.

In sum, we believe a scholarly review and analysis of these cases, in the *Journal of Ancient History*, will contribute greatly to understanding of the laws and practices of that enigma of history, late twentieth-century America.

(Note: This proposal demonstrates what a misleading view one would get of our culture and legal system from a few selected and unrepresentative cases.)

Copyright and Protection for Ideas

Copyright Myths and Realities

YOU CAN IGNORE A SUBPOENA IF YOUR NAME isn't spelled correctly on it. It's okay to hunt on property that doesn't have a posted "No Trespassing" sign. And you can't be sued for libel for reporting what someone else said so long as you correctly attribute the statement.

Myths, old wives' tales, and other misunderstandings like these abound in the law. But there are probably more misunderstandings in current circulation about copyright than any other area of law.

In the century since Mark Twain noted that "only one thing is impossible to God, to find any sense in any copyright law on this planet," copyright laws have only become more complex, and copyright myths more abundant. This is particularly so given the changes in U.S. copyright law in the last two decades.

Let's examine a few of the prevailing myths.

Myth 1. You have to do certain things (such as publish a copyright notice and get the copyright registered) in order to obtain a copyright. A few years ago, this was partly true since works published without a copyright notice

157

went into the public domain. But it has never been a requirement that one register a work in order to have a copyright, and since 1989 even notice has not been required.

A copyright is nothing more than the right of the author of a work to control its publication, adaption, display, or performance for a limited period of time. Under current law, that right springs into being automatically when a work is created (in the words of the Copyright Act, when it becomes "fixed in tangible form"). So once you write your manuscript, type your screenplay, film your movie, or record your song, you have a copyright in that new creative work.

A copyright *notice* (the © symbol, year of first publication, and your name, printed on the work in question) is no longer essential but simply serves to warn off potential infringers. *Registration* of the copyright with the Copyright Office of the Library of Congress is essential only if you wish to sue someone for infringement.

Myth 2. Some newly printed works are copyrighted (like a newspaper's "copyrighted article") and others aren't. The fact that a newspaper editor, acting out of habit and pride in a particular story, places a copyright notice on that story and not on others doesn't mean the other stories are fair game for copying. Nowadays, as noted above, every newly created work is automatically copyrighted.

Copyright notices like the ones used on special newspaper articles are almost a kind of advertising. They send the message, "This is an especially important story." And like "No Trespassing" signs, they warn potential lawbreakers about something everyone should know anyway— that you can't trespass on others' real property or infringe on others' intangible intellectual property.

Myth 3. Copyright is primarily for authors of literary works. While the Constitution authorized copyrights to be granted to authors, it was left for Congress to define "authors." And Congress has decided that authors include photographers, artists, mapmakers, architects, musicians, and writers of computer software, among others.

As a result, much of the economic significance of copyrights today relates to nonliterary work. Rights to musical compositions and performances (like Lennon/McCartney songs and Michael Jackson albums) and to computer software (like WordPerfect and Lotus 1-2-3) probably cumulatively outweigh the market value of rights to literary works like John Grisham's novels.

Myth 4. Copyright is reserved for creative works of significant merit—like Grisham's books, Spielberg's movies, and Beatles' music. In one sense, the purpose of copyright law is to encourage creation of meritorious works—to "promote the progress of science and the useful arts" in the Constitution's words. But copyright extends to all original works, regardless of merit.

Scripts and videotapes of *All My Children*, letters announcing the Publisher's Clearinghouse sweepstakes, the taped chatter of baseball play-by-play announcers, photographs published in *Hustler*, daily traffic reports on radio (if they are taped and hence "fixed in tangible form"), and even your son or daughter's letter from college asking for more money, all qualify as copyrightable creative works.

So, also, many business publications and productions enjoy copyright protection. A restaurant's menu, a mail-order retailer's catalog, a company's employee manual, an instructional video, and a manufacturer's product designs and written manufacturing procedures all qualify for copyright. Hence, copyright infringement claims may figure in many business disputes, when competitors, ex-employees, or others copy or imitate a firm's copyrighted works.

Myth 5. Copyright is structured for big business, and little guys have no practical copyright rights or power. Although publishers do benefit most from copyright protection, the "work for hire" doctrine actually gives one important leg up to freelance writers and artists (although not to employees who create works for their employers).

Nonemployee writers and artists who sell their work are presumed, in the absence of an agreement to the contrary, to retain the copyright in the work. Thus a freelance writer can sell a story to a newspaper but retain the right to adapt it for a magazine article, a book, or a screenplay. A freelance artist who allows a customer to reproduce an image in one form (e.g., a particular publication) generally retains all remaining rights and may sell rights to reproduce it in other forms.

Myth 6. Only direct copying of copyrighted works is forbidden. Copyright protection extends beyond the author's exact words or the artist's precise expressions.

In the famous J. D. Salinger case decided in 1987, for example, the biographer Ian Hamilton attempted to paraphrase Salinger's copyrighted letters. Where Salinger had written "like a dead rat," Hamilton used the phrase "resembling a lifeless rodent." Salinger had written "grey and nude," and Hamilton paraphrased, "ancient and unclothed." These and similar close paraphrases were held to be infringement because Hamilton had infringed on Salinger's "sequence of thoughts, choice of words, emphasis and arrangement"—that is, the essence of his creativity.

Similarly, several years ago the celebrity artist Jeff Koons, mimicking a photograph he had obtained in an airport gift shop, created a sculpture, *String of Puppies*, portraying a couple sitting on a park bench holding eight puppies. Despite the differences in artistic media and Koons's professed desire to comment on pop culture, the Koons sculpture was held to infringe the copyright of the photographer who took the original photograph.

Myth 7. If a work is copyrighted, all copying is forbidden. Both the apparent meaning of the word *copyright* and the message that the powerful publishing, music, and movie industries would like to send to consumers are deceptive. *Copyright* originated centuries ago as the "copieright," meaning the right of a book publisher to be the exclusive first publisher of a manuscript (then called a "copie"). Historically, a copyright did not mean that all copying was forbidden but rather only that certain rights essential to bring the work to market (such as the right of first commercial publication) could be exclusively granted and legally protected.

In recent decades the photocopy machine has brought a new meaning to the word *copy* and greatly eased reproduction of printed works. But it is less clear than popularly thought that all photocopying of copyrighted works constitutes infringement. Even before photocopy machines, handwritten and other kinds of copying of portions of copyrighted works for personal use were widespread and generally permitted.

The Supreme Court in the 1984 *Sony Betamax* case permitted personal home copying of television broadcasts, thus indicating that other kinds of personal copying may also be permitted. A related question—business photocopying for research uses—is still hotly debated. Although several decisions held that the practice constitutes infringement, each case depends on its own facts.

The myths mentioned above are only a few of those that surround copyright law. Years ago, such misunderstandings may have been relatively inconsequential. But in today's world, given the increasing value of copyrights and the increasing number of persons owning and using copyrights, all persons involved in communications and artistic work ought to get beyond the myths and better understand copyright issues.

Fair Use and the Salinger Biography

Copyright law is a protection, not a hazard, for writers—right? Wrong. It is both.

Copyright can be a hazard whenever a writer quotes from or paraphrases the writings, published or unpublished, of another. J. D. Salinger, the famous author whose name seems always accompanied by the adjective "reclusive," brought this home when he successfully enjoined the publication of an unauthorized biography.

Salinger's biographer, Ian Hamilton, discovered a number of revealing letters written by Salinger, which the recipients had donated to several university libraries. Hamilton quoted extensively from these letters in preparing his manuscript, thus creating a revealing portrait of "the reclusive J. D. Salinger."

Salinger, however, obtained galley proofs of the biography. In reading the galleys he learned for the first time of the availability of his letters. Immediately, Salinger registered seventy-nine of his unpublished letters for copyright protection. That was his right; authors can register copyrights in their works at any time, even years after they were written, and even if they no longer possess the writings.

Once the copyrights were registered, Salinger complained to Hamilton and his publisher, Random House, about their use of the letters. In response, they revised the book, converting much of the quoted material into paraphrase, and quoted directly only about 200 words. Salinger nonetheless still complained of the paraphrases and sued to prevent publication of the biography.

Salinger won. The federal Court of Appeals for the Second Circuit, in New York, ruled that Hamilton's biography infringed Salinger's copyright in his private letters. The court directed an order in 1986 preventing publication of the second version of Hamilton's biography, which had the working title, *Salinger: A Writing Life*.

The appeals court noted that copyright law (which has its origins in the Constitution) protects only the "expressive content" of a writing, not the facts or ideas it contains. In the court's judgment, Hamilton's biography went over the line. It not only reported the facts and ideas contained in Salinger's letters but also borrowed and exploited Salinger's creative expression.

Hamilton eventually published a book about Salinger, but it was a much different book than he had intended. Indeed, as finally published in 1988, the book, *In Search of J. D. Salinger*, chiefly concerned Hamilton's attempts to uncover the facts of Salinger's life, including Hamilton's excursions into copyright law.

The Second Circuit court decision, *Salinger v. Random House*, illustrates the fine line writers must follow in making use of the writings of others.

First, lengthy *direct quotation*, like that used by Hamilton in his initial manuscript, clearly constitutes infringement. That is why Hamilton and Random House voluntarily revised the manuscript to remove almost all of the direct quotes, once Salinger registered his copyright.

Second, brief, selected direct quotations may or may not constitute infringement. Generally, such short quotations are protected by the *fair use* doctrine, which permits limited use of copyrighted material.

However, fair use is quite limited with respect to quotations from unpublished works, like Salinger's letters. And the court stressed in the *Salinger* case that fair use is a *qualitative* as well as a quantitative standard. If the quotations from the letters are what "makes the book worth reading," then even brief, selected quotes may constitute infringement.

Third, *paraphrasing* from copyrighted material can constitute infringement, too. The trial judge in the *Salinger* case found Hamilton's paraphrasing acceptable, but the appeals court disagreed, pointing to many of Hamilton's word-for-word paraphrases of Salinger's letters.

For example, where Salinger wrote "like a dead rat," Hamilton used the paraphrase "resembling a lifeless rodent." Salinger's phrase "grey and nude" became Hamilton's "ancient and unclothed," and Salinger's "applauding madly" became Hamilton's "claps her hands in appreciation." Similarly, Salinger in one letter wrote of Wendell Willkie, "He looks to me like a guy who makes his wife keep a scrapbook for him." Hamilton, in his revised manuscript, used the same simile with different words, writing that Salinger "had fingered [Willkie] as the sort of fellow who makes his wife keep an album of his press clippings."

The appeals court found that such close paraphrases, though not infringing Salinger's precise words, nonetheless infringed his "sequence of thoughts, choice of words, emphasis, and arrangement" and thus infringed Salinger's copyrighted creative expression.

The *Salinger* decision illustrates that copyright law is a hazard to a writer and can even lead to court orders preventing publication whenever the writer directly or indirectly infringes the "creative expression" of another.

Writers must be diligent, therefore, in using copyrighted (or copyrightable) sources to ensure that as they report facts or ideas from these sources, they do not borrow the original writers' words, arrangements, sequences, emphases, or literary devices.

Copyright Lesson

[Note: We are listening in on a journalism school legal seminar, taught in the late 1980s by a professor who learned copyright law a decade or more earlier.]
PROFESSOR. Welcome, class, to today's seminar on copyright law. We are fortunate to have with us today a distinguished panel of lawyers, journalists, biographers, historians, and publishers, all of whom have experience with recent copyright suits.

Let me begin with some copyright basics. Copyright law, of course, is much less controversial than the laws of libel or privacy. It affords great protections to us as writers.

A copyright is a grant of exclusive rights in a creative work. This work can be an article, a book, a screenplay, a piece of artwork, a movie or television show, or some other original creative work.

Of course, before a copyright comes into being, certain formalities must be followed. For instance, the writer must put a copyright notice on his work, he must publish it, and he must register the copyright with the Copyright Office in the Library of Congress in Washington, D.C.
LAWYER. Excuse me, Professor. A copyright comes into being automatically when a work is created, even in the absence of the formalities you mentioned. Registration of the copyright with the Copyright Office helps in the event of disputes and is required before you can sue on a copyright, but it is not otherwise required.

Under the 1976 Copyright Act, publication isn't required for a copyright to come into being. And because of an international copyright convention that the United States has ratified, a copyright notice isn't even required, although it is still a good idea.

PROFESSOR. Ah, thank you, Mr. Lawyer, for that technical clarification. Now I'd like to leave the technicalities and address copyright concerns of journalists and writers of nonfiction works.

We must first distinguish between facts, ideas, and expressions. The Copyright Act protects only an author's particular *expression* of an idea or fact, not the idea or fact itself.

So no one can copyright facts. A historian can use original sources and confidently write about past events such as the story of the Watergate scandal without fear of copyright infringement.

MAGAZINE EDITOR. Professor, even historical writing and reporting can involve copyright infringement. In 1979, *The Nation* magazine obtained an advance copy of President Ford's memoirs and published an account of his pardon of President Nixon for the Watergate crimes. The story was historically accurate and quoted in places from Ford's own explanations.

But Ford's publisher sued the magazine, and ultimately won in the Supreme Court, on the ground that the magazine, by using the quotations, went beyond reporting facts and infringed the copyright on the Ford memoirs.

PROFESSOR. Hmm. Well, wasn't that a special case because *The Nation*'s story preempted *Time* magazine's serialization of the Ford memoirs?

But that leads me to the long-established fair use doctrine, a doctrine that can be very helpful to those who need to quote or use small portions of copyrighted material.

A copyright gives the creator a bundle of exclusive rights in his creation—including the rights to reproduce the work, prepare derivative works, and distribute copies of the work. The copyright owner can prevent others from copying or other infringing uses of his work.

But that does not mean that all use of the copyrighted work by others is forbidden. The law specifically allows "fair use"—a permissible limited amount of copying.

"Fair use" has always been an important aid to journalists and nonfiction writers. It permits quotation of excerpts from a book in a book review, and quotations from key sources so long as they are small in size compared to the whole copyrighted work.

BIOGRAPHER. Professor, some of my colleagues have been burned by court decisions that have construed "fair use" quite narrowly. It seems that almost any use of copyrighted material, even by biographers, is being held to constitute infringement.

For one thing, the *amount* of copyrighted material that is used isn't the test for fair use. *The Nation* used less than 1 percent of Ford's memoirs, but the Supreme Court said that was too much because it included key passages—the ones that made the book "worth reading."

And the J. D. Salinger case is even worse. Salinger sued Random House several years ago, when it was about to publish an unauthorized biography of him. The author, Ian Hamilton, had quoted from Salinger's private letters, which were publicly available in several university library collections.

But Salinger registered his copyright in the letters—many years after he had written them—and successfully sued. The federal appeals court in New York prevented the book from including quotations from the letters, or even paraphrases of them. The decision essentially prevented publication of Hamilton's biography.

PROFESSOR. Well . . . ah, wasn't the *Salinger* case unusual because it involved unpublished letters, which are given greater copyright protection than published works? Anyway, one court decision by one federal appeals court really shouldn't be taken as the end to the time-honored fair use doctrine.

INVESTIGATIVE REPORTER. It's more than just one case, Professor. And the court that's involved is the Second Circuit U.S. Court of Appeals in New York City, which has jurisdiction over all the major publishing houses.

As a reporter, I'm bothered by the decision involving a book on U.S. foreign policy written by Jonathan Kwitny, an award-winning investigative reporter. Kwitny quoted from a manuscript by a former U.S. embassy official in Teheran. The book, *Endless Enemies*, portrayed the official unfavorably. But from a standpoint of avoiding a libel suit, Kwitny did everything right. His book was scrupulously accurate and even gave the official's story in his own words.

But because of *The Nation* and *Salinger* cases, the official saw that he had a better legal weapon than a libel suit. He sued for *copyright infringement*, even though his real concern was not copying of his writing but the *unfavorable portrayal* of his actions. He won—in a federal district court in the Second Circuit.

HISTORIAN. Professor, I agree with my fellow panelists. Even my profession is being hurt by the Second Circuit decisions. The Second Circuit said it would have enjoined a book about the history of the Church of Scientology and its founder, L. Ron Hubbard, because it quoted from private copyrighted Scientology writings—which were essential to telling the story.

That book avoided an injunction only because of a procedural blunder by the copyright owners. I understand some of the judges dissented quite vigorously, but the majority held to a very rigid view that even refused to recognize any First Amendment rights to quote newsworthy copyrighted materials.

PUBLISHER. I, too, am very concerned, Professor. These recent copyright decisions have turned copyright law on end so that in many instances it now *inhibits* authors more than it protects them.

In my profession, scores of manuscripts are currently being rewritten because of these new decisions. Few of them are coming out any better for the additional work, since we are eliminating the quotations that give the manuscripts their color, liveliness, and authenticity.

To us in the publishing world, these decisions seem topsy-turvy. They are allowing disgruntled subjects of books a powerful censorship tool—one that would be inconceivable in the legal fields of libel, privacy, and prior restraint.

PROFESSOR. (*Glancing at clock.*) Excuse me, Mr. Publisher and other panelists. Our class time is now almost up.

(*Shuffling and examining notes.*)

Let me now conclude . . . that our copyright laws are based on the U.S. Constitution, which allows Congress to secure exclusive rights to writers in order to "promote the progress of science and useful arts."

I am sure, in conclusion, that those of us in the writing and publishing fields are very much appreciative of the special recognition and protection afforded our creative work by copyright law.

DISTINGUISHED PANEL. [*Silence.*]

The Nature of Copyright and Users' Rights

Almost any writer or artist has warm fuzzy feelings about copyright law. It is seen as one of the few special privileges given to writers and other creative folk. It seems to put the government's imprimatur on creative work and even holds open the promise, perhaps some day, of profit from one's writing or artistry. This vision is about as realistic as most warm fuzzies.

For one thing, copyright has always primarily protected publishers rather than authors because of the economics of the publishing business. Beyond that, however, several modern trends in copyright law actually inhibit or threaten the values that copyright law was designed to protect—the advance of knowledge and learning.

If that seems too abstract to be a practical concern, consider whose interests have been affected adversely by these developments: journalists, biographers, historians, writers, researchers, librarians and library users, and even sports fans.

The Nature of Copyright: A Law of Users' Rights by L. Ray Patterson and Stanley W. Lindberg is an outstanding contribution to the literature on copyright. It not only describes these adverse trends but also provides the full historical and analytical perspective to explain what has gone wrong.

One of the basic problems is that copyright law by nature is special-interest legislation. The Founding Fathers may have had pure do-gooder instincts when they framed the copyright clause of the Constitution. But in each of the copyright acts since the first one in 1790, Congress has responded to special-interest groups.

The 1976 Copyright Act, the current law, is the most extreme example. Industry lobbyists—book publishers and the motion picture, recording, and computer software industries in particular—essentially hashed out the act on their own and handed it to Congress for enactment. The results were changes in the law that solve industry concerns but ignore other user and writer concerns and, in some cases, even inhibit free speech.

The problem has been compounded by courts that misunderstand copyright principles. To oversimplify one of Patterson and Lindberg's main themes, courts have often mistakenly viewed copyright as an inherent property right of authors and publishers rather than as a limited grant by the government designed to promote the advancement of knowledge. Viewing copyright solely as a property right, courts have often reached extreme rulings that distorted the balance of interest among writers, publishers, and users.

The combined effect of the legislation and the court rulings has been to narrow the *use* of copyrighted materials far more than would be appropriate to serve the advancement-of-knowledge purposes.

Consider these developments:

- Subjects of unfavorable biographies and news reports can, under a series of court decisions in the 1980s based on copyright law, restrain any but the most minimal quotations and paraphrasing from their own unpublished writings. These rulings, restrictively construing the copyright *fair use* doctrine, stem from the copyright-as-property theory, which the authors persuasively argue is contrary to history, constitutional policy, and congressional intent. (A ruling in November 1991 by the Second Circuit federal appeals court for the first time found a challenged book to be within the "fair use" safe harbor. But the opinion did not reject the court's prior restrictive rulings. That was ultimately accomplished by legislation originally sponsored by Senator Paul Simon (D. Ill.) and others, which made it clear that fair use can be made of unpublished as well as published works.)
- Since the 1976 act, copyright formation no longer requires formalities. A copyright basically springs into being on the completion of any creative work, even if the creator did not seek or desire a copyright. The effect is that large amounts of published material have been unnecessarily removed from the public domain for the copyright period (life of the author plus fifty years, or seventy-five years for corporate works).
- Copyright now extends to electronic "works" even if they have no creative author, if the public has no effective access to them, and if they will never enter the public domain. For example, a sports team, a broadcaster, or a celebrity can copyright (and thus monopolize commercial use of) a live football game, a local newscast, or a live entertainment program—but never make the programs commercially available for purchase, and even erase the tapes soon after broadcast. This frustrates the essential copyright quid pro quo—the implicit bargain by which the government grants a copyright monopoly in return for the work being made available commercially and eventually being surrendered to the public domain.
- Publishers are aggressively seeking to expand their rights by insisting on payment for all copying including noncommercial copying for personal use. Although there is still little legal support for this position, it is beginning to be popularly perceived as if it were a settled requirement of the law. The public could thus be herded into a fee-

per-use environment—a situation more reminiscent of the discredited English stationer's copyright than the purpose of the U.S. constitutional copyright.

These and other problems of the current copyright situation are carefully and dispassionately brought out in the Patterson-Lindberg book. The authors, professors of law and English respectively at the University of Georgia, urge what might be called a *back-to-basics* approach—a return to first principles, including:

- Recognition that copyright is a limited grant designed for a public purpose, to encourage creativity and advance knowledge, not an unlimited private property right.
- Recognition of the difference between the *copyright* and the copyrighted *work*. This abstraction greatly affects, for example, personal use—a person's right to make free noncommercial use (including copies) of materials he owns.
- Reestablishment of the copyright "bargain" by which all creators of copyrighted works make their works available to public purchase and eventual preservation in the public domain.
- Maintenance of a balance among the rights of authors, publishers, and users. This would involve increasing the rights of both individual authors (recognizing some right of ensuring the integrity and paternity of one's work) and users (recognizing expanded fair and personal use rights).

The book is written in a style far more analytical than alarmist. This is both its strength and its weakness. It is a strength because we need such a comprehensive historical and analytical review of copyright policies in general and user interests in particular. This book will be necessary reading in the public debate on copyright for years to come, for it refutes many of the assumptions and lays bare many of the theories that have guided copyright policymakers to date.

The authors' analytical style is a weakness, too, however, for it may preclude the wider readership the message of the book deserves. (Not many lay readers will find enticing a book that dwells on distinctions such as those between derivative and independent rights or between ownership of a copyright and ownership of a copyrighted work.)

What is happening to copyright today is just as important to free speech and the dissemination of information and comment as developments in more familiar areas of media law such as libel, privacy, access, and censorship. The problems of modern copyright law can benefit, as these other areas have, from the attention and concern of the broader media and public community.

Parody and Fair Use

Comedians Mark Russell and the Capitol Steps beat singers Michael Jackson and Dolly Parton. *Mad* Magazine and the *Harvard Lampoon* won over Leonard Bernstein, Irving Berlin, Cole Porter, and George and Ira Gershwin. Home Box Office, Comedy Central, and the NBC television network were also victors.

No, the forum was not a Hollywood Bowl gala for a new combined Grammys/Emmys/National Magazine Awards. It was the considerably less glamorous—but perhaps more important to the entertainment industry—United States Supreme Court.

The Court ruled in a case titled *Campbell v. Acuff-Rose Music, Inc.*, which might be thought of as *Roy Orbison v. 2 Live Crew*. The owners of the rights to Orbison's classic 60s song "Oh, Pretty Woman!" sued the '90s rap group 2 Live Crew over that group's parody piece, "Pretty Woman."

And, yes, the issue was so central to many entertainers that it actually set comedians against songwriters, and satirical magazines against legendary composers. All of the persons and groups listed above, and others (including some usual suspects such as the ACLU and a ubiquitous group of "concerned law professors"), weighed in with advice submitted in friend-of-the-court briefs.

The Court's decision, in essence, adopted the position urged by the comedians and satirists. It is a landmark decision that recognizes the social and literary value to parody and frees creative persons from some of the legal straitjackets imposed by some earlier copyright decisions.

The ruling is important not only to those who specialize in parody but also to all writers, artists, and communications professionals—both commercial and noncommercial—who at times utilize references to or parodies of existing copyrighted works.

The case was about two very different pretty women.

Orbison's song glamorized an idealized "pretty woman." The singer first idolizes the woman:

> Pretty Woman, I couldn't help but see,
> Pretty Woman, that you look lovely as can be
> . . . Pretty Woman, say you'll stay with me.

Then he is disappointed when she rebuffs him:

> Pretty Woman, don't walk on by,
> Pretty Woman, don't make me cry.

And finally he cheers when she appears to change her mind:

> Is she walking back to me?
> Yeah, she's walking back to me!

The 2 Live Crew version uses some of Orbison's music and key words, but the overall story concerns, to say the least, a different "pretty woman." The group begins by using lines and accompanying music from Orbison's song:

> Pretty woman walkin' down the street
> Pretty woman girl you look so sweet.

But the picture soon changes:

> Big hairy woman you need to shave that stuff
> . . . Big hairy woman all that hair ain't legit
> 'Cause you look like 'Cousin It.'

The following choruses depict a "bald-headed woman" and a "two-timin' woman." And the song concludes not with delight in the woman's turning to the singer, but a different feeling about the woman who is revealed to be pregnant:

> Two timin' woman you's out with my boy last night
> Two timin' woman that takes a load off my mind
> Two timin' woman now I know the baby ain't mine.
> Oh, two timin' woman
> Oh pretty woman.

At first blush the subject matter of this case might seem ill-suited for nine conservative middle-aged and elderly jurists, and least of all its reclusive bachelor member from New Hampshire, Justice David Souter.

But in a unanimous opinion in 1994, written by Justice Souter, the Court took 2 Live Crew's parody song quite seriously and ultimately concluded it could qualify as "fair use" of Orbison's copyrighted song and hence not a copyright infringement.

Perhaps to maintain his conservative New England moorings, amid the disturbing reality of '90s rap music and bald-headed two-timin' big hairy women, Justice Souter even managed to invoke on behalf of the rap group an 1841 decision by the legendary Justice Joseph Story of Massachusetts.

The court reached its ruling by carefully applying the established tests for fair use in copyright law (which had indeed originated with Justice Story in 1841). But in doing so, the court broke new ground in two key areas:

- It set aside the previous law's *presumption* that all commercial uses of a copyrighted work are unfair. This presumption—which the Supreme Court itself created a decade earlier—has been deadly, since almost all creative work done in this country is done for some commercial benefit. Indeed, in the ruling, Justice Souter acknowledged the pervasiveness of the profit motive, by quoting Dr. Samuel Johnson's pronouncement that "[n]o man but a blockhead ever wrote, except for money."
- It recognized the social, political, and creative value of parody and even broadly construed the kinds of parody that might be useful and protected.

Parody is a derivative art. In Justice Souter's words, "Parody's humor, or in any event its comment, necessarily springs from recognizable allusion to its object through distorted imitation." Copyright law has often seen derivation as improper—as it is in many cases—but the Court's sophisticated analysis noted that some derivation is necessary in legitimate parody. This alone was a key ruling.

Additionally, Justice Souter's opinion treated the 2 Live Crew parody seriously and thus vindicated the principle that art (including parody that deserves protection) is not limited to certain socially approved forms or concepts but can be found, and ought to be protected, in many other places.

Though he admitted that the justices "might not assign a high rank to the parodic element" in "Pretty Woman," Justice Souter noted that the 2 Live Crew song sought to make an important comment and ought to be allowed to parody Orbison's song to do so:

"2 Live Crew juxtaposes the romantic musings of a man whose fantasy comes true," Justice Souter wrote, "with degrading taunts, a bawdy demand for sex, and a sigh of relief from parental responsibility. The later words can be taken as a comment on the naivete of the original of an earlier day, as a rejection of its sentiment that ignores the ugliness of street life and the debasement it signifies." The court held that 2 Live Crew was entitled to use the technique of parody, with its "joinder of reference and ridicule," to convey this message.

In specific terms, the Court held that the 2 Live Crew parody song was not clearly a copyright infringement and may be fair use under copyright law. The case was sent back to the trial court for further hearings on whether the use is fair in fact.

United States law has usually been very protective of writers, artists, and commentators. With a number of restrictive copyright fair use decisions in the 1980s, it seemed to be turning away from that protectiveness and heading toward somewhat draconian rules that limited creativity. But with this ruling, perhaps like Orbison's pretty woman, the law may be turning back.

Rights in Ideas

Art Buchwald won his "theft of idea" case against Eddie Murphy and Paramount Pictures over the original authorship of the movie *Coming to America*. So can you, too, win the credit and profits you feel you deserve for your ideas?

It's not that easy. The Buchwald case was a rare one, which involved special circumstances present in very few "idea" cases. "Theft of idea" cases make up a legal growth industry—not only because of the increasing number of the suits but also because of the huge potential liability when successful films and television shows are involved. A cynic might conclude that these suits bear out the adage that failure is an orphan, while success has a hundred fathers.

Because they fall within a void in the law—an area unprotected by traditional intellectual property concepts such as copyright—the suits are brought under theories such as misappropriation, breach of contract, implied contract, unjust enrichment, and breach of a confidential relationship.

Buchwald's *Coming to America* suit illustrates what it takes to have a successful theft of idea case: a protectable idea, a legal commitment, and strong evidence of deliberate appropriation of the idea.

Protectable Idea. The first requirement for a successful suit is an idea that is both concrete and novel. Most litigants fail to overcome this hurdle. Their ideas are unwritten, amorphous, common, or predictable.

The originality requirement, in particular, is a hard one to meet. A writer who claimed credit for the idea behind the movie *Fort Apache, the Bronx* lost even though his script contained many of the same scenes as the movie. The court found that the "depictions of bribes, prostitution, purse-snatching and neighborhood hostility to law enforcement" were not novel, but rather "stock material for most police stories."

Similarly, treasure hidden in a snake-ridden cave and other jungle adventure scenes were all considered predictable stock literary devices— "simply too general to be protectable" in the words of a court that dismissed a case against the makers of *Raiders of the Lost Ark.*

By contrast, Buchwald's idea—a political satire involving a black Third World leader who goes through major changes during a visit to the United States—made it over the novelty and concreteness thresholds. His eight-page screen treatment was written and contained sufficiently concrete detail and specificity. Most important, the testimony showed that it had real novelty—enough to spark and keep the attention and interest of Paramount creative executives and Murphy's managers.

Legal Commitment. Even with a sufficiently novel and concrete idea, a plaintiff will usually get nowhere without some legal commitment from the publisher who has allegedly stolen the idea. Almost all successful idea claims contain some evidence of *agreement*, explicit or implicit, in the dealings between the originator of the idea and the recipient.

For this reason, although hundreds of unsolicited ideas are sent each year to television networks and movie studios, it is practically impossible to build a successful case on an unsolicited idea. Regular recipients of unsolicited ideas follow precautions designed to disavow any commitment to the idea originators.

The best protection for the author of an idea, and the element found in most successful idea cases, is a written agreement in which the recipient agrees to use or consider the idea. Buchwald had such a written contract, an agreement under which Paramount acquired a limited-time option to his story rights. Paramount even extended the option three times in separate agreements.

This contract became the linchpin of Buchwald's claim. It provided that Buchwald would be paid for any motion picture "*based upon*" his idea. Thus, when the jury ultimately found that *Coming to America* was "based upon" Buchwald's original screen treatment, Paramount became obligated to Buchwald under the contract.

Appropriation. The last hurdle—actual theft of the idea—is also difficult for most claimants to prove. It requires tracing the final film, book, or show back to the plaintiff's original idea. Ideas and other intellectual processes, however, rarely leave trails.

Again, Buchwald's case was unique. His idea was discussed repeatedly over a period of two years with agents and representatives of Eddie Murphy, the planned star, as well as a number of Paramount writers and executives. There was concrete evidence that Paramount and Murphy knew of his idea and that they liked it a lot. So when Paramount and Murphy developed a remarkably similar movie not long afterward, the inference was unmistakable that the new movie plot was "based upon" Buchwald's original screen treatment. As a result, the court ruled that Buchwald was entitled to damages for breach of contract—making Buchwald phenomenally successful as a theft-of-idea plaintiff.

Of course, Buchwald never got the percentage he expected or thought he deserved from the profits of *Coming to America*. The ruling in Buchwald's favor on the merits was merely the prelude to the even harder fought damages phase of the case, and the eventual award of $900,000 to Buchwald and his co-plaintiff Allain Bernheim in 1992 (and their $1 million settlement in 1995) was disappointing to them and their contingency-fee lawyer who battled a succession of Paramount lawyers for seven years.

But the settlement, at least, could keep Buchwald well stocked with the fine cigars he enjoys, while he contemplated his next idea—and the difficulties of proving and winning a theft of idea case.

Advertising

Comparative Advertising Regulation

COMPARISON IS ONE OF THE MOST BASIC AND effective persuasive techniques. But in advertising, it is also one of the most risky. The risks increased further in 1989, when a new statute went into effect, broadening the federal law that forms the basis for legal battles over comparative advertising.

Comparative advertising is still relatively new. But it has already produced numerous high stakes legal battles, such as the never-ending "aspirin wars" among pain-reliever manufacturers and the bitter legal fight that enabled U-Haul to put one of its major competitors out of business.

The legal basis for most of these disputes has been a provision of the federal trademark law, the Lanham Act. The provision, Section 43(a), prohibits misleading statements in advertising. As written in the original Lanham Act in 1940, Section 43(a) made it illegal for someone to misrepresent his own goods or services.

Until the 1970s, that was sufficient to cover practically all unfair competition cases. The evils most often seen in advertising during that period were sales claims about the goods being advertised. But in the 1970s, aggressive comparative advertising campaigns became prevalent. Instead of simply boasting of their own product, or comparing it to a mythical "Brand X," advertisers began directly bashing the competition.

Like its contemporary descendant, the negative political commercial, product comparison advertising often proved to be devastatingly effective. Advertised product comparisons provide the drama and competition that appeal to basic elements of human psychology. Moreover, the negative images of comparative ads seem to be more readily learned and retained than the positive ones of traditional advertisements.

Manufacturers of the unfavorably portrayed products have predictably cried "foul" to comparative ads. And often they have sued in court, invoking the Lanham Act, Section 43(a). The suits have proven to be powerful and effective tools in the regulation of advertising.

Many major consumer products companies have preferred suit under Section 43(a) rather than alternative out-of-court remedies, such as proceedings before the National Advertising Division of the Council of Better Business Bureaus. A Section 43(a) suit, unlike other remedies, can allow a victimized firm to enjoin the complained-of advertisements, discover its rival's files purporting to back up the advertised tests or comparisons, and obtain money damages.

In effect, Section 43(a) suits turn the tables on the comparative advertiser, by focusing not on the product comparison but on a comparison of advertiser's claim with the true facts—often including the advertiser's own test results and data. Some advertisers find this focus uncomfortable.

For example, when a cigarette manufacturer was sued by a competitor over its claim of having the "lowest tar of all cigarettes," it was hard-pressed to explain away the fact that another brand had half the tar. Its ad was enjoined.

Even misleading but literally true comparisons can be hazardous. In one of the many suits over pain reliever ads, Anacin's manufacturer claimed that Maximum Strength Anacin was strongest "in the pain reliever doctors recommend most" (aspirin). But discovery in the lawsuit brought by Tylenol's maker revealed that Anacin's own staff knew that the ad conveyed the misleading impression that Maximum Strength Anacin was the strongest formula for *any* over-the-counter pain reliever. The ad was enjoined.

In another case, a comparative advertising suit by U-Haul has been credited with putting Jartran, one of its major competitors, out of business. Jartran's price comparison ads made misleading comparison of low

Jartran promotional rates with higher regular U-Haul rates, when in fact Jartran's regular prices were higher than U-Haul's. A court awarded U-Haul $40 million in damages against Jartran, a company that at the height of its comparative ad campaign had annual revenues of $80 million.

But as powerful as Section 43(a) has been as a means of regulating comparative advertising, prior to the late 1980s it had not lived up to its full potential. Its original wording presented a stumbling block. It seemed to make actionable only false statements about the advertiser's *own* products, not false statements about the *competitor's* products. Many courts adopted this narrow view.

The suits usually went ahead anyway. Lawyers learned to characterize the message in comparative advertising in such a way so that the complained-of claims referred to the advertiser's goods. Thus, if BadCo's commercials portrayed GoodCo's product as ineffective, GoodCo— which was really concerned about what was said about *its* product— would sue, claiming that BadCo falsely represented *BadCo's product* as the only effective product on the market.

Although most suits proceeded under these sometimes awkward characterizations of the advertising claims, the narrowness of the statute undoubtedly discouraged and restricted many comparative advertising suits. In recognition of this problem, Congress in 1988 took up Section 43(a) as part of its general revision of the federal trademark laws and expressly extended the section to cover *all* false advertising. The revised section, which became effective in late 1989, specifically allows suit against anyone who misrepresents "his or her or *another person's* goods, services or commercial activities." The revision, according to a Senate report, was designed to bring the statute in line with Congress's original intent to further energize the "federal law of unfair competition" that was created by Section 43(a).

In light of this broadened federal law of unfair competition, advertisers must craft their creative work with even more attention to the risks of potential litigation and the requirements for truthful and nonmisleading advertising claims.

Use of Trademarks in Advertising

The Olympic tradition that was celebrated and practiced in Barcelona in the summer of 1992 may stretch back to the ancient Greeks. But the "licensing" of the Olympics bears a distinctly late twentieth-century flavor.

It's doubtful that in ancient times the games depended on commercial licensing ties. At least, no archaeologist has reported finding notices of "Spartan Chariot Works—the official chariot-maker of the First Olympiad" or "Plato—official philosopher of the Olympics."

Indeed, even the early *modern* Olympic games had few licensing and marketing ties compared with those of recent years. Licensing has been a growth business of the later part of this century, a product of strong trademark laws, the triumph of national multimedia marketing, and a consumer-driven society. Not only with respect to the Olympics but also all aspects of sports, entertainment, and consumer businesses, licensing has become an important, even expected, marketing tool.

Licensing, of course, is the sale of certain trademark rights by which the trademark owner (for instance, the International Olympic Committee) allows another (for instance, Pepsi-Cola), to use its trademarks (the word *Olympics* and the famous five-ring symbol) in marketing.

Licensing creates some interesting conflicts, in both the advertising and the news arenas, over what a nonlicensee can publish about licensed events. The Barcelona summer Olympic games generated a few of these conflicts even before they began.

Credit card issuers Visa and American Express were locked in a bitter advertising battle, and Visa took advantage of its Olympics sponsorship, even going so far in its advertising as to name American Express and highlight AmEx's purported deficiencies.

American Express struck back, during the winter Olympics and before the summer games, with advertising that came close to suggesting a connection between American Express and the Olympics. During the winter games, American Express ran television and print advertisements that showed Alpine scenery and invited cardholders to visit "the French Alps for all winter fun and games." Visa cried foul and complained that American Express was trying to suggest Olympic sponsorship (even though the ads did not use the word *Olympics* or the five-ring Olympic symbol). Again before the summer games, American Express ran advertisements touting the AmEx card's usefulness in Barcelona and Spain. One ad concluded, "And remember, to visit Spain, you don't need a visa."

The AmEx ads fall under the category of *ambush marketing*—advertising that attempts to preempt a competitor's licensing advantages.

Other Olympic ambush campaigns were conducted in 1988 by Pepsi (which highlighted its connection with Magic Johnson, even though its rival Coca-Cola was the sole Olympic soft drink sponsor) and Reebok and Converse (which pointed to athletes who use their products, even though Nike was the official Olympic footwear sponsor).

These carefully crafted ambush campaigns probably avoid infringement of the International Olympic Committee's rights. Even so, however, the committee and its official sponsors threatened suit, complained to media organizations, and took other steps to stop or at least restrict the campaigns.

The legal framework underlying these disputes is garden-variety trademark law, and the issue is the same as that in any trademark dispute: *Are consumers confused?*

Just as one seller cannot use a trademark that is closely similar to a rival's—and thus "pass off" its goods on consumers who think they are buying the other brand—an advertiser cannot suggest an official sponsorship that he does not have.

Under these principles, where a firm does seek to improperly wrap itself in the good will of a sports event or team, or entertainment figure, without official sanction, it can be enjoined in court. Owners of major sports and entertainment trademarks are often extremely diligent in seeking to enforce their rights, in view of the enormous value of many of the trademarks and associations.

Major league baseball, for example, has been very protective of the team trademarks it has controlled for the last decade. Anyone who incorrectly claims or suggests, and commercially utilizes, an official connection with the St. Louis Cardinals, the Chicago Cubs, or any other major-league team may find himself in receipt of a cease-and-desist letter (or, in extreme cases, a summons) from major league baseball.

That is not to say that every publication that uses or involves a licensed event is unlawful. In a number of cases, trademark owners have gone farther than the principles of free speech will permit in attempting to restrict *any* use, even legitimate noncommercial use, of their trademarks.

For example, the Boston Marathon committee granted an official sponsorship to one of the commercial Boston television stations in 1991. When a rival station announced plans to also televise the event, the "official" station objected and sought an injunction against its rival.

The court refused to grant an injunction, noting that the event was held outdoors and in public, and anyone was free to photograph it and comment on it. All the second station could not do was claim official sponsorship or use the marathon name or trademarks in a way that suggested sponsorship. The same result has held when television stations have sought to protect exclusive rights to parades and other public events.

These conflicts between trademark owners and licensees, and others who wish to televise, discuss, and use licensed materials, are likely to continue and increase in coming years. Fifty years ago, almost as in ancient Greece, the licensing value of trademarks was minimal. Today it is enormous and likely to continue growing in today's global market.

Publicity Rights in Advertising

Right of Publicity sounds like a typically confusing legal concept. But a few cases explain it vividly:

- *Forum* magazine can't use Cher's photo in its advertising to suggest that she endorses the magazine, when she doesn't.
- Photographs in Christian Dior advertisements can't portray a model who closely resembles the late Jacqueline Onassis because that might falsely suggest that Ms. Onassis had endorsed their product.
- Frito-Lay's radio commercials can't be recorded by a singer who closely imitates Bette Midler, who herself refused to sing for the commercials.
- A manufacturer of portable toilets can't name its products "Here's Johnny," without the consent of Johnny Carson (which he's not about to give). Adopting the slogan "World's Favorite Commodian" will only make things worse.

That's the right of publicity. Since its beginnings in the 1960s, it has evolved into a strong legal protection for celebrities, preventing others from appropriating their names, likenesses, signatures, voices, and other personal attributes.

In the 1980s the right expanded enormously. With the *Midler* and *Onassis* cases, it was construed to cover not only *direct* appropriation of celebrity names and likenesses but also the subtle *indirect* appropriations involved in look-alikes (the *Onassis* case) and sound-alikes (the *Midler* case).

And the right seems to be expanding still. Many celebrities in the entertainment and sports worlds, and even political figures and persons involved in newsworthy events, are asserting their alleged rights of publicity. And producers of advertising promotions and editorial parodies, for their part, are learning to be cautious in mentioning, portraying, or evoking celebrities.

Consider several of the most extreme cases. Singer Tom Waits won a $2.5 million verdict based on a "sound-alike" Doritos radio commercial. Louisiana chef Paul Prudhomme sued over a Folgers television commercial that depicted a portly bearded chef. The descendants of Malcolm X attempted to exploit his publicity rights. And even Rodney King, the Los Angeles police beating victim who became a celebrity of sorts, has exploited his salable right of publicity.

And the Ninth Circuit U.S. Court of Appeals held that an advertisement that parodied Vanna White and *Wheel of Fortune*—by portraying a blonde shapely robot as Vanna's successor some years hence—could constitute an infringement of Vanna White's right of publicity. White's case eventually went to trial and a jury awarded her $403,000.

One begins to wonder if and how this right is limited. In our celebrity-filled world, isn't this expanding right threatening to chill a whole range of speech? Is the creative technique of parody being sacrificed to the economic value of the purity of a celebrity's image?

Enter Judge Alex Kozinski. A brilliant Reagan-appointed jurist, who has a independent libertarian streak in his conservative political philosophy, Judge Kozinski opened up new insights into the right of publicity, and how far it could or should extend, when he dissented from the appeals court's decision to allow the *Vanna White* case to go to trial.

In a forceful opinion, describing and analyzing numerous right of publicity claims, Judge Kozinski focused on the policy issues implicated by broad constructions of the right of publicity. He argued that in the *White* opinion at least—and by implication in other decisions as well—courts have been far too protective of rights of publicity and have failed to recognize the significant free speech issues at stake. The entire Kozinski opinion, a model of judicial clarity and cogency, is worth reading by anyone interested in the subject. But a summary and a few excerpts will give its flavor.

Initially, he cited some of the extreme cases in which owners of trademarks and rights of publicity have attempted to prevent others from using their "rights." He noted that many worthy books, movies, films, songs, and music could not have been written if intellectual property rights were so narrowly construed. Intellectual property is meant not just for owners but also *users*, he notes.

He took the popular book *Presumed Innocent* as an example. Scott Turow's copyright prevents others from copying it or making a movie out of it. But the basic story line—an idealistic young prosecutor on trial for a crime he didn't commit—is free for anyone to use, even if the idea came from *Presumed Innocent* and even if the new work reminds readers of Turow's book.

"All creators draw in part on the work of those who came before, referring to it, building on it, poking fun at it; we call this creativity, not piracy," Judge Kozinski explained. "Creativity is impossible without a rich public domain. . . . Overprotection stifles the very creative forces it's supposed to nurture."

He concluded that the opinion in *Vanna White v. Samsung*, allowing White to proceed with her right-of-publicity claim based on the advertisement with the robot, was such a mistaken "overprotection": "It's now a tort for advertisers to *remind* the public of a celebrity. Not to use a celebrity's name, voice, signature or likeness; not to imply the celebrity endorses a product; but simply to evoke a celebrity's image in the public's mind. This Orwellian notion withdraws far more from the public domain than prudence and common sense allow."

Legal concepts often tend to develop into absolutes, and this is especially so with the concept of *property*. In recent years, copyright, right of publicity, and other forms of intellectual property have been increasingly construed as absolute property rights.

Judge Kozinski argued that intellectual property rights *aren't* "absolute guarantees protected against all kinds of interferences, subtle as well as blatant." They are, rather, policy accommodations of competing interests, which incorporate by various means the rights of *users* as well as those of creators and owners. Without users' rights, these concepts will "impoverish the public domain, to the detriment of future creators and the public at large."

"Intellectual property rights aren't free," he argued.

They're imposed at the expense of future creators and the public at large. Where would we be if Charles Lindbergh had an exclusive right to the concept of a heroic solo aviator? If Arthur Conan Doyle had gotten a copyright in the idea of the detective story, or if Albert Einstein had patented the theory of relativity? If every author and celebrity had been given the right to keep people from mocking them or their work? Surely this would have made the world poorer, not richer, culturally as well as economically.

The Kozinski dissent also raised problems of conflicts between a broad right of publicity and the federal copyright law and then went on to discuss First Amendment rights relating to the right of publicity.

"I doubt even a name-and-likeness-only right of publicity can stand [under the First Amendment] without a parody exception," he wrote.

The First Amendment isn't just about religion or politics—it's also about protecting the free development of our national culture. Parody, humor, irreverence are all vital components of the marketplace of ideas. The last thing we need, the last thing the First Amendment will tolerate, is a law that lets public figures keep people from mocking them, or from "evoking" their images in the mind of the public.

Judge Kozinski obviously wrote his opinion with a special audience in mind: the nine jurists who work in the large marble building at First Street and Maryland Avenue in Washington, D.C. In at least one prior First Amendment case, the *Masson v. The New Yorker* libel case, the Supreme Court granted review in a case in which Judge Kozinski dissented and ruled generally consistently with his opinion.

Shortly after Kozinski's opinion, moreover, the Supreme Court decided to consider a case, concerning a song by the rap group 2 Live Crew, that raised the issue of parody rights in copyright. And when the Supreme Court ruled the following year in the *2 Live Crew* case, its decision reflected a clear understanding of the issue highlighted by Judge Kozinski's opinion—the dangers of too-broad publicity and other intellectual property rights.

Broadcasting

Licensing of Broadcast Spectrum

CONSIDER PSLS — PERSONAL SEAT LICENSES, the innovative stadium-funding mechanism used in professional sports. PSLs are sold to fans, who then have the right to buy game tickets for particular seats. PSLs are valuable and transferable, and they permit stadium developers to reap direct benefit from fans' competition for season tickets.

Now consider ESLs—*Electromagnetic Spectrum Licenses*. ESLs share many characteristics with PSLs:

- If you want to be in the game—that is, to be a spectrum user—you will need a license.
- License costs vary depending on location. The most desirable locations (on the spectrum) cost more, the marginal locations less.
- Licenses are valuable and likely to increase in value. In the past the market has assigned value to the de facto rights involved (the renewal expectations of season ticketholders and of radio and television station licensees, for example). Once formalized, these rights are likely to continue to increase in value.

185

- Licensees' costs will not end with the initial license purchase. License owners may even have to pay for the right to transfer them to someone else later on.
- Most buyers recognize the need for licenses, though some resent having to *buy* licenses for rights that they formerly got for free.
- Licenses seem to be the wave of the future, because they fairly allocate a scarce resource and bring an attractive financial windfall to the seller (or, in the eyes of some economists, a recognition of the value that has been conveyed without cost in the past).

In short, just as a PSL gives a fan a right to purchase tickets to future games in a certain location, an ESL gives its owner the right to future use of a particular piece of property—a portion of the public airwaves. Both licenses are, in essence, *the initial right to occupy and use a certain space.*

Licenses of electromagnetic spectrum do exist and are likely to increase in the future. Since the early 1990s, the Federal Communications Commission (FCC) has auctioned off rights to use certain spectrum locations. That is, it has sold Electromagnetic Spectrum Licenses.

ESLs, like PSLs, can be big moneymakers. PSLs brought in many millions in Charlotte, North Carolina, and St. Louis to finance new stadiums. They have been considered and used for other new stadiums, in Nashville, Cincinnati, and San Francisco. Similarly, in just nine months in 1994 and 1995, the federal government raised almost *$9 billion* by selling off commercial rights to use certain spectrum frequencies. And the government has not yet even *attempted* to sell its most valuable spectrum rights.

The concept of selling spectrum licenses seems somewhat strange to us. Our communications system was based for more than fifty years on an entirely different model—the idea that space on the electromagnetic spectrum could *never* be sold. Conventional wisdom has held that spectrum is a precious resource that must be held in public hands, like our national parklands.

When policymakers in the 1930s first examined the new medium of radio, this was their very first conclusion: the airwaves through which radio waves traveled are owned by the public. And they reached a second conclusion that, as a result, radio broadcasting (and other spectrum uses) should be conducted by private parties who would be permitted ("licensed") to use portions of spectrum, in return only for their agreement to serve the *public interest.*

For years, our entire over-the-air communications system has been founded on these two oddly inconsistent conclusions: (1) The airwaves are too valuable to be sold; (2) therefore, we must give them away.

Under the federal Communications Act, the Federal Communications Commission was directed to award licenses giving the right to use the airwaves to particular users, for limited time periods, and conditioned on adherence to the principle of use in the public interest.

To this end, the FCC awarded and renewed spectrum licenses based on comparative hearings that assessed each applicant's perceived ability to serve the public interest. The comparative hearing process developed predictable problems. *Public interest* came to be interpreted in somewhat narrow and bureaucratic ways, and decision makers often had to make fine and forced distinctions in deciding between competing applicants.

The same spectrum allocation rules and processes applied to other spectrum uses—frequencies used by police and emergency radio communications; airplane and ship radio; wireless and beeper transmissions; CB, ham, and walkie-talkie hobbyists; and the like. These uses usually took a backseat in policy discussions; broadcasting has always been the crown jewel and focus of our communications system.

The also-ran uses, however, suddenly took on more importance when lucrative cellular telephone services began around 1980. Cellular franchises were extremely valuable and in demand, and the public interest standard did not help very much in choosing among applicants. So the FCC made some allocation decisions based on a relatively new method—lotteries.

The cellular lotteries, however, encouraged speculation and applications by unqualified applicants (who, if they won, would simply cash in by selling their license to a real cellular operator). In the meantime, particularly under the deregulation-oriented FCC appointed by President Reagan, a whole new set of thinking developed about *broadcasting* regulation. Some of this new thinking grew out of empirical observations about a half-century of broadcasting history.

Radio and television station licenses have developed, in effect if not in theory, as practically irrevocable property rights; denials of renewals of broadcasting licenses are rare. The marketplace certainly sees broadcasting licenses as a kind of reliable property right; television and radio franchises are regularly sold for prices far in excess of the physical property conveyed. Additionally, the once-bright promise that broadcasting would be conducted in the public interest dimmed over time, as economic competition, advertiser needs, and viewer preferences developed as the real drivers of broadcasting content.

Accordingly, based on disappointment with the cellular lottery speculation and the dimmed realities of public interest broadcasting, regulators began listening to economists who argued that rights to use valuable airwaves need not, and perhaps ought not, be given away—especially if the public interest quid pro quo was turning out to be illusory. Instead, spectrum rights could be *auctioned*.

In an auction, the high bid serves as the allocation principle, and the applicant offers money payment, rather than simply the promise of operating in the public interest, in return for its right to use spectrum. Moreover, the payment, established by legitimate market forces, would flow to the *government*, not private speculators (as it did after many of the cellular lotteries.)

Congress was initially reluctant to authorize spectrum licenses but took a tentative first step toward auctions in its 1993 Omnibus Budget Reconciliation Act. That act permitted spectrum auctions at the FCC's option, but only for a five-year experiment, and not for broadcasting licenses.

The spectrum auctions that have been conducted under this authority have been spectacular successes, in terms of commercial participation and funds raised. The first spectrum auctions were conducted in July 1994 to allocate spectrum to be used for advanced paging and messaging services. These auctions raised almost $2 billion, far more than had been expected.

The next auctions, which began in late 1994 and were completed in early 1995, involved frequencies for new wireless personal communications services in large cities. These auctions brought in $7 billion for the government. Further auction rounds were scheduled.

Every method of spectrum allocation entails problems. Comparative hearings often lead to decisions based on inconsequential or forced distinctions between applicants. Lotteries permit speculation by unqualified applicants. Auctions—*surprise!*—favor deep-pocket applicants and hence freeze out minorities, small businesses, and other traditionally favored applicants.

Spectrum license auctions, like the sale of football PSLs, serve a useful function in allocating a much-demanded limited resource and in producing funds for the original resource owner. Given its spectacular

$9 billion start, the spectrum auction experiment will likely be continued beyond the initial five-year period, and auctions will probably become a permanent and accepted technique for allocating spectrum.

The really big decision about spectrum auctions, however, lies ahead. At some point policymakers will have to confront the explosive issue that Congress initially deferred: Should we ever abandon comparative hearings for radio and television licenses and simply auction them off, too?

Broadcasting and Press Freedoms

In the 1970s, the new medium of promise was television. TV sets had been commercially available for about twenty years. Broadcast content had shifted from Lucy and Howdy Doody to Cronkite's news, *Laugh-In*'s sophistication, and public television's cultural programming. Television journalism had begun to present a serious challenge to print.

With respect to law and public policy, however, the Supreme Court, in 1969, upheld Congress's determination to treat broadcasting differently from all other communications media. As a result, this medium of promise was saddled with intrusive governmental restrictions, including significant limitations on content, controversy, and creativity.

By the mid-1990s, the new medium of promise was the computer. Personal computers (which had been available for about twenty years) had improved tremendously in usability, speed, and capabilities. Computer content had shifted from simple games and writing projects to electronic research and publishing and worldwide discourse on the Internet. Instantaneous, creative, fact-based, multimedia, worldwide, electronic, person-to-person communication was becoming a reality.

And with respect to law and public policy? Congress attempted to treat computer communications differently from all other communications media. Fulfillment of the future promise of this medium may well be prevented or limited by laws written in this stage of maturation of computer communications.

If, according to Santayana's famous pronouncement, those who do not study the past are condemned to repeat its mistakes, before we begin regulating computer communications we ought to study the development of the regulation of broadcasting—and even the Supreme Court's whole philosophy with regard to new and different communications media.

Though broadcasting policy evolved over many years, one of the crucial steps occurred in 1969 with the Supreme Court's decision in *Red Lion Broadcasting Co. v. Federal Communications Commission.* There, the Court upheld the *fairness doctrine*, a government rule that, in essence, imposed a government-controlled editorial policy on every broadcaster in the nation. The rule controlled how all controversial issues would be handled on radio or TV—with balanced amounts of time allocated to each "side" of an issue (as determined in hindsight by the agency) without regard to the broadcaster's own news or editorial judgment.

The rationale for *Red Lion* was that because broadcasters transmitted their signals over the electromagnetic spectrum, which Congress deemed to be a public resource, broadcast outlets were presumed scarce and broadcasters had to be required to act "in the public interest." Congress and the FCC would enforce "public interest" broadcasting, using the fairness doctrine and other techniques, including:

- the personal attack rule, which governs attacks on the character of an identified person or group made during discussion of a controversial issue;
- political advertising requirements, which permit political candidates special access, rates, and freedoms in their broadcast advertisements;
- an absolute ban, during normal waking hours, of legal nonobscene content, which is nonetheless judged by the FCC to be "indecent" and hence potentially harmful to children;
- advertising and program requirements for children's television; and
- other content controls including restrictions on certain kinds of news, documentary and fictional programming involving such things as staging, warnings, and frightening events.

All of these restrictions applied to broadcasting would have been illegal if applied to print. The Supreme Court's 1974 *Miami Herald v. Tornillo* decision explicitly rejected any "fairness doctrine" for print as inconsistent with "First Amendment guarantees of a free press as they have evolved to this time."

Why, then, do we permit different regulations on broadcasting and print? Why doesn't the First Amendment as it has evolved to this time apply to broadcasting?

These are good questions, which the Supreme Court has never adequately answered. In *Red Lion,* the Court stated: "Differences in the characteristics of new media justify differences in the First Amendment standards applied to them." This statement, however, derived from a much different statement in *Joseph Burstyn v. Wilson*, a 1956 decision that first recognized motion pictures as a form of free expression: "Each method [of expression] tends to present its own peculiar problems. But the basic principles of freedom of speech and the press, like the First Amendment's commands, do not vary. These principles . . . make freedom of expression the rule."

The shift from *unvarying* First Amendment principles and commands, in 1956, to *varying First Amendment standards*, in 1969, was a significant and drastic change. It permitted a First Amendment double standard—different freedoms from content regulation in different media. Simply put, each medium became a law unto itself.

Since *Red Lion*, this double standard has been expanded to media that, unlike broadcasting, are not even arguably scarce, like cable television (which is subject to many broadcasting and special regulations) and direct satellite broadcast services (which, though not scarce, are subject to many broadcasting regulations).

Is *Red Lion* still effective on the eve of the twenty-first century? Yes and no. Though it has never been overruled and is still formally "good law," in reality *Red Lion* no longer rules the jungle of broadcasting policy; it is a lame and discredited pussycat of a policy.

First, *Red Lion's* scarcity rationale is demonstrably erroneous in our modern media world, with ubiquitous, diverse, and expanding broadcast outlets and programming. If anything, *print* is the scarce resource: Has anyone seen a two-newspaper town recently? Second, the fairness doctrine itself—the rule defended and upheld in *Red Lion*—was abolished during the Reagan administration. Since its abolition, current events programming has flourished, and there is far more coverage of all sides of all controversial issues than ever before.

What remains of *Red Lion* is the double standard of media regulation—the "each medium is a law unto itself" principle that exalts form and fears over consistency as to content.

The next medium in line for possible "law unto itself" treatment is computer communications. In particular, Senator James Exon (D. Neb.) proposed the Communications Decency Act applying broadcast-style intrusive regulations rather than print-style freedoms to the content of the Internet and other computer networks and communications. Congress passed the Act in 1996. Other initiatives to regulate the content of computer communications have been made.

If the story of broadcasting regulation since *Red Lion* has taught us anything, it is that we must be wary of the argument that because a new medium is different from familiar ones, it must be regulated differently.

Of course every medium is different; this is a truism. To understand why we regulate on this basis, we must recognize another truth: *Every new medium of communication seems revolutionary to those accustomed to the status quo. We often seek to control new media out of fear, not need.* As one commentator put it, new technologies are often born in captivity. This has happened with print, with motion pictures, and with broadcasting.

One policy analyst has vividly illustrated the problem. With current technology one could conceivably set up five television sets in one room, each connected to a different input device: broadcast TV, cable TV; a VCR; direct satellite TV; and a TV signal transmitted over a telephone line. It could be arranged to have each set simultaneously portray the same content, say, a movie with some sexual content. Because of the current philosophy of regulating different media differently, even though each set would show the very same picture and sound, *four different regulators' standards* would apply. Content that was proper and legal on one or two of the sets could be illegal on adjoining sets.

Perhaps we are hardened to this example because we are accustomed to intrusive regulation of broadcasting. But varying regulation based on the means of transmission can endanger print, too. Modern electronic communications are leading to a convergence of media. Print and images (such as are contained in traditional newspapers) may be transmitted electronically. If the "law unto itself" model remains in effect, newspapers transmitted over the airwaves could be subjected to broadcasting regulations such as political advertising rules, and newspapers transmitted by cable could face controls such as public access requirements.

This system does not make sense. Content is content. Content that is legal in print should be legal in television, on radio, and over telephone lines or computer networks. Allowing policy to be set based on fears of new media leads to inconsistency, government censorship and intrusion, and waste of promise and potential.

History teaches that fears of new media are inappropriate and the benefits of new media spring from use, creativity, and freedom, not from controls and regulations.

Print was feared by many when the printing press was invented. But today we revere not "printed by authority" newspapers but rather the creativity and ideas, born of true press freedom, like those found in Benjamin Franklin's *Poor Richard's Almanac,* Horace Greeley's *New York Tribune,* and William Lloyd Garrison's *Liberator.* In books we learn most not from government-edited or -censored orthodoxy but from products of freedom and controversy, like *Huckleberry Finn* and *Leaves of Grass,* and works of writers like H. L. Mencken, James Joyce, and Allen Ginsburg.

Movies were feared as presenting unique dangers of corruption and evil when they began, and both direct and indirect regulation ensued. But who would seek to reject the creativity and freedom in today's movie-making, in Hollywood and hundreds of other locations, in favor of a return to government boards of censors, blacklists, and witchhunts, and inflexible industry codes written in the dark shadow of government threats of censorship?

Our system of regulating based on the *medium of transmission* rather than the *content of the message* should be abolished in favor of a unitary policy, recognizing full First Amendment freedoms for all media. This is the policy the Supreme Court alluded to, before *Red Lion,* when it noted, "The basic principles of freedom of speech and the press do not vary."

Computer communications will not, any more than television or other media, bring paradise on Earth. Every medium does present unique problems and disappointments as well as promises. But the computer medium has great potential for enhancing person-to-person communications, for making facts and resources readily available, for promoting discussion, thinking, and progress, and for enhancing the availability, convenience, and content of all other media.

This full potential cannot and will not be realized unless we break down legal and regulatory distinctions among media and afford full First Amendment freedoms to all communications, regardless of the particular medium on which they are carried.

Political Television Commercials

Strange as election campaigns seem to many of us, they must seem stranger still to owners and operators of television and radio stations. Political broadcasting rules—those special laws that govern news and commercials relating to election campaigns—are as out of whack with normal publishing and broadcasting principles as candidates' promises are with reality. For example:

- Station owners—who generally control whether, when, and how to broadcast a program or commercial—are stripped of many of these normal powers.
- Screenings for libel, indecency, and overall propriety—which broadcasters normally conduct, in some fashion, for every bit of airtime from their opening national anthem to their last nighttime Vegamatic commercial—are, essentially, *prohibited.*
- Even the supposedly immutable rules of supply/demand economics are suspended; commercial time that is most heavily in demand by favored customers must be offered for sale to onetime or sporadic customers at an artificially low price.

The looking-glass world of political television rules plainly doesn't make sense from the viewpoint of normal editorial and advertising practices. But that's no surprise, for the rules were written by Congress and interpreted in large part by the Federal Communications Commission—both entities more attuned to the needs of candidates (and, perhaps, voters) than those of broadcasters.

If you are puzzled why the content of your television screen seems so different from normal during an election campaign, the political television rules are likely to blame. A brief synopsis of the rules and what they mean:

Equal Opportunities Rule. Section 315 of the Communications Act requires stations to give candidates for office equal opportunities (not "equal time," a phrase often used) on the air. This rule applies to both commercial and noncommercial time. If one candidate is shown on an interview program for a half hour, for example, the opposing candidate is entitled to a similar amount of free time, at a time period likely to reach an equivalent audience. Or if one candidate buys commercials during one popular prime-time show, the opponent is entitled to buy equivalent commercial time.

The rule doesn't apply to news programming. This has led to disputes regarding whether political debates are exempt news events and whether documentary shows like *60 Minutes* and *20/20* and interview shows like

Donahue qualify as news programming. The law now recognizes debates as news events; accordingly, minor party candidates can be excluded from the debates. Regularly scheduled documentary and news interview shows are generally held exempt from the equal opportunities rule.

The rule applies in any case where the candidate "uses" broadcast time. Usually that refers to a free broadcast or a commercial in which the candidate's voice or image appear. (At one point, this was interpreted to mean that any showing of old Ronald Reagan movies during one of Reagan's political campaign would give rise to equal opportunity rights of his opponents.)

The station isn't required by this rule to give any candidate free time—but if it gives *any* candidate free time, then it must accord that same privilege to all candidates in that race. Publicly announced, legally qualified candidates who are on the ballot or committed to running as write-in candidates qualify for the benefits of this rule. (This includes fringe as well as major party candidates.) And candidates bear the burden of raising their claims for equivalent time.

No Censorship, No Liability Rule. Once broadcast stations accept paid advertising from candidates, they may not censor it—even if they desire to apply their normal standards of libel, decency, or good taste. In fairness, since the law bans broadcasters from exercising editorial control, it also gives broadcasters immunity from any liability resulting from the broadcast. (The candidate and others behind the commercial, of course, are liable.)

Under this rule, stations have been required to air political commercials with antiabortion messages that contain graphic footage of abortion procedures. One court, however, held that one such commercial was so "patently offensive according to contemporary community standards" and unsuitable for viewing by children that the station could restrict it to late-night hours. Stations may attempt to run disclaimers before potentially offensive political commercials that they cannot control, but even this is legally hazardous; stations must disclaim evenhandedly.

Sponsorship Identification Rules. Federal communications law requires that broadcasters reveal in connection with each commercial that it was a paid commercial and who paid for it. Federal election law also requires the preparer of the commercial to include in each commercial an announcement specifying who authorized it, if the payor is someone other than the official campaign committee.

Lowest Unit Charge Rule. Easily broadcasters' least favorite rule, this one requires station owners to charge candidates their lowest advertising rate during the forty-five days before a primary election and sixty days before a general election. The law specifies how the lowest unit charge is calculated and—surprise—it gives candidates a big discount indeed. Candidates get the same rates as the station's most favored commercial advertiser, considering all of that commercial advertiser's volume discounts—regardless of how much or how little time the candidate buys.

In effect, this rule allows candidates to dominate the television screens during the preelection season (even, for example, during a new television season's most popular and lucrative prime-time shows) and pay far less than the market-driven commercial advertising rates for such time.

Reasonable Access for Federal Candidates Rule. In theory, a station can avoid many of these rules with respect to candidates for state office by simply refusing to sell the candidates airtime or to portray them on non-news programs. But not so for candidates for federal office. A special rule requires broadcasters to provide some time to candidates for federal office, including some during prime time, if the candidates request it. The stations are not required to give federal candidates free time, however.

Many, if not most, of these rules seem anachronistic in an age of broadcasting deregulation and increasing skepticism of the old idea that the "scarcity" of broadcast stations requires broadcast content regulation. But while the Fairness Doctrine and many other broadcasting content controls have disappeared in recent years, there are few moves to discontinue these political broadcasting controls. After all, the only persons who can change these rules are the ones who benefit most from them.

11

Fair Trial,
Free Press

Fair Trial Right: Impartial, Not Ignorant, Jurors

LET'S EAVESDROP ON A CONVERSATION AMONG officials of the Court of Conventional Wisdom during the summer of 1994:

JUDGE. How can we *possibly* find twelve jurors for the O. J. Simpson trial?

COURT CLERK. One thing's for sure—we can't have anyone who knows *anything* about the case on the jury!

LAW CLERK. This case has had saturation publicity. We'll need to find twelve people who were on vacation in Siberia during June. But even that might not work—they might hear something about the case after they return.

COURT CLERK. I've got it! Let's pick only jurors who don't own a TV or radio or subscribe to newspapers or magazines. There must be twelve people like that in the Los Angeles area—maybe in a homeless shelter somewhere.

JUDGE. No, that wouldn't do, either. They might eventually hear some-one talk about the case.

COURT CLERK. Is it too late to gag the press?

JUDGE. Some of us wish we had that power, like the judge in Canada who totally banned any reporting of a big trial in Quebec this spring. But the Supreme Court won't let us do it here, because of the First Amendment.

LAW CLERK. How about selecting only jurors with *very* low IQs? That way, they won't know or care about the news and they'd probably forget anything they did hear. Also, they'll follow the rules we give them and not think independently.

JUDGE. Hmm, maybe we can make it work. Let's look for twelve homeless persons, with very low IQs, who were on vacation in Siberia, and who never listen to or talk about the news. But I'm still worried—if one of them somehow listens to or thinks about the news, then we couldn't have a fair trial after all!

Happily, such a search for totally ignorant jurors will never take place, except in the mind of many citizens (and commentators) who mistakenly believe the prevalent conventional wisdom that the only qualified juror is a totally ignorant juror.

That's not the law. The Sixth Amendment provides that the accused shall be entitled to a speedy public trial "by an *impartial* jury," not an *ignorant* jury.

Impartiality is different from ignorance. Jurors can be impartial without being ostrich-like ciphers who totally lack interest in public affairs. And fair trials *are* possible despite broad news coverage, even the blanket coverage in the apprehension and preliminary hearing of O. J. Simpson.

The jury trial system adopted by the framers of the Bill of Rights from English common law was originally built not on juror ignorance but on juror knowledge and intelligence. When juries were first used in England, 800 to 1,000 years ago, jurors had to be knowledgeable in the facts of the case in order to be selected. As society matured and cities grew, that requirement was eventually dropped, but all jurors were still expected to be knowledgeable, active participants in the judicial decision-making process.

By our nation's early days, juries were expected to get the facts totally from the evidence at trial. And so the issue of prejudicial pretrial publicity arose—most notably, in the sensational treason prosecution of Aaron Burr, archenemy of Thomas Jefferson, during Jefferson's second presidential term.

Burr's lawyers claimed that only jurors unfamiliar with the parties or the incident could fairly decide the case. But Chief Justice John Marshall, who presided at the trial, rejected that claim, excluding only jurors who had "strong prejudices." Marshall refused to exclude jurors who had heard some of the facts and had some opinions because to do so "would exclude intelligent and observing men, whose minds were really in a situation to decide upon the whole case according to the testimony."

Arguments such as those by Burr's attorneys, claiming that juror impartiality required juror ignorance, have been raised again and again. But the Supreme Court has consistently held, as Chief Justice Marshall did, that jurors may be impartial without being ignorant. In *Murphy v. Florida* in 1975, for example, the Court held that juries are not tainted by a juror's "mere familiarity with [the defendant] or his past." For a juror to lack impartiality, it takes "an actual predisposition" against the defendant, the Court held.

Why do we permit jurors who have some prior knowledge of the case? One reason is that we believe in jurors' fairness and ability to set aside their prior knowledge and decide the case on the evidence. But another reason is that the "remedy" of having ignorant jurors would be worse than the problem it would cure. As Mark Twain noted in a pointed critique of the ignorant juror model, this model "compels us to swear in juries composed of fools and rascals, because the system rigidly excludes honest men and men of brains. . . . [The system presumes that] ignoramuses alone could mete out unsullied justice."

Even those who agree that jurors need not be ignorant to be impartial still often criticize the press for the volume and intensity of its coverage of spectacular crimes and incidents.

The thinking seems to be that even if pretrial publicity is not fatal to trial fairness, it should somehow be minimized, and it is the duty of a responsible press to do so. Many commentators like to elevate this thinking to the level of an alleged conflict between the right of fair trial and that of a free press and urge the media to "act responsibly" so as to not eventually lose their free press rights.

Even apart from the basic misunderstanding of juror impartiality, this position misconstrues the nature of press freedom and government responsibility for fair trials. The First Amendment guarantees freedom of the press in absolute terms, without any trial-publicity exception. And the "rights in conflict" metaphor, while vivid and clever, is fundamentally unsound.

As former Justice Hans Linde of the Oregon Supreme Court has noted, constitutional rights, by their very nature, do not conflict with one another:

> What is a constitutional right? It is a claim that runs against the government—usually not a claim that the government do something *for* you or me, but that it refrain from doing something *to* us. The constitution prescribes how government is to behave and how not. The constitution does not make rules for private persons.

Hence, the government must protect the rights *both* of free press and of fair trial. As Justice Linde explained:

> If the Cleveland press has a right under the Sixth Amendment not to be censored, the government is constitutionally forbidden to censor it. If Sam Sheppard has a right under the Sixth Amendment not to be convicted by a prejudiced jury, the state is constitutionally forbidden to obtain or act upon such a conviction. Its obligation is to try him properly or not at all. The defendant has no constitutional right against the press.

Once we reject the rights-in-conflict metaphor, we focus on the real issue of the right of a fair trial: the government's responsibility to use every means at its disposal—short of abridging any other constitutional rights—to preserve trial fairness. The techniques available are numerous:

- Voir dire of the jury panel, by which lawyers fully probe for potential juror prejudice and challenge for cause any jurors who appear prejudiced
- Preemptory challenges, by which lawyers for both sides exclude jurors without giving any reasons
- Jury instructions, in which jurors are instructed on the need to disregard external knowledge and opinions and decide the case on the evidence
- Sequestration and other techniques by which jurors are isolated from media reports and other non-courtroom influences during the trial
- Continuances or changes of venue, if needed, to move the trial to a time or place when publicity and juror opinions are less intense

- Restraints on out-of-court statements by court personnel, including police, prosecutors, and even defense attorneys during the course of the trial or pretrial proceedings

Are these techniques sufficient in cases of highly publicized crimes and prominent defendants?

Well, they have worked so far—in spectacular and celebrated cases ranging from the trial of Aaron Burr in 1807 to modern-day trials such as those of O. J. Simpson, the Watergate defendants, accused mass murderers John Wayne Gacy and Jeffrey Dahmer, and celebrities including Mike Tyson, William Kennedy Smith, Claus von Bulow, and John DeLorean.

Yes, these techniques will work to preserve the right to a fair trial. And they will work far better than a system in which "ignoramuses mete out justice" or a system in which one constitutional right is sacrificed to the cause of another.

Fair Trial, Free Press in Practice

Does the free press endanger fair trials? This question is not confined to celebrity crimes and stories in the national media. It can arise in a particular community with respect to local cases and local media.

The question was posed in the St. Louis area in 1987 with respect to events in and out of three separate courtrooms across the metropolitan area:

- In St. Louis City, a mistrial was declared at the opening of the capital murder trial of Anthony J. Leisure, after publication of a *St. Louis Post-Dispatch* article previewing the trial and mentioning Leisure's prior related murder conviction.
- A juror in the concluded forty-four-month civil trial in Belleville, Illinois, of the Sturgeon, Missouri, dioxin spill revealed to the *Post-Dispatch* that she and other jurors had read and listened to media accounts of the trial.
- In St. Louis County, in the case of the 1986 murder conviction of Walter Harvey, hearings began on the effect of revelations that several jurors had reconnected their hotel television set during the trial and watched KSDK-TV news accounts of the trial.

These cases highlight a tension between two valued rights, press free-dom and fair, impartial justice.

Fair trials require jurors who are both impartial and fair—jurors who have open minds and who will decide the case solely on the evidence at trial. To best achieve this end, while maintaining press freedom, the legal system attempts to separate jurors from publicity about the trials they decide.

In each of the three cases, this separation of the jurors from media accounts of the trial somehow failed. This is a problem. Jurors are not supposed to listen to news accounts of the trial or take information about the background of the case into the jury room. But it is not automatically a miscarriage of justice every time a juror reads or hears a news account about his or her case.

The separation of jurors from news accounts is a kind of safety mechanism—a way of protecting jurors' impartiality and limiting their decision to one based on the trial evidence. This safety mechanism can fail without necessarily causing an unfair trial. It still must be determined whether the jurors' impartiality and fairness were actually affected. The three St. Louis cases illustrate this principle.

The Belleville dioxin trial was the most dramatic example. The case took three and one-half years to try—the longest trial in American his-tory. Hardly anyone seriously believed that the jurors could or would to-tally exclude all outside accounts of the trial during the long pendency of the case. And certainly no one was eager to retry it.

What, then, of the revelation, several days after the verdict, that sev-eral jurors read or listened to news accounts of the trial during their six-week-long deliberations? It appeared to reveal definite juror miscon-duct—disobedience of the court's specific instructions.

By itself, however, this does not constitute unfairness in the trial. By all accounts, and as the split nature of their verdict showed, the jurors took their task seriously and tried to be fair and impartial. The trial judge refused to reverse the trial verdict solely because of the jurors' reported attention to the news.

Similarly, in the Walter Harvey murder trial, despite more deliber-ate misconduct by the jurors, it still had to be decided if the miscon-duct really tainted the trial outcome. For that highly publicized, double murder trial, jurors were brought in from Kansas City to try the case in Clayton, Missouri. They were sequestered in a hotel and their television wires were cut to remove the possibility of their seeing news accounts of the trial.

Yet, two jurors reconnected the wires, turned on the television, and (with several other jurors) viewed portions of two KSDK-TV reports on the trial. One of the things they learned from the TV report, before they made their sentencing recommendation, was that Harvey had been convicted in a prior trial.

After the trial, when those activities by the jurors were revealed, the trial court held a hearing and determined that the juror misconduct did not affect the outcome. (For example, it was not clear if the jurors understood what was broadcast, and despite hearing of Harvey's prior conviction, they went on to recommend the least severe sentence.) The Missouri Court of Appeals later reversed this ruling in part, requiring further hearings to more fully explore the issue. So again, the issue is whether juror viewing of television reports *actually prejudiced* the trial.

The Leisure case involves slightly different circumstances. Leisure was set to be tried on capital murder charges in a car bombing incident. As jury selection began in St. Louis City Circuit Court, the *Post-Dispatch* published a brief article, which, among other things, mentioned that Leisure had been previously convicted of murder in another car bombing.

Jurors are routinely sequestered in capital cases in Missouri, but because jury selection had not been completed, some prospective jurors may have read the article. Because of this, and to prevent any taint to the trial, the court declared a mistrial and rescheduled the trial.

Heated rhetoric and accusations often accompany so-called free press—fair trial controversies. In the three cases, particularly the Leisure case, accusations of both journalistic and judicial irresponsibility were heard.

But the common thread of these cases should really caution against simplistic finger-pointing. The task of separating jurors from the news is awkward, with some built-in problems due to human nature.

When the jury system began in England hundreds of years ago, jurors were selected because of their knowledge of the case and witnesses. Now we often expect the other extreme—jurors totally ignorant of all the surrounding facts and issues. In fact, the law does not require jurors to enter the courtroom with blank minds but only with fair and impartial minds.

Separating jurors from news coverage is one means to achieve impartiality but not the only way. Such separation attempts may create their own problems; the mystique of a total news blackout may operate like the designation of forbidden fruit and increase jurors' desire for outside facts.

Moreover, in the Harvey and dioxin cases, the courts may ultimately rely on jurors, with their sense of fairness and impartiality, to set aside the news accounts and rule solely on the evidence at trial. (Judges, for example, do this routinely.) If this is the result, then perhaps news blackouts are not essential after all.

The irony of many fair trial—free press debates is that lawyers and journalists both usually assume more impact from news accounts than actually occurs. Americans are not avid newspaper readers, and jurors do not analyze the news with a lawyer's critical eye. As one federal appeals court noted several years ago, concerning some of the most widely publicized cases of recent history, the Watergate scandal and the Abscam prosecutions, "many, if not most, potential jurors are untainted by press coverage."

Cameras in the Courtroom

During the late 1970s and the 1980s, media groups on several different occasions sought a rule opening Missouri courtrooms to cameras and tape recorders. In one petition, the Missouri Freedom of Information Council argued that expanded media coverage of the courts would allow modern technology "to bring the courts to the people."

Each of these efforts was unsuccessful. And the biggest obstacle to cameras in court seemed to be the perception that courts and television, like oil and water, do not mix. For many, particularly conservative midwestern judges, broadcast journalism and its tools and techniques seemed incompatible with judicial decorum and deliberation.

One of the media's standard responses has been to cite the experience of the many states that reinstated cameras in the courtroom during this time period. Their experience indicated that hypothesized undesirable changes in behavior in front of courtroom cameras—"playing for the cameras" or for the home TV audience—does not occur. If anything, participants in televised trials are usually on better behavior than those not under electronic scrutiny.

But perhaps the most telling evidence of the compatibility of cameras in court, moreover, is the day-to-day experiences that the courts have already had with television technologies, even in Missouri. There is no question anymore whether courts and television will mix. The only issue is whether, as the uses of video technologies expand *within* the courthouse, television will also be used to convey courthouse proceedings to the society *outside.*

Already television cameras, television pictures, and video and sound recordings are regularly used in countless ways in connection with court proceedings.

- Videotape evidence is a routine part of both civil lawsuits and criminal prosecutions. Undercover criminal investigations, both highly publicized federal operations like the Abscam and DeLorean prosecutions and many nonspectacular local investigations, use hidden television cameras as a standard investigatory tool. Videotape evidence from such investigations is recognized by the courts as reliable and admissible—and visually damning to hapless defendants caught before a camera. In civil cases, pretrial depositions are frequently videotaped and played at trial when the witness cannot attend the trial. Indeed, videotape depositions have become preferred to the pre-video method of readings from printed transcripts.
- Professional video presentations are also used in trials. One of the most potent tools of the personal injury plaintiff's bar is the day-in-the-life film, a video presentation showing how the plaintiff's injury affects his daily life. Formerly the province of those able to afford expensive filmmakers, such presentations are now available to anyone with a modern videotape camera.
- Video presentations and seminars are regularly used in the training of lawyers and judges. Video legal education seminars, some transmitted by satellite, put thousands of lawyers and judges in touch weekly with national legal experts. And the most sought-after trial practice seminars are those that allow the participants to perform before a camera and later review and critique their performance on videotape.
- Special video connections in certain courtrooms in Missouri allow prisoners to "appear" in court by video, without being physically transported to the courthouse. In authorizing this setup, the general assembly implicitly recognized the usefulness of television as a modern replacement to presence in the courtroom. That, of course, is

what proponents of cameras in the courtroom claim, in a somewhat different context—that television cameras in court can be the eyes and ears of citizens who cannot personally attend court.

- Some entire trials have been conducted on videotape. A state trial court in Erie County, Ohio, has been conducting prerecorded video trials since 1975. In these cases, all of the major elements of civil trials—opening statements, testimony of witnesses, and closing arguments—are videotaped (often in different out-of-court locations), edited together (with all objectionable testimony deleted), and finally presented to the jury on a television screen. The full prerecorded trial is also available to the appellate court for review. The judicial report on prerecorded trials is enthusiastic and favorable: "Technology can save the jury trial."

- Similarly, in some major complex trials, trial testimony of witnesses is videotaped so that it will be available in case witnesses die and a retrial is required after appeal.

- Television and recording technologies, just as they are regular parts of American life, have become regular parts of American trials. Videotapes and sound recordings are used as evidence in cases dealing with disputes over television broadcasts, recorded music, and films, and as demonstrative tools in many nonmedia cases.

- Not least of all, the video consciousness has entered the courtroom, too. Television has affected not only the intellectual background of citizens but also their attention spans, their values, and their expectations of the legal system. Any effective courtroom participant must know and understand these realities of the video age.

Thus, in a very real sense, television pervades courtrooms, as it pervades every other place in our society, even if the doors are locked to bar the actual entry of cameras.

Ultimately, the Missouri Supreme Court did permit cameras in court on an experimental basis in 1992 and a semipermanent basis in 1994. However, the state entered the modern era *very* cautiously. One expert in the field called the Missouri plan "among the most timid" nationwide.

The Missouri rule, formally known as Administrative Rule 16, included a number of restrictions on use of cameras in courtrooms, many of which drew immediate criticism. Some of the rule provisions imposed *substantive* restrictions on usage of cameras in court. For example:

- *Limited Number of Cameras.* Only one video camera, one still photographer, and one audio line will be allowed in a courtroom, no matter how newsworthy (or noncontroversial) the trial. Hence, pooling arrangements will be required—presumably even if only two media outlets cover the trial.
- *Fixed Video Camera.* The television camera must be operated from a fixed position in the courtroom.
- *Sensitive Matter Exclusion.* Cameras are not permitted in juvenile, adoption, domestic relations, or child custody hearings. If the trial judge consents, however, cameras may be permitted in the trial of a juvenile who is prosecuted as an adult.
- *Witness Opt-Outs.* Certain kinds of witnesses—including *all* witnesses in criminal cases—are given the right to prohibit photography or audio recording of their testimony. Witnesses given this right include victims or witnesses of a crime, police informants, undercover agents, relocated witnesses, and juveniles. And photography and recording of the testimony of other witnesses who do not fit in these categories may nonetheless be prohibited at the discretion of the trial judge.
- *Prohibited Subjects of Photography.* No photography or audio recording will be permitted of jurors, prospective jurors, jury selection, private conferences between the judge and attorneys or among attorneys, or "material on counsel table."
- *Hallway Interviews.* Broadcast reporters (but apparently not print reporters) are prohibited from recording interviews in the hallways in front of the courtroom.
- *Trial Judge Discretion.* The trial judge is allowed to impose other restrictions as he sees fit or even prohibit cameras altogether.

The rule also imposes *procedural* restrictions—what might less kindly be called "red tape"—on reporters or photographers who wish to use cameras in the courtroom. Among them:

- *Media Coordinators.* Arrangements for use of cameras and audio equipment in courtrooms must be made through a single media representative, appointed in advance. This requirement, designed to prevent technical media issues from becoming a burden on the trial judge, is typical.

- *Equipment Approval.* The media must obtain advance judicial approval for the audio and video equipment used, apparently to ensure that it will not be disruptive.

Altogether, these restrictions make the Missouri rule "among the most timid and most restrictive of all the states that have allowed cameras in court," according to journalist Fred Graham. Graham, former Supreme Court reporter for the *New York Times* and CBS News, and later chief correspondent for the cable television court TV network, commented on the Missouri rule at a conference sponsored by the Missouri Bar's media law committee.

Graham was especially critical of the witness opt-out procedure. By requiring the trial judge to give witnesses a kind of "warning" that they can avoid camera and audio coverage, the rule essentially *encourages* such opt-outs, Graham asserted. And he argued that there is no need for allowing opt-outs. He also criticized some of the procedural hurdles the rule imposed.

Graham's concerns are more than the one-sided views of a journalist. Even some of the judges and bar leaders who participated on the state supreme court's special advisory committee expressed bafflement at why the court wrote the rule so restrictively. Some fear that the restrictions would discourage use of cameras in Missouri courtrooms.

Perhaps the greatest deficiency of the Missouri rule, however, is simply its orientation toward restricting coverage in an attempt to avoid problems. This, in a sense, has been the focus of courts and the organized bar since the mid-1950s, when the traditions of yellow journalism, played out during the infancy of broadcasting, led to sensationalistic and disruptive trial coverage using cameras.

In the eighties and nineties, the maturity of the technology and of the journalism profession have largely set to rest those old bugbears of journalistic disruption and sensationalism. But the caution in the bench, though understandable given the historic perspective, continues to prevent a full entry into the age of electronic journalism.

The problem with this cautious perspective is simply that it can prevent us from enjoying the *benefits* of electronic journalism in the crucial area of court and legal coverage. Just as C-SPAN and televised town meetings have dramatically increased interest in and understanding of the legislative process, cameras in the courtroom have the potential to greatly increase citizen understanding of the courts and perhaps even self-understanding and reform in the participants in the judicial system itself.

Technologies, like television, cannot be confined or limited only to certain functions approved from on high. Just as television accomplishes useful tasks *within* the court system, it can—and should be encouraged to—carry out the important and useful function of reporting and televising courthouse news to the society outside.

The Business
(and Education)
of the Press

Student Press Rights

WHEN A CONSERVATIVE SUPREME COURT struck down progressive child-labor legislation in 1905, Justice Oliver Wendell Holmes asserted in dissent that the Constitution "does not enact Mr. Herbert Spencer's *Social Statics.*"

In 1988, the Supreme Court upheld the Hazelwood, Missouri, School District's censorship of a high school newspaper and, in essence, concluded that the Constitution did not enact the liberal educational philosophy of Jean Jacques Rousseau, either.

The Court's decision in *Hazelwood School District v. Kuhlmeier* was a setback to press freedom in high schools. Yet the *Hazelwood* decision, in its intent and analysis, is primarily a ruling about education, and the educator's control over the high school curriculum. It is a reaffirmation of the great power (and responsibility) that has been committed to public school boards in our country.

The issue before the Supreme Court in the *Hazelwood* case was "whether the First Amendment requires a school to tolerate particular student speech," namely, two controversial student-written articles from the triweekly Hazelwood East *Spectrum* that were deleted by the school's principal in 1983.

The *Spectrum* was written and edited by students in the high school's Journalism II class, under supervision of a teacher and following policy guidelines set out by the school board. Over the years, it had published articles on many timely and controversial topics, including drugs, cults, runaways, desegregation, and teenage dating.

In the spring of 1983, the *Spectrum* staff prepared a series of articles on teenage pregnancy, the impact of divorce on children, and juvenile delinquency. Several of the stories were based on, and included quotations from, interviews with Hazelwood East students, including three pregnant students and several students whose parents had recently divorced.

The articles were approved by the *Spectrum's* faculty advisors. But shortly before scheduled publication, when they reached Robert Reynolds, the school's principal, he ordered the articles pulled. Reynolds explained that he considered the articles on pregnancy and divorce "too sensitive" for "our immature audience of readers." He also thought the articles invaded the privacy of the students and parents portrayed in the articles and were unfair by not including the parents' views.

Three student members of the *Spectrum* staff did not accept Reynolds's action or reasoning. They photocopied and distributed the banned articles and sued the school district in federal court in St. Louis, charging that the school action violated their First Amendment rights. The case was heard by Chief U.S. District Judge John F. Nangle, who in 1985 ruled in favor of the school district. The students appealed to the U.S. Court of Appeals for the Eighth Circuit, which, in a 2–1 decision, reversed Judge Nangle's ruling and held that the school's action was illegal.

The Supreme Court accepted certiorari and heard the case in the fall of 1987. The Hazelwood dispute was the first case to reach the high court concerning the freedoms and responsibilities of students who write and edit their school newspapers.

In its decision, the Court first noted that publication of the *Spectrum* was heavily intertwined with the school's curriculum. *Spectrum* was written and edited by students in the school's Journalism II class. It was published and heavily subsidized by the school district. School policies gave student editors freedom only within the limits of "responsible journalism." The journalism advisor and principal routinely reviewed page proofs before publication.

The Court also scrutinized the actions of Hazelwood East principal Robert Reynolds in censoring the articles, which concerned students' experiences with pregnancy and divorce. Reynolds appeared concerned with fairness to those mentioned in the articles and what he perceived as inappropriateness of the sexual subject matter of the pregnancy story to some of the school's younger students.

On this factual predicate, the Court then began its legal analysis. The Court initially disagreed with the appellate court's characterization of *Spectrum* as a "public forum" because the Hazelwood authorities had not, by policy or practice, opened *Spectrum* to indiscriminate use by the general public.

Then the court took on the real issue: does the Constitution allow administrative censorship of a high school newspaper like the *Spectrum*?

Two different legal principles could have applied on this issue. One is the principle accepted since *Tinker v. Des Moines School District* in 1969 that students "do not shed their constitutional rights to freedom of speech or expression at the schoolhouse gate." This generally allows students to express their views at school in a nondisruptive way.

The other principle is that public schools are allowed reasonable authority in the areas of curriculum, discipline, and educational standards in order to carry out their educational mission. This generally gives school officials broad discretion to educate children according to their best judgment.

Either of these doctrines could be used to different results in the *Hazelwood* case. Viewed as student expression, the *Spectrum* articles would be upheld. Viewed as standard-setting in a matter of curriculum, the principal's censorship would be upheld.

Justice Byron R. White, writing for the Court majority, had little problem determining how to view the Hazelwood situation. Since *Spectrum* was "school-sponsored," "supervised by faculty," and "designed to impart particular knowledge or skills to student participants and audiences," the Court held that it "may fairly be characterized as part of the school curriculum." Not surprisingly, the Court held that "educators are entitled to exercise greater control" over such curricular expression like the *Spectrum* articles than over noncurricular expression.

The Court distinguished the *Tinker* rule as applying to noncurricular expression, such as "personal expression that happens to occur on school premises." Justice White set forth three reasons why curricular expression is subject to regulation: (1) to ensure that students learn the lesson being taught; (2) to avoid exposing immature students to inappropriate material; and (3) to clarify what messages carry the school's sanction, or "imprimatur."

In addressing *how* this curricular expression can be regulated, Justice White stated that school officials need only show that their actions "are reasonably related to legitimate pedagogical concerns." In constitutional law, courts following "reasonableness" standards generally defer to any official action short of arbitrariness or bad motives.

Under this new standard (which the Court indicated will apply to all "student speech in school-sponsored expressive activities"), the Court found the Hazelwood censorship permissible. Simply put, the student expression occurred as part of the school curriculum, and the principal's censorship was reasonably related to legitimate educational concerns.

Advocates of press freedom and student rights were understandably concerned with the censorship permitted by the *Hazelwood* decision and some of the broad reasoning it employed. In particular, the Court's emphasis on protecting "immature" high school students from inappropriate material and its concerns over perception of the school district's sponsorship seem considerably overdone. Immature students can be shielded from inappropriate material by many means short of blanket censorship. And public perceptions of school sponsorship should not determine student press rights.

However, the essence of the court decision is that local school districts have broad authority over their own school curriculum, even when the curriculum at issue is preparation of a school newspaper. In two ways the decision is less radical and less harmful to legitimate First Amendment concerns than it may seem at first blush.

First, the ruling is limited both in the newspapers it covers and in the censorship it permits. *Spectrum* was a school-paid, school-directed, for-credit publication, with a tradition of clearance by school officials. The *Hazelwood* ruling, because of its focus on curriculum, presumably would not apply to school newspapers that lack significant curricular ties or have been given student editorial freedom.

Censorship even of curricular newspapers, moreover, must be based on "legitimate pedagogical concerns." This could become a significant barrier to officials who would blue-pencil every bit of dissent and individuality from the student press. In school libraries, for example, the Supreme Court has prohibited educators from removing books for narrowly partisan or political purposes.

Moreover, the decision applies only at the high school level or below. The court explicitly held that it was not deciding whether the "same degree of deference" to the administrative decisions was appropriate at the university level. Many other precedents hold that college students must be permitted far more latitude in expression than high school students.

Second, the *Hazelwood* decision properly upholds local school officials' right and responsibility to control school curriculum matters. Journalism is a class at Hazelwood East, and realistically there should be no constitutional violation just because it is taught under an official-directed rather than a student-directed program. These are matters of educational philosophy, not constitutional rights.

Justice Holmes was correct in 1905 when he claimed that social Darwinism had not been enacted by the Constitution. And the Supreme Court was probably correct in the *Hazelwood* case for concluding that the Constitution did not enact any particular educational philosophy, either.

Perhaps students learn journalism best when they learn it by practice, making editorial decisions (and mistakes) themselves without any censorship from higher-ups. Perhaps some other method is better. The *Hazelwood* decision simply says that when a student newspaper is set up as part of the school curriculum, this educational choice is for the local school board and is not dictated by the Constitution.

In a way, this is more consistent with traditional notions of press freedom than a ruling favorable to the students would have been. It has often been said that freedom of the press is freedom of those who own a press. Professional journalists enjoy only such freedom as their publishers give them, and student journalists have now learned this lesson, too.

Ultimately, the most important aspect of the *Hazelwood* case may not be the legal principle established but rather the way school districts interpret it and proceed with their student newspapers in the future.

The Supreme Court, like the presidency, is a "bully pulpit," and some may interpret the *Hazelwood* decision as an exhortation for school officials to censor student journalism. This would be a mistake. Censorship is a crude and un-American tool, rarely effective and often counterproductive. In most situations, a school official who contemplates censorship is one who has failed to teach students effectively in the first place.

The *Hazelwood* decision simply *allows* censorship of school newspapers that are set up as part of the curriculum. It neither requires school newspapers to be set up this way nor requires the censorship power to be exercised. Nothing in the decision prohibits school districts from giving students editorial responsibility, either through a firm no-censorship policy or a noncurricular school newspaper.

One of the best arguments for giving student journalists editorial control over their publications is that one learns responsibility only by exercising responsibility. Now, the Supreme Court has firmly handed local school districts the responsibility for appropriate journalism education. As school officials exercise that responsibility, one hopes they will learn that wise and effective education of youth is best achieved by adherence to the constitutional principles including press freedom that exist in adult society.

Reporters as Professionals

Reporters, take heart. Gingrich and Clinton may deride you, local officials may misuse you, and the public may mistrust you. But a federal court has now certified that you (or, more precisely, *some* of you) are *artistic professionals*. It's official that you're not drones, and the court has judicially established that you:

- use initiative and responsibility,
- act intelligently and creatively,
- possess knowledge and expertise,
- work using independence and judgment, and
- write with style, artistry, and clarity.

In short, *you've got respect*. You are indeed a winner! Sort of. You may find this respect hard to bank on—because your paychecks will decrease as your "respect" increases.

Let's examine how you got all this respect. During the New Deal, in 1938, President Roosevelt proposed, and Congress passed, the Fair Labor Standards Act, a measure designed to set minimum employment standards. Among other things, it required workers to be paid time and one-half for overtime work. The law was directed at the evil of abuse of laborers but extended well past the factory gate. So executive, administrative, and professional workers were exempted, to ensure that the measure did not sweep *too* far.

The question soon arose: are news reporters "professionals" (exempt from the Act) or not (and therefore covered by it, and entitled to overtime pay)? Even in the early days the answer was unclear. Robert Jackson, an assistant attorney general when the act was submitted to Congress, opined that reporters were professionals. But early Department of Labor interpretations distinguished between exempt (i.e., "professional") editorial writers and analysts and nonexempt "legmen" and "rewrite men" reporters.

For fifty or so years, the department interpretations were generally followed, with the result that reporters were considered nonprofessional workers. Reporters swallowed their pride and accepted overtime pay and awards. Publishers grumbled, vowing (not entirely convincingly) that they viewed their reporters as respected professionals.

Publishers and broadcasters continued to challenge the designation of reporters as nonprofessionals. In a 1990 case involving WDFW-TV in Dallas, they won one key concession from the federal Court of Appeals for the Fifth Circuit. The court admitted that the Department of Labor's 1940-era interpretations were outmoded and that modern journalists were quite capable of original, creative, professional work.

Nonetheless, when it examined the work of reporters, producers, directors, and assignment editors at WDFW, the court found that they more closely followed the 1940s "legman" and "rewrite man" models than that of a modern creative journalistic professional. For the most part, the court found, WDFW news personnel went about their daily work in ways "dictated by management" and produced stories "neither analytic nor interpretative nor original."

In 1994, publishers scored a bigger victory. In *Sherwood v. Washington Post*, a federal trial court in Washington, D.C., examined *Post* reporter Robert Sherwood's work and work habits and concluded that he was a true "artistic professional." (Reporters can't qualify as "managerial" or "administrative" professionals, but the law permits writers to qualify as "artistic" professionals if their primary duty consists of work requiring "invention, imagination or talent.")

The court in the *Sherwood* case found that Sherwood, a thirty-year veteran reporter, carried out his reporting duties with considerable independence, initiative, creativity, and expertise. Parts of the court's opinion strain a bit (for example, when the decision on which portions of an interview to include in a story is held up as an example of Sherwood's "responsibility" with respect to "important decisions about his writing"). But by and large, the decision accurately depicts and characterizes the duties and conduct of a topflight reporter on a topflight newspaper.

Even more so than the court in *WDFW*, the *Sherwood* court rejected the fifty-year-old Labor Department interpretations as relics of a long-past "Front Page" era, when stories were "short, simplistic and over-dimensional," totally unlike the original, analytical, and creative content of modern *Post* stories.

Because it is firmly based on facts of modern-day major-newspaper reporting and distinguishes and rejects the aging Labor Department interpretations, the *Sherwood* decision may well represent a turning point. Cases of this nature will always depend on the facts of the particular case, and especially on whether reporters are truly given independence (as at the *Post*) or whether they are directed in narrow tasks (as at WDFW).

But *Sherwood* (and even *WDFW*) indicates that reporters will no longer be automatically viewed as nonexempt workers. Given the changes in the journalism profession since the 1940s, it is increasingly likely that reporters will be considered "artistic professionals"—with full rights to both the pride and the lower pay that come with that status.

Book Publishing Contracts

The suit between Joan Collins and Random House, tried in early 1996, was remarkable. Not just because the actress managed to convince a jury that she was a legitimate aspiring writer. Not just because the jury disregarded the literary experts who supported the publisher's rejection of her manuscripts. The Collins case was most remarkable because it exemplified a rare occurrence of the book publishing world—an author winning a contract dispute with a publisher.

Collins is best known as a star of *Dynasty*, a prime-time soap opera, and is the sister of Jackie Collins, a writer of popular pulp novels. Joan Collins entered into a book contract with Random House in 1990, at the height of her popularity, and in the following three years produced two lengthy—but reportedly disorganized and amateurish—manuscripts, "The Ruling Passion" and "Hell Hath No Fury." Random House rejected Collins's manuscripts, even after several years of work, on the grounds that they failed to meet the "complete manuscript" requirement of her contract.

Random House sued Ms. Collins for return of advances paid to her and her agent, and the trial in New York City caught the attention of the public and the press, apparently because of the author's prominence and the many dismal evaluations of her manuscripts and her literary ability. At trial, a Random House executive called the first manuscript melodramatic and "incoherent" and even Collins's own lawyers did not defend it as a great literary work. In his summation at trial, Collins's lawyer Donald Zakarin said his client generally wrote about "money and sex, and power and sex, and intrigue and sex."

Collins, whose legal clout and jury appeal apparently made up for what her writing ability lacked, prevailed at trial. The jury found that the publisher had breached its contract by failing to accept and publish the first of her two manuscripts. The jury verdict's would allow Collins to keep her $1.2 million advance and perhaps receive more from the publisher.

The trial was covered on the Court TV cable channel, and the verdict was reported not only in the print and broadcast tabloid media but even on the front page of the *New York Times*.

Unfortunately for authors, the Collins case is not typical of most author-publisher contract disputes. Author-publisher contracts are notoriously one-sided. A typical book publisher enters into contract negotiations possessing an established reputation, significant working capital, an editorial staff, a production network, market understanding, marketing power, a recognized nameplate, and the ability to easily walk away from any single proposed book project. A typical first-time author, for his or her part, usually enters into contract negotiations with two things: a rough book outline (or an unfinished manuscript) and *desperation* for a publishing contract.

Thus, except for those few well-established authors or celebrities with unquestioned literary skills or selling power, most authors must defer to the publisher on most book contract issues. But while unknown authors cannot expect to do as well as Joan Collins, either in negotiations or in litigation, all authors can benefit from an understanding of the key contract issues and a willingness to address those issues. Here's an overview of some key book contract issues:

Rights. One of the first provisions in a book contract is the grant of rights, the provision by which the author permits the publisher to publish the work. This provision is obviously necessary, since the author by law owns the copyright to his or her work and must grant permission for the publisher to print and sell the work.

However, most book contract rights clauses extend far beyond the minimal necessary grant of rights. An author's overall copyright embraces many specific rights—hardback rights, paperback rights, serial publication rights, North American publication rights, European publication rights, translation rights, electronic publishing rights, and rights to adapt the book into movies, plays, television programs, or musicals. Most publishers' standard book contracts seek to obtain *all* of these rights for the publisher and then give the publisher control over how those rights are exploited.

It's often not appropriate for the publisher to take over all rights, particularly if the author or his or her agent is capable of independently negotiating secondary publications and adaptations of the work—for example, foreign translations and publications, and adaptations of the work into audiovisual productions. In such cases, authors can often negotiate with their publishers a narrowing of the rights grant to the publisher and, hence, a broader retention of rights.

In particular, in today's electronic and multimedia environment, authors should be especially careful in granting electronic publishing rights. Even as sophisticated organizations as the Walt Disney Corporation and the Philadelphia Orchestra have been embarrassed in recent years by their past sloppiness in preserving or delineating video and electronic rights.

Manuscript Requirements. Joan Collins's agent, the late Irving "Swifty" Lazar, knew that manuscript acceptability might be a problem with Collins's books, and he negotiated a special contract provision, which required Random House to pay Collins upon her submission of a "complete manuscript." That is a break from most book contracts, which require the publisher to pay only upon receipt of a "satisfactory" manuscript. Under such standard contracts, an author who receives an advance is obligated to pay back the advance if his or her manuscript is not acceptable.

Whether a manuscript is "acceptable" under the standard provision can often lead to disputes, but in most such disputes, the author has little practical power. Undoubtedly, the great majority of authors who are told their manuscripts are not acceptable either give up or revise the manuscript until it is suitable. Given the legal costs involved, the subjectivity of the "acceptability" standard and the editorial judgments involved, and the deference that publishers and editors could expect from courts in most cases, few authors ever find it in their interest to bring the kind of legal challenge that Collins mounted.

Royalties. The royalty provisions of just about any book contract send a clear signal to new and noncelebrity authors: *Don't quit your day job.* Royalty schedules vary from publisher to publisher and within different publishing sectors (for example, the trade, educational, and scholarly sectors). Generally, however, authors' royalties run 10 to 15 percent of the wholesale or retail price of the book, less returns (unsold copies returned by bookstores to publishers), and are usually paid on a delayed quarterly or semiannual basis. If an author has been paid an advance, he or she will not receive royalty checks until the calculated royalties exceed the amount of the advance.

Indemnification. From an author's perspective, the most dreaded provision of a standard book contract is the "indemnification" or "hold harmless" clause. This provision requires the author to pay the publisher's expenses—including any damages awards in court—if the publisher incurs any legal liability based on the content of the book. Authors and writers' groups have been critical of these provisions, claiming that they illogically shift the burden of defending a work from deep-pocket publishers to impecunious writers and, hence, encourage editorial timidity.

Some publishers view author indemnification as essential and nonnegotiable. But in recent years many others have demonstrated flexibility. Some publishers will, if pressed, eliminate the indemnification clause. Others have at times agreed to share responsibility for legal exposure. Some publishers agree to cover the author on their insurance contracts, perhaps with the author covering part or all of the increased insurance cost.

Hence, although indemnification remains a sticking point in many book contracts, for the increasing number of authors who are concerned about this point and who are willing to raise it and negotiate it in a spirit of give-and-take, solutions can often be worked out.

Credits and Marketing. Authors and editors care about how their names are displayed, how credits are given in subsequent editions, and how their works are marketed. These topics, however, are rarely adequately addressed in standard book contracts, perhaps because these issues of burning concern to authors are of little or no concern to publishers.

As a result, a surprising number of disputes (some litigated, some negotiated, some just sulked over) have arisen regarding the narrow area of authorship credit, particularly where multiple authors or editors are involved. Most of the disputes could have been avoided if the authors or their counsel had attended to the issues at the negotiation stage and set forth clear guidelines for credits in the contract.

These examples illustrate a few of the many book publishing contract concerns, which deserve the careful attention of all authors. Whatever the nature of an author's work, experience, and level of celebrity, the book publishing contract that the author negotiates and signs may well determine whether his or her authorship develops into a satisfying experience—or one that is as unsatisfying as a plotless and incoherent Joan Collins novel.

Distribution Rights

Junk mail.
"Throwaway" newspapers.
"Junk faxes."
Junk e-mail messages ("spam").
Auto-dial telephone solicitations.
Newsrack blight.

Welcome to the newfound "problem" of unsolicited information and communications. If you *like* sending or getting unsolicited mail or communications, you'd better not admit it. As the disparaging language used for these forms of communications indicates, unsolicited communications are very much out of favor. To the dismay of both pro-free speech activists and several whole industries dependent on unsolicited communications, there is a growing and popular move on to restrict various techniques of unsolicited distribution of news, information, and advertising.

Legislators love restricting unsolicited communications (at least so long as their own newsletters and mailings aren't affected). Anti-junk-communications laws permit—indeed *encourage*—lawmakers to limit the distribution of news and advertising vehicles, to embrace the beloved values of personal privacy, and to accomplish these objectives with no governmental budget impact. Many private organizations also find it desirable to fight to ban unsolicited communications.

Some anti-unsolicited-communications efforts are not new. The direct marketing field has long faced various efforts to ban or restrict junk mail. Newspapers have had to constantly defend their right to place newsracks in public places against challenges based on clutter, safety, and aesthetics. And free-distribution newspapers—"throwaways" in the familiar pejorative—are often attacked as litter and a nuisance.

The newest twist involves anti-unsolicited-communications laws specifically aimed at modern electronic communications. When the telephone auto-dialing device became popular, for example, Congress passed the Telephone Consumer Protection Act of 1991. This act banned automated telephone calls for telemarketing purposes.

That same act also banned—almost as an afterthought, with no hearings or testimony—unsolicited faxes, which have been labeled as (you guessed it) "junk faxes." This provision, a favorite of class-action lawyers because of a $500-per-transmission penalty, has served to chill the development of fax newsletters and circulars.

And concern about unsolicited communications has spread in the on-line and cyberspace worlds. One highly publicized advertisement by two immigration attorneys, widely distributed by e-mail to thousands of participants to many Usenet newsgroups, received widespread condemnation as a misuse of the Internet. And America Online (AOL) sued a direct marketer under a novel theory, claiming that the marketer's mailing of tens of thousands of e-mail advertising messages overloaded AOL's system and constituted improper use of the AOL system, which was illegal under several federal computer statutes.

Unsolicited communications aren't new. The revolutionary activists of colonial days were pioneers in unsolicited communications. As the Supreme Court noted in a famous passage in a 1938 case involving pamphleteering, pamphlets and leaflets "have been historic weapons in the defense of liberty, as the pamphlets of Thomas Paine and others in our own history abundantly attest."

In that case, the Supreme Court recognized and protected the right of protesters to distribute their leaflets, pamphlets, and other written works—even to those who did not want them. The Court stated, "Liberty of circulation is as essential to [freedom of the press] as liberty of publishing." In a subsequent case, the Court held that the right to pamphleteer even extended to *anonymous* pamphleteering, and in 1995 the Court reaffirmed that holding to invalidate election-law regulations that required electioneering flyers and advertisements to be marked with the creator's name.

Because of this history, the right to distribute publications is clearest in the case of political pamphleteering and solicitations for "causes" (especially civic and religious appeals). But most court decisions have recognized that the right also extends to newspaper publishers and their efforts to sell and distribute their publications.

Accordingly, cities may not restrict placement of newsracks on public sidewalks merely for perceived aesthetic reasons or because of a dislike of newsbox clutter. Since the right to distribute newspapers through newsboxes is of constitutional stature, only a "compelling state interest"—which usually doesn't exist—will suffice to support a ban. Similarly, throwaway newspapers may not be banned as litter or nuisances or as aids to burglars; courts have recognized that these papers (even if they primarily consist of advertising) are cousins to Thomas Paine's pamphlets and convey the kind of information and ideas on which our system thrives.

Similarly, efforts to curtail junk mail as a nuisance or privacy invasion have not succeeded. One federal judge dismissed a plea to bar use of public records for junk mailing lists with the explanation that "[t]he short, though regular, journey from mail box to trash can . . . is an acceptable burden, at least so far as the Constitution is concerned."

The right to distribute, however, seems to lose force the farther one gets from traditional printed publications. Fifty years ago, in the context of the budding new technology of sound amplification, the Supreme Court struggled with what Justice Felix Frankfurter described as "new technological devices . . . and attempts to control them in order to gain their benefits while maintaining the precious freedom of privacy." The Court initially held, in a closely split decision, that loudspeakers were "totally indispensable instruments of effective public speech. . . . the way people are reached" and hence constitutionally protected. But soon afterward the Court retreated, holding that this new technology, with its opportunity for "aural aggression" could be banned outright.

In the same way, courts and legislators have viewed aural communications over telephone lines, and other electronic communications, as somehow different from the distribution of pamphlets and newspapers and, hence, subject to bans or significant restrictions. Bans on use of autodialing devices in telemarketing have been upheld by several courts, primarily on the grounds that they regulate commercial speech rather than classic political speech.

Similarly, the provision of the Telephone Consumer Protection Act that prohibits unsolicited fax advertisements has been upheld as a reasonable regulation of commercial speech. A more open question is whether the ban on unsolicited faxes can extend even to fax newspapers and newsletters—publications that are essentially electronic siblings of the traditional free-distribution community newspapers. These issues have been raised in suits in St. Louis and Indianapolis, among other places.

Another twist on the electronic distribution issue is presented by America Online's claim, made in federal court in Virginia, that a direct marketer violated a federal criminal statute when it overloaded AOL's system with unsolicited e-mail messages. The suit charged that Cyber Promotions sent unsolicited e-mail advertisements to more than 100,000 addresses on AOL's network and then compounded the problem by designating a computer within AOL's domain as the sending computer to which all undeliverable e-mail messages would be returned. AOL claimed that the messages, and particularly the return of undeliverable mail, violated two federal computer laws, as unauthorized and fraudulent use of a computer system.

Though unique and unlikely to set any broad precedent, the AOL case illustrates that distribution limitations are likely to be sought at some point against every new medium. E-mail messages can hardly be considered personally intrusive, aurally offensive, or invitations to crime or criminals; yet the phrase "junk e-mail" and the rhetoric that it must be stopped are prevalent.

As in many areas, on the right of distribution, our law is settled only as to things that no one fights over anymore: Thomas Paine's right to distribute pamphlets urging independence of the colonies from King George III. Like the Supreme Court fifty years ago, when confronted with the new technology of sound amplification, policymakers today are divided in how new distribution technologies should be treated—as analogous to Paine's pamphlets (and hence constitutionally protected) because they are media for communicating ideas or, alternatively, as carriers of "junk," potential nuisances, and means for sensory and electronic "aggression" (which do not deserve constitutional protection).

The analogies chosen, and the decisions made in this area, may turn out to be critical to the future of the communications media affected. Distribution of ideas and information—including distribution to those who would not otherwise seek them out—is, in many ways, the most crucial step in the process of communication, particularly for those who seek to influence or persuade others.

13

The Internet and Electronic Information

Information as Property

THE INFORMATION AGE HAS ARRIVED, AND IT IS working its way into American law.

In the 1980s and 1990s, the pursuit of knowledge, ideas, and information of value has been the new Gold Rush. As if to confirm this new reality, the United States Supreme Court, in the case of former *Wall Street Journal* reporter Foster Winans, ruled that information must be treated as a kind of property—a form of wealth.

The Supreme Court, in a broad ruling, upheld Winans's federal criminal conviction for stealing information that belonged to his employer. The decision has implications well beyond the unusual case of Winans and his inside-trading circle. The Winans decision marks off new legal boundaries within the white-collar working world and will affect all business persons who regularly deal in the intangible property of information, words, and ideas. It unmistakably ushers American law into the Information Age—an age in which information, words, and ideas constitute a significant and valuable form of property.

Just as the Industrial Age transformed the law relating to labor, interstate commerce, and industrial organization, the new Information Age will bring about a blossoming of the law of information and ideas. Legal battles in the Information Age will increasingly revolve not on men and materials but on the use of words and knowledge.

Millions of Americans work in knowledge jobs, in finance, government, publishing, research, consulting, computer science, and scores of other fields. In these jobs, productivity and success are based on the intangibles of information, words, and ideas.

Winans, who wrote the *Journal*'s popular "Heard on the Street" column, was a paradigmatic modern knowledge worker. His only tools were his pen, notepad, and computer terminal, and he produced only words on newsprint. His job was to gather, synthesize, and disclose useful information—specifically, recommendations and predictions regarding stocks and the market.

Winans misused his job-related knowledge. He schemed to profit by personally trading in the stock market and by giving friends stock tips, based on his advance knowledge of the next day's "Heard" columns. The column usually affected the market in the stocks it discussed, so profits came readily based on these tips.

Winans was not strictly a corporate insider under the securities law because he did not use inside information obtained from companies in whose stocks he traded. Nonetheless, the use of advance information about the "Heard" column violated the *Journal*'s employee manual, which asserted that "all material gleaned by you in the course of your work . . . is deemed to be strictly the company's property." Thus, when prosecutors brought criminal charges against him, they charged him under unique, creative theories, partly based on the *Journal* manual.

The key theory, which the Supreme Court unanimously approved in upholding Winans's conviction, was that Winans stole valuable, confidential information from the *Journal*. The gist of this theory was the *theft of information* from the *Journal*, not (as in an insider trading prosecution) the improper use of information in the stock market.

In determining whether Winans had acted criminally, the Court initially looked to the *Journal* employee handbook. The Court recognized that no criminal consequences could flow merely from the *Journal*'s ethical rules. But the manual went further than admonitory rules. It classified information obtained on the job ("all material gleaned by you in the course of your work") as "*company property.*"

Because of that property designation, the Court concluded, the

Journal's publication schedule and the contents of the "Heard" column prior to its publication were "confidential business information," and the *Journal* had an "intangible property right" in keeping the information confidential.

From this conclusion that the *Journal* had a "property right" in confidential information, the other steps to Winans's conviction followed. Winans had used the information for his own purposes and thus deprived the *Journal* "of its right to exclusive use of the information." Simply put, Winans had stolen property from the *Journal*. In this regard, the Supreme Court's decision treats Winans just like a bank employee who embezzles funds or a thief who steals an automobile.

The radical aspect of the Winans decision is the broad extent to which it recognizes property rights to information in the workplace. In Winans's case, the information at issue (the *Journal*'s publication schedule and advance notice of the content of the "Heard" column) became valuable property solely because the Journal's employee policies made it confidential.

Until this decision, legal protection for "confidential" information in the workplace extended only to the relatively limited information recognized as trade secrets. Even in knowledge industries, access to classic trade secrets is limited, often to employees working under detailed written employment agreements.

But now it appears that whatever an employer designates as confidential may become the employer's legally protected intangible property. This is a major extension of the legal protection for information in the workplace because millions of employees have access to such information and there are few written guidelines concerning its use or abuse.

The Winans decision will probably lead to more litigation, to refine the limits on confidential information and prevent misuse of the new powers given to employers. It will also open the courthouse door to more disputes over the many valuable "intangibles" within today's many industries.

The legal concerns of the knowledge industries are extensive and include not only workplace confidentiality but also trade secrets, copyright, rights to ideas, contractual claims relating to use of information, rights of publicity, libel, and rights of privacy. Some of these doctrines are yet in their infancy, and all will likely be extensively probed and developed in coming years.

For now, the Supreme Court has signaled that the protective custody of the law can and will expand, as appropriate, to embrace those intangible but valuable rights that constitute the lifeblood of the Information Age.

Price Tags on Information

It's today's big story and it can't be avoided—the coming Information Age; the Information Superhighway; our Interactive Future; the Dawn of Multimedia. If you are a media and an information addict, you probably *like* the idea of the coming Information Age.

As you see it: The more information, the better. The quicker and more convenient the delivery of information, the better. The more channels of information, the better, because of the greater choices, diversity, and independent sources of information. In sum, the more that information is valued in the marketplace, the better.

The new information technologies, you reason, can only increase the quality, quantity, and breadth of distribution of news and information. In this new world, information consumers will be like kings and queens, and the world's information their riches.

Hold on, Dr. Pangloss. It's time to look beyond those rose-colored pixels on your computer screen.

Yes, information will be valuable in the new electronic information marketplace. Yes, the market for information will expand, corresponding to the expansion in channels of delivery and the greater ease of delivery. But will these developments mean easy (and less expensive) access to valuable information? Or will they lead to a new cost-based system in which much valuable information, though technically available to all, moves on a tollway rather than a freeway? In short, will the Information Age broaden information dissemination and use or promote development of information fiefdoms? These are key questions, and the answers are not yet clear.

Much will depend on laws pertaining to proprietary rights in information—that is, on the extent to which particular kinds of valuable information are recognized as someone's protectable private property. In this regard, the information era has already begun, for in numerous areas, lines are being drawn, claims staked, and battles fought over proprietary rights to information.

It's not that information rights are always uncertain. Most aren't. No one disputes that the *St. Louis Post-Dispatch* owns its library of current and past articles and features; that the *St. Louis Business Journal* owns its compilations of local business activity; or that A. G. Edwards and Company owns its analysts' research and reports. Any or all of these databases, and thousands like them, are potential moneymakers in the information age, and properly so. Nor does anyone dispute that federal government publications, Supreme Court decisions, and creative works no longer under copyright protection are free and available for anyone to copy, distribute, or use.

In between these two areas of certainty, however, important battles are being fought and crucial policy decisions made. A few examples:

Rights of Use, Quotation, and Analysis. Aided by narrow judicial readings of the copyright *fair use* doctrine in recent years, some publishers are asserting newly broadened rights to control (i.e., charge for) use and quotation of their copyrighted or other proprietary works.

A newspaper, for example, may seek to charge a publisher for its use in an advertisement of a short passage from the newspaper's review of one of the publisher's books. A celebrity may attempt to charge for any use or republication of his image or quotations in any moneymaking context. An analyst of information may attempt to charge for republication of his newsworthy conclusions. Each of these examples is real. Each is an attempt to move a boundary line—the boundary between information that is free and that which is not free—in the direction of making more information private property.

In a pay-per-item information age, this boundary shift could have a broad impact. It could cost users of traditionally free information and also affect editorial freedom and accessibility of news.

An example: A small consumer-oriented newsletter, *The Insurance Forum*, has for years published summaries of ratings of insurance companies by the A. M. Best Company and other rating agencies. The newsletter's annual ratings summary issue alerted industry observers to changes in ratings systems and criteria, changes in individual firm ratings, and the differences in judgments of various rating services. It was a selective industry-wide version of the typical news item, "Ratings service lowers [or raises] company's rating."

For years, this went along fine, and *The Insurance Forum* encountered no problem. But in 1993, A. M. Best Company first threatened and then sued the publication, claiming that even the newsletter's editorial use of Best's ratings constituted copyright infringement. Best's claim was marginal but arguable under copyright precedents and serious, given the economic muscle and political clout of Best and similar publishers. Ultimately, the dispute was settled—with *The Insurance Forum* backing down in the face of Best's lawsuit.

Though this was a relatively minor dispute—unless you were editor of *The Insurance Forum*—it typifies the kind of boundary disputes that are increasingly being fought by aggressive advocates of greater proprietary rights in information. The cumulative result in these boundary disputes is likely to affect the emerging electronic information technologies and the relative interests of information providers and users.

Commercially Valuable Government Records. In many ways, electronic records are more valuable than paper records. The ability to search, organize, and manipulate data electronically provides enhanced value. As a result, many governmental records that in paper form had limited commercial value now in electronic form have greater commercial value. And, yes, attempts are being made to exploit that commercial value.

A case in point: Now that the Missouri statutes are available in electronic form, the "owner" of the statutes, the Missouri General Assembly, has seen dollar signs. Rather than make the electronic version of the statutes broadly and widely available for minimal copying costs (as the state Sunshine Law requires for state records), some members of the legislature have sought to *limit* channels of distribution and charge for copies at *higher-than-cost* commercial rates.

The obvious motive is profit—the electronic statutes are commercially valuable, since they permit lawyers, researchers, and others to more rapidly and effectively research legal issues. So the legislature wants to make money. Its technique: First, restrict access by prohibiting public copying à la Sunshine Law. Second, authorize one or more commercial intermediaries to purchase the electronic statutes from the state and resell them to users. Third, set prices to the intermediaries, or royalty arrangements, at levels so that the state will make money off of the sales.

The legislature has even gone so far as to attempt to claim a copyright in the statutes so that it can prevent nonauthorized electronic copying (i.e., copying at cost by the taxpayers, for whom the statutes were created) and channel all use of the electronic statutes through its designated commercial agent or agents.

The legality of these restrictions on access to public records, and in particular the attempt to copyright the state statutes, is questionable and will be challenged. But attempts like this to exploit potential commercial value in government information are going on in many areas and are likely to continue and increase.

The Information Age stories we read about every day call up images of microchips, fiber optics, computers, and video screens. But considering the way information owners and providers are preparing for the new age, a better symbol may be the cash register.

Who Owns Information?

Everyone agrees that the modern Information Age can and will change the ways we live and work and that, therefore, the legal structure of the new technologies will be important.

So it is appropriate for many people to raise questions about the legal rules that will govern play in the new information superworld—questions relating to ownership of information, access to information, controls on intrusion into personal information, and rights to use information.

But it is important, too, that the questions asked are the *right* ones. And that is the problem with much of the academic theorizing about legal rules for the Information Age, including much of the discussion in Anne Wells Branscomb's book *Who Owns Information? From Privacy to Public Access.*

Though the author does an excellent job of explaining many of the information policy issues that arise under both new and old technologies—and does so from the firm factual footing so often missing from works about privacy and technology—she displays an unfortunate predilection to presume that laws should *limit* rather than *expand* use of information and technologies.

Profit (from information ownership) and protection of the privacy of information about individuals (again through recognition of ownership-like rights in information) seem to be the author's touchstones. These goals, of course, are furthered by *restrictions* on information access and use. The potential individual and social benefits from information *use* are, to the extent they are considered, treated as merely secondary considerations.

The subject of *Who Owns Information?* is plainly ripe. Issues concerning technology, privacy, and rights in information have been discussed for years, but recent rapid progress in computer and communications technologies makes them seem more urgent. And, thankfully, our recent experiences with advanced technologies give us some practical experience so that we are no longer addressing these questions merely in the abstract.

Abstraction has long been a problem in this area. As far back as the famous 1890 Warren-Brandeis *Harvard Law Review* article on "The Right to Privacy," and continuing with many modern academic theorists, the legal and journalistic literature has overflowed with abstract theories built upon a germ of fact and a lot of speculation. It is speculated that computers will create a central Big Brother; therefore, computer usage must be restricted. Or that database linkages will destroy all personal privacy; therefore, such linkages should be restricted. Or that readily available government information and computer records will be abused; therefore, access to such information should be limited. And so on goes the speculation of technological horribles and the extreme legal theories to match.

The Branscomb book at least examines *facts*. It reviews specific situations in which information is used, and restricted. It presents *specific case studies* from all sides of the issues and examines those case studies, for the most part, quite fairly.

This is the fascinating part of the book and the one most useful to those who are concerned about technological legal policy. A few examples:

- Branscomb explains (in a chapter titled "Who Owns Your Name and Address") how a citizen's completion of the low-tech Postal Service change-of-address card actually sets in motion a chain of events that within a few days makes that information available to almost all national mail-order merchants—even those the resident never dealt with before.
- In her chapter on medical history information, she uses case studies to explain not only the harm and embarrassment caused to individuals whose medical condition is involuntarily disclosed (such as Arthur Ashe and hemophiliac AIDS victim Ryan White) but also the public health usefulness of third-party analysis and tracking by name of individual medical data. Though this use of data would seem anathema to most people when presented in theory, it nonetheless

is relatively common and can help eliminate diseases, reveal health problems, and even assist individuals in their ordinary medical care.

- She explains the competing considerations attendant to low-cost government distribution of government-compiled data or higher-cost distribution through commercial intermediaries. Experience at agencies like the Securities and Exchange Commission and the Environmental Protection Agency has demonstrated that both ways have some advantages. Citizens and public interest groups generally favor low-cost government distribution. But the public also wants lower taxes and more efficient government services, and the use of commercial data distributors can improve service and provide revenue to the government agency.

In analyzing these facts and case studies, Branscomb takes an even-handed approach, despite her own apparent bias toward restricting information use. For example, rather than expressing knee-jerk horror to the Postal Service's automatic turnover of change-of-address information to the mail-order industry, she urges only that policymakers understand the existing system in making judgments about whether and how name-and-address information should be restricted.

For its facts, case studies, and thoughtful recitals of many of the competing policy considerations, *Who Owns Information?* is a valuable contribution to the popular debate on legal rights in the Information Age.

Specific facts and information about new technologies need to be understood and discussed. Pure theorizing usually leads to extreme, impractical, and inflexible solutions. Solutions are likely to be more restrained, practical, and flexible—wiser and better suited to the real world—when they are based on an understanding of how, in practice, information is actually created, distributed, used, and abused.

Unfortunately, however, *Who Owns Information?* slides into oversimplification and overtheorizing in the preliminary answers it suggests to the problems of the Information Age. Branscomb appears fixated on the intellectual property model of "ownership" in rights in information as the framework for addressing new information technology problems.

Repeatedly she turns to information ownership as her preferred solution to many different issues. Whatever the issue—even such totally unrelated problems as unsolicited catalog mailings, use of modern photographic technology, or access to computerized government records—

she suggests that (a) someone ought to be able to control or limit these activities and (b) the controls should be based on some new theory of information ownership or "proprietary rights."

Ownership of information and information rights, however, can never serve as a neutral framework for resolving information policy issues. The ownership model inherently leads to restrictions on information access and use. Indeed, Branscomb suggests that no fewer than twelve distinct rights (and one duty) would grow out of her new proposed "law of information assets."

Branscomb's model of putting information under private lock and key would be a profoundly mistaken policy choice for a society that has so far prospered because of freedom of access and use of information. Calling to mind as it does the "a man's home is his castle" and "what's mine is mine" thought patterns, the ownership model is particularly ill-suited for intangible things like information that exist apart from a particular physical possession and may be simultaneously and productively used by many different people in many different ways. (Even Branscomb admits, "Information is by its nature intended to be shared.")

Though some intangibles—inventions and creative expression—are legally protected under patent and copyright laws, those laws create only *limited-period* ownership rights and do so for the specific purpose of *encouraging* socially beneficial acts of creation. The ownership-of-information idea Branscomb suggests is quite different; for the most part, her proposals would *permanently* restrict use of information, *without* any return social benefit, since the information already exists. Existing intellectual property laws that encourage creation and eventual broad dissemination of works hardly justify new laws that permanently restrict use of existing information.

Even beyond the imperfect parallels to intellectual property, the information-ownership model is flawed because its ultimate effect would simply be to divide potential users into *information-haves* (the commercial and governmental entities that have the power, money, or profit potential that permits them to acquire information rights) and *information-have-nots* (individual citizens, civic and public interest organizations, and certain businesses like the press whose information needs are broad and diffuse rather than tied to specific profit potential).

In suggesting that our legal system should provide for ownership-type rights in information in order to solve complex and competing issues of information access, use, and controls, Branscomb falls into the seductive trap of expecting a single neat all-encompassing theory to bring order to the wild and unruly world of information creation, assembly, and use.

Infophobes, technophobes, and privacy-focused alarmists have long feared a technological Big Brother who intruded into every citizen's life. And those who stand to profit most from new potentials and demands made possible by modern technology fear that laws of freedom of information access and use will lower the value of their work. These are valid concerns in theory.

But as the facts and case studies set forth in Branscomb's book demonstrate, in practice the new information technologies have contributed in many ways to individualism, decentralization, a better quality of life, and increasing personal and economic opportunities. If we are, as Branscomb notes, "in the process of developing a new paradigm for our information society," we had better make sure that the new paradigm addresses the realities of the Information Age.

We really ought not focus solely on the theoretical possibility of a meanie Big Brother who spies on us or steals from us. For we also face the very real danger of an oversensitive Big Sister whose well-intentioned but poorly thought-out laws and policies could unduly limit, restrict, or put too high a price tag on our use and enjoyment of liberating technologies.

Law of Cyberspace Messages

The law of cyberspace. What is it? Naturally, experts differ. Some say cyberspace—the world of communication via computers—is a totally new legal world, which current legal rules cannot control. Others say it represents only a new environment in which existing rules will work just fine. Both sides make valid points—the old rules will apply, although they will need at times to be adapted, revised, and even stretched to cover new methods and techniques of communications.

We don't have the full picture yet. Sure, e-mail use is increasing, barriers are being broken in Internet access and navigation, and more and more people are regularly using powerful personal computers. But any new medium requires time before it achieves its full potential—and the legal issues won't all emerge until that potential is achieved. We can speculate, however, on some of the legal issues and realities of the computer-communications world.

Your Place, My Place, or Memphis? Computer linkups such as electronic mail and the Internet allow parties to communicate easily and practically instantly with persons who are far away. From Aspen, Colorado, you can send messages to a business correspondent or personal friend in England, exchange digitized artwork or photographs with an artist in Florida, and sell merchandise to a Korean company.

All this makes cyberspace seem like the ideal method of communication. Until you consider that those very same communications could lead to a libel suit in London, an obscenity prosecution in Pensacola, and impoundment of your goods in Seoul.

The legal issue is *jurisdiction.* By sending communications into other countries and states, you may be viewed as having committed torts or entered into contracts in those jurisdictions and hence may be subject to faraway courts.

In 1994, for example, prosecutors in Memphis secured an obscenity conviction against a California couple who ran a pornographic computer bulletin board. Because a Tennessee resident had access to the material and complained about it, the prosecution was based on the Bible Belt community standards of Shelby County, Tennessee, even though the defendants operated in California.

Your Law, My Law, or English Law? The jurisdiction issue presents even more problems when the communication is international. Suppose—as often happens with e-mail—you come to feel very comfortable with computer communications, and you develop a direct, even acerbic, e-mail style. In communicating with correspondents in England, you make a few sharp comments about a common acquaintance. The target of one of your remarks catches wind of it and then sues you for libel—in the Queen's Bench court on Fleet Street in London.

This cross-national libel suit sends you a double whammy. Not only may you have to defend yourself in another country, but your case may be governed by English law, which, unlike our law, affords few protections for free speech. Put another way, you may well lose a libel suit in England that you could have easily won in the United States.

At least one British cyber-libel suit has already been filed, by a British scientist against a researcher in Geneva, based on statements made on the

Usenet forum. (British libel law is strict even by European standards.) Suits in Britain against U.S. nationals for statements made on the Internet about British citizens (or even Americans who do some business in England) are inevitable. Indeed, wealthy and litigious plaintiffs have long preferred to sue journalists and writers in London whenever possible. In such cases, if the court takes jurisdiction, American defendants may have little recourse other than the hope that U.S. courts will rule, as some have, that English law is so one-sided and insensitive to free speech concerns that its libel judgments should not be enforced in America.

Carriers, Editors, Publishers, or Distributors? Not only individual communicators but also the various on-line providers that facilitate computer communications face potential cyberspace liability.

On-line services such as CompuServe, Prodigy, and America Online are obvious deep-pocket targets of persons offended by cybertalk or conduct. But are the on-line service operators liable for the actions of their customers or participants? The first few cases that addressed these issues decided them based on rough analogies to non-cyberspace publishing.

In an early case, for example, Cubby, Inc., a publisher of an on-line newsletter, sued CompuServe over an allegedly libelous statement that appeared on a rival's on-line newsletter, *Rumorville*, which was distributed over CompuServe. The court dismissed CompuServe, reasoning that it was an "electronic news distributor" and hence more like a news distributor than a publisher. (Distributors are liable for defamation only if they know or have reason to know of the defamation, and CompuServe concededly did not know of it.) Part of the court's reasoning was that CompuServe does not edit the services it distributes.

Other courts have taken different approaches to drawing a line in cyberspace between publishing and distributing information. In a case brought by *Playboy* magazine, for example, a court held that a computer bulletin-board operator could be liable for copyright and trademark infringement because he allowed customers to download computer graphic files based on photographs in *Playboy*. And a troubling decision in a case involving the Prodigy on-line service held Prodigy to a higher standard of care because Prodigy conducted rudimentary screening of materials it transmitted—somewhat like the newsstand operator who sells some, but not all, available magazines.

The *Cubby*, *Playboy*, and *Prodigy* decisions raised as many issues as they settle. What standard should apply to services that exercise editorial control (like Prodigy), and how much screening really constitutes editorial control? What level of editorial screening creates—or mitigates—the on-line provider's legal responsibility? Will monitoring be required for copyright or privacy violations, even if not for libelous statements—and what further problems will that monitoring create?

Several of these issues were addressed in the Telecommunications Act of 1996. One provision of the act protected on-line services from civil liability based on their actions restricting or enabling limits on access to objectionable material. One of the express purposes of this exemption was to overrule the *Prodigy* case because that decision had discouraged rather than encouraged content monitoring. With this legislation, on-line providers will in the future have the same immunity as other passive conduits (such as telephone companies have) with respect to the content they transmit.

Publishing, Speaking Privately, or Just Relaying Messages? As with on-line providers, the role in which original writers of cyber-communications will be cast is currently uncertain. Just as an on-line service may be like a newsboy, a publisher, or a telephone company, a writer could be analogized to an ordinary citizen, a journalist, or a messenger.

It makes a difference which analogy is selected. In libel law, for example, the protections afforded journalists may not apply to private one-on-one communications, like a credit-reporting agency's report about a business firm's creditworthiness. Application of this public/private distinction in cyberspace could be difficult. For example, is a communication considered private based on its actual or its intended readership, based on the means of transmittal, or based on its content?

The initial determinations here could have far-reaching effects—particularly if cyberspace became subject to the more restrictive rules of private business communications rather than the free-speech-based rules of public communications.

Rights, Authorizations, and Licenses. Let's assume a computer communicator wants to do everything right. He carefully avoids defamation and privacy violations and attempts to secure proper authorizations, and make proper payments, for any copyrighted material he uses. That intent may be easier to form than to follow.

The multimedia capabilities of cyber-communications will lead to sticky problems in securing authorizations. Let's assume, for example, that our communicator wants to sent some digitized music, art, and photographs as part of his message. If his music constitutes a performance of another's musical composition, he needs to secure a license from the composer to make the recording. If he is transmitting a previously recorded work, he needs a license from ASCAP (the American Society of Composers, Authors, and Publishers) or BMI (Broadcast Music, Inc.). If he is somehow synchronizing the music with the artwork or photographs, he needs a synchronization license available through a special clearing agency. He will also need authorizations from the owners of the copyrights of the art, photographs, and any significant amount of text that he transmits.

Music rights are particularly complex, so this example exaggerates the difficulties involved in obtaining rights in a typical situation. But for all media, it is still far easier to *use* copyrighted works in computer communications than it is to secure proper authorizations to do so.

First Editions, Revised Editions, Undiscovered Editions, and Untraceable Republications. Traditional publishing, and even broadcasting, can be readily fixed in time, content, and authorship. Computer communications are more malleable. A message or bulletin-board posting can be updated or changed many times after its first publication and hence be viewed by many different readers with many different contents. Or, conversely, a communication sent into cyberspace can rest there undisturbed for a great length of time—and then, much later, be read, distributed, changed, and retransmitted.

When, then, does a statute of limitations begin to run—from the initial publication, the revised publication, or the discovery of the publication? When and how must a publisher correct a mistaken communication—especially if, by the time the corrected second edition went out, the first edition had already been reproduced by readers and retransmitted throughout an untraceable network? Finally, in a medium where copying and adulteration of another's work is easy, how will liability for improper publications be divided between original authors and revisors?

In the ephemeral world of cyberspace, these questions, like many others, will present challenges for courts and policymakers.

Internet Jurisdiction

Try out the Internet's three-step courthouse hyperlink: (1) create a business Web page, (2) post it on the Internet, in search of customers and sales, and (3) *hypertravel instantly* to a distant city to face a disgruntled customer in court.

This may be only *slightly* exaggerated. A series of rulings in 1996 indicates that parties that use the World Wide Web to advertise may become subject to suit wherever the Web reaches. The initial 1996 rulings are far from definitive, since the issue was just then presenting itself to courts. But the early cases had a clear trend: those parties that use their Web pages to actively solicit sales throughout the nation may become subject to the powers of courts in the home states of the customers they are soliciting.

The technical legal issue is one of *personal jurisdiction*—that is, whether it is fair and just, and thus permissible, for a court in one state to exercise power over a citizen of another state. The general rule is that if Joe Hardsell, a citizen of Missouri, has taken sufficient actions in New York (perhaps by actively selling to customers in New York) so that he derives benefits from New York, then he can reasonably anticipate that he may be sued in New York, and New York courts may exercise jurisdiction over Joe.

As in many other areas of law, the general principles are clear, but how they apply in particular circumstances is often open to dispute. And since Internet publishing is a new circumstance, for which there are no precedents and many possible analogies, it has been unclear to what extent Internet publishing and advertising would subject the publisher to jurisdiction around the nation.

Several important rulings were issued on these points in 1996, as Internet commerce multiplied to the extent that many Internet business disputes reached the courts. In most cases, the rulings have permitted distant courts to exercise jurisdiction over web publishers and advertisers.

One case involving the Blue Note jazz club in Columbia, Missouri, indicates that one can publish on the Web without submitting to jurisdiction nationwide. But this "safe harbor" from nationwide jurisdiction may be a fairly narrow one.

The Columbia Blue Note jazz club posted an Internet page. Among other things, the Web page provided information about the club and a schedule of upcoming events. It also generously noted that it was not affiliated with the well-known club of the same name in New York: "The Blue Note's Cyberspot should not be confused with one of the world's finest jazz club[s] [the] Blue Note, located in the heart of New York's

Greenwich Village. If you should find yourself in the big apple give them a visit." This disclaimer contained a "hyperlink" to the New York Blue Note's web pages.

The New York club didn't take kindly to the Columbia club's page, even with the free plug. The owners of the New York club, who owned a federal trademark registration for "Blue Note" and who have attempted to franchise their club, sued the Columbia club for trademark infringement—in federal court in New York City. (After the lawsuit was filed, the Columbia club cut back its reference on its Web page to the Greenwich Village club; it deleted the effusive endorsement, removed the hyperlink, and retained only a dry disclaimer of any association between the two clubs.)

The Columbia club fought jurisdiction in New York; hence, the New York judge had to decide whether mere publication of an Internet page by a business in Missouri was sufficient to give a New York court power over the defendant. The court framed the issue as whether the creation of a Web site "which exists either in Missouri or in cyberspace—i.e., anywhere the Internet exists" constituted an offer to sell the Columbia club's services in New York. Based on the circumstances—including the key fact that one could not even obtain tickets to the Columbia club over the Internet—the court concluded that New York courts did not have jurisdiction. Just putting information about the Columbia club on the Internet was not enough to create jurisdiction elsewhere, the court held.

The Blue Note case, if followed, appears to identify a minimal level of Internet activity—essentially, mere posting of information—that will not invoke the jurisdiction of a faraway court. But most of the early cases and rulings in this area have indicated that where more than just posting of information is involved—that is, where the Internet pages carry over into *active solicitation* of sales—jurisdiction will vest in distant states.

For example, a federal court in Connecticut asserted power over an Internet advertiser that used its Web pages to actively solicit sales nationwide, including in Connecticut. There, the advertiser used both its Web pages and its 800 number to solicit sales. In finding jurisdiction, the court focused on the fact that the Internet advertisements were available to more than 10,000 Internet users in Connecticut, on an around-the-clock basis.

In other cases and pronouncements, courts and policymakers have tended to view an Internet publisher or advertiser as intentionally intruding into all the states for the purpose of making sales, and hence subject to jurisdiction. These precedents include:

- An opinion issued by Hubert H. Humphrey III, the attorney general of Minnesota, stating that "[i]ndividuals and organizations outside of Minnesota who disseminate information in Minnesota via the Internet and thereby cause a result to occur in Minnesota are subject to state criminal and civil laws." The opinion analogized the posting of an Internet page outside of Minnesota to a bullet shot over a jurisdictional border into Minnesota.
- A federal appeals court ruling that a CompuServe subscriber who used the service to offer his "shareware" software to prospective customers was subject to jurisdiction in CompuServe's home state, Ohio. The court found that the subscriber had, in essence, used CompuServe as his distribution agent for a nationwide sales campaign.
- Another appeals court ruling, upholding the criminal prosecution in Memphis of the California-based operators of a computer bulletin-board system offering pornographic computer graphic files. The court rejected the argument that a postal inspector in Memphis traveled in cyberspace to California to pluck the files from the California computer. Rather, because the bulletin-board operator marketed its membership nationwide and exchanged passwords for fees from Tennessee residents, it had subjected itself to the jurisdiction of courts in Tennessee.

Additionally, in one unusual case that is suggestive of the *international* jurisdictional ramifications of Internet publishing, a federal court in New York enforced an injunction against the Italian publisher of *Playmen* magazine, which posted a *Playmen* page on the Internet from its headquarters in Italy. Although the Italian publisher was subject to New York jurisdiction because of the prior injunction, and hence the ruling did not directly concern jurisdiction, the court ruled that an Internet posting in Italy constituted a "distribution" of materials in the United States. The court pointedly rejected the publisher's analogy that calling up its page on a computer in the United States was akin to flying to Italy, getting off the plane, and buying a magazine at a newsstand in Italy.

These rulings suggest that as the Internet accelerates the speed and activity of business communications, and effectively shrinks the distance between businesses and their customers, it may also expand the legal jurisdictions to which its business users are subject.

Facts and Promise of the Internet

The initial decision on Internet free speech, following passage of the Communications Decency Act of 1996, received much attention and was applauded throughout the free speech community. But the lasting effect of the decision by a three-judge panel of federal judges in Philadelphia, and a similar decision a few months later by a court in New York, probably lies less in the opinions of the judges than in the factual record masterfully presented by the litigants in the Philadelphia case.

ACLU v. Reno, the Philadelphia case, appears to represent constitutional litigation at its best—a case promptly filed and intelligently litigated in a highly regarded forum, by lawyers and litigants cognizant of the pioneer factual and policy issues before the court. Although the case went to the U.S. Supreme Court—hence meaning that the lower court decision will ultimately become something of a historical footnote—the way the case was presented and considered in Philadelphia was destined to affect all further proceedings, including those in the Supreme Court.

In particular, the factual record in *ACLU v. Reno* (as well as its companion case *American Library Association v. U.S. Department of Justice*) made a key difference in the ultimate decisions of constitutional policy regarding free speech on the Internet. Legal cases are usually won or lost on the facts, and even with regard to cutting-edge issues in constitutional policy, facts matter tremendously.

The American Civil Liberties Union and other pro–free speech litigants in the *ACLU v. Reno* case realized this truism and organized for the court an impressive set of testimony, demonstrations, and exhibits, all focused on showing the need for free speech on the Internet, and the folly and futility of Congress's Communications Decency Act of 1996, with its ban on "indecent" and "patently offensive" Internet speech.

The attention to facts began with the list of plaintiffs in the case. The plaintiffs in the ACLU action included a number of organizations like Planned Parenthood and Stop Prisoner Rape whose serious Internet content arguably fell within the act's broad "indecency" and "patently offensive" categories. The American Library Association led a group of writer, librarian, and publisher plaintiffs in the companion case. The list of plaintiff organizations alone signaled the breadth of interests and social groups that would face chilled or restricted communications under the Communications Decency Act.

The plaintiffs' presentation of testimony and exhibits at trial was equally artful. The leadoff witnesses on the first day of trial in early 1996 included an officer of a company that makes software to enable parents to control receipt of content from the Internet, a psychologist and minister, and the directors of legitimate Web-based information services whose good works would be curtailed or inhibited by the act. Other witnesses included the director of the Carnegie Library, an information technology consultant from Harvard, the publishers of public-interest Web pages, and Internet marketing and publishing experts.

Essentially, the plaintiffs presented at the trial, through knowledgeable, credible, and mainstream witnesses, the wealth and promise of materials available on the Internet, the futility and overbreadth of the Communications Decency Act censorship tool, the private-sector parental control and choice alternatives to government censorship, and the human face of Communications Decency Act censorship.

Both sides utilized courtroom demonstrations of the Internet. The plaintiffs used their demonstrations to explain fully the workings of the Internet, including the nature of Internet publishing and the techniques by which content is found, made available, accessed, and screened. The government took a narrower approach, focusing primarily on the particular perceived problems that motivated Congress to pass the act.

The plaintiffs' approach effectively blunted several of the government's points. For example, when the government demonstrated the possibility that children could stumble onto indecent material, the judges understood that this was simply one manifestation of the broader Internet phenomenon of "accidental retrieval of irrelevant search results." And the government's expert was forced to admit that the "odds are slim" that a user would come across a sexually explicit site by accident. In effect, the plaintiffs' full demonstration of the Internet defused the shock value and set in context the possibility that children occasionally would stumble onto indecent material.

The testimony, exhibits, and courtroom demonstrations led the three-judge court to make a number of factual findings that, in the aggregate, significantly advanced the cause of Internet free speech. Among these findings:

- The Internet permits six different kinds of communications, including one-to-one messaging (such as e-mail), one-to-many messaging (such as listserv), distributed message databases (such as Usenet newsgroups), real time communications (such as Internet relay chat), real time remote computer utilization (such as telnet) and remote information retrieval (such as FTP and the World Wide Web). With this explanation, the Internet appears more like a postal service than a television broadcaster—a crucial point in the legal analysis and analogies.

- The Internet is inherently decentralized and is not susceptible to centralized content controls. Moreover, a large percentage (perhaps 40 percent or more) of Internet content originates outside the United States.

- Internet "publishing" is unique. Publishers do not so much *send or distribute materials* (or force material on others) as they make it *available* to readers who must actively *seek it out* in order to receive it. From the provider's perspective, once the provider posts content on the Internet, it cannot prevent anyone, in any community, from accessing that content. From the user's perspective, communications do not "invade" an individual's home or appear on someone's computer screen unbidden; the user must affirmatively reach out for information.

- The government's proposed solutions concerning "indecent" and "patently offensive" content on the Internet appeared practically unworkable or ineffective. (The government suggested that adults who wished to have access to "indecent" or "patently offensive" content could be required to utilize credit card verification, adult password verification, or "tagging" of "indecent" sites.)

- Private solutions to the problem of protecting children from inappropriate material are much more promising. Screening software is already available that helps parents screen out not only indecent sexual material but many different categories of materials of potential concern to parents—for example, violence, profanity, racism/ethnic impropriety, militant/extremist positions, drugs and drug culture, gambling, and different levels of nudity.

- To the extent that it can be analogized to other media, the Internet is significantly different from broadcast media. This is a key legal point, since precedents in the area of broadcasting permit restriction of "indecent" broadcast content because of the presumed intrusiveness of broadcasting into the home and the need for protection of children from this intrusive medium. The court found, however, that there were "significant differences between Internet communications and communications received by radio or television. . . . The receipt of information on the Internet requires a series of affirmative steps more deliberate and directed than merely turning a dial. A child requires some sophistication and some ability to read to retrieve material and thereby to use the Internet unattended."

- The Internet holds incredible promise. In the words of the court's findings of fact:

It is no exaggeration to conclude that the content on the Internet is as diverse as human thought. . . . The Internet provides an easy and inexpensive way for a speaker to reach a large audience, potentially of millions. The start-up and operating costs entailed by communication on the Internet are significantly lower than those associated with other forms of mass communications. . . . Unlike traditional media, the barriers to entry as a speaker on the Internet do not differ significantly from the barriers to entry as a listener. Once one has entered cyberspace, one may engage in the dialogue that occurs there. . . . The Internet is therefore a unique and wholly new medium of worldwide human communication.

From these and other facts, the three-judge panel in Philadelphia found that the Communications Decency Act unconstitutionally abridged the freedom of speech and of the press. The lengthy separate opinions by Chief Judge Dolores K. Sloviter of the U.S. Court of Appeals for the Third Circuit and Philadelphia district judges Ronald L. Buckwalter and Steward Dalzell contain thoughtful and cogent analysis of the Internet and its place in the jurisprudence of free speech. The three-judge panel in New York, in the case of *Shea v. Reno*, reached similar conclusions a short while later—but without the same detail in the fact findings.

The opinions of these six judges will ultimately be overshadowed by the Supreme Court's ruling on Internet free speech issues. Their factual findings, however, significantly affected the outcome of the case. Those facts, which went a long way to compelling the conclusion that Internet communications ought not be unduly restricted, held one of the keys to the outcome of the important policy issue of Internet freedoms and regulation.

Ultimately the Supreme Court affirmed the Philadelphia court's ruling, in large part because of its conclusion, based on the trial court record, that the World Wide Web is "comparable, from the reader's perspective, to both a vast library, including millions of readily available and indexed publications, and a sprawling mall offering goods and services." These facts were clearly key steps along the way to the Supreme Court's conclusion that the speech restrictions of the Communications Decency Act had to give way to society's "interest in encouraging freedom of expression."

This is all as it should be. Facts are, and ought to be, the foundation of policy. Throughout the history of communications law in our nation, from the days of colonial pamphlets to the epoch of electronic communications and entertainment media, judicial recognition of the facts of media use and potential—their ability to inform, educate, inspire, challenge, and set off debate and discussion among our citizens—has opened the way to new and broader approaches to free expression.

The Internet, like past new media, presents at its inception great new promise for personal and public enrichment. Our First Amendment system, so open to encouraging open communication, promises us the opportunity to utilize the new medium to the fullest. What are finally needed to bring these promises together—to permit the medium to be most fully and effectively used—are citizen, professional, and policy-maker visionaries who can focus on the key facts and frame the proper legal construct so that the medium's potential can be exploited, its abuse minimized, and the public discourse broadened and enhanced. In *ACLU v. Reno* and the other initial Internet test cases, the plaintiff organizations and leaders, and the six judges, rose to the challenge and delivered.

Notes

Select Bibliography

Notes

1. First Principles

The First Amendment and Its Purposes

Background on English and colonial practices: Fredrick S. Siebert, FREEDOM OF THE PRESS IN ENGLAND, 1476–1776: THE RISE AND DECLINE OF GOVERNMENT CONTROL (U. Ill. Press 1952); Chester J. Antieau, RIGHTS OF OUR FATHERS (Coiner 1968); Robert A. Rutland, THE BIRTH OF THE BILL OF RIGHTS: 1776–1791 (Collier-Macmillan 1955); Leonard W. Levy, EMERGENCE OF A FREE PRESS (Oxford U. Press 1985). Jefferson letters: Thomas Jefferson, WRITINGS, pp. 916, 983–84 (Library of America 1984). Hand quotation: Irving Dillard, editor, THE SPIRIT OF LIBERTY: PAPERS AND ADDRESSES OF LEONARD HAND (Knopf 1974). Eighth Circuit quotation: *Price v. Viking Penguin, Inc.*, 881 F.2d 1426, 16 Media L.Rptr. 2169 (8th Cir. 1989).

Freedom of Speech

Right to use offensively worded public protest messages: *Cohen v. California*, 403 U.S. 15 (1971). Ruling that protests may extend into public school classrooms: *Tinker v. Des Moines Independent Community School District*, 393 U.S. 503 (1969). Decisions that upheld the right of the Nazis to march: *Collin v. Smith*, 578 F.2d 1197, 3 Media L.Rptr. 2490 (7th Cir.), *cert. denied*, 439 U.S. 915 (1978); *Village of Skokie v. National Socialist Party of America*, 69 Ill.2d 605, 373 N.E.2d 21, 3 Media L.Rptr. 1704 (1978). Flag burning protest cases: *Texas v. Johnson*, 491 U.S. 397 (1989); *United States v. Eichman*, 496 U.S. 310 (1990). Ohio contemporary art museum case: The 1990 prosecution of the Cincinnati Contemporary Art Center and its director, Dennis Barrie, based on an exhibition featuring the work of photographer Robert Mapplethorpe. *See* Charles-Edward Anderson, *Mapplethorpe Photos on Trial*, ABA JOURNAL, Dec. 1990; Robin Cembalest, *The Obscenity Trial: How They Voted to Acquit*, ARTNEWS, Dec. 1990; Jayne Merkel, *Report from Cincinnati: Art on Trial*, ART IN AMERICA, Dec. 1990; Dennis Barrie, *The Scene of the Crime*, ART JOURNAL, Fall 1991. Florida rap band prosecution: The 1990 prosecution of 2 Live Crew in Broward County, Florida. *See* Charles-Edward Anderson, *2 Live Crew Acquitted*, ABA JOURNAL, Dec. 1990; Lisa Jones, *The Signifying Monkees: 2 Live Crew's Nasty-Boy Rap on Trial in South Florida*, VILLAGE VOICE, Nov. 6, 1990. The exception to the trend signified by the acquittals of Barrie and 2 Live Crew was the conviction of a Broward County record

251

store owner for selling the 2 Live Crew album, "As Nasty as They Wanna Be." *See* Peter Plagens, *Mixed Signals on Obscenity*, NEWSWEEK, Oct. 15, 1990; *Record Store Owner Guilty*, ABA JOURNAL, Dec. 1990. *See generally* Nat Hentoff, THE FIRST FREEDOM: THE TUMULTUOUS HISTORY OF FREE SPEECH IN AMERICA (Delacorte 1980).

Freedom of the Press

Motion pictures held protected as a medium of communication: *Joseph Burstyn, Inc. v. Wilson*, 343 U.S. 495, 1 Media L.Rptr. 1357 (1952). No compelled publications of politicians' responses to editorials: *Miami Herald Publishing Co. v. Tornillo*, 418 U.S. 241, 1 Media L.Rptr. 1898 (1974). Abolition of the "fairness doctrine": *see Telecommunications Research and Action Center v. FCC*, 801 F.2d 501, 88 ALR Fed. 527, 13 Media L.Rptr. 1881 (D.C. Cir. 1986); *Syracuse Peace Council v. FCC*, 867 F.2d 654, 16 Media L.Rptr. 1225 (D.C. Cir. 1989); and *Arkansas AFL-CIO v. FCC*, 11 F.3d 1430, 22 Media L.Rptr. 1001 (8th Cir. 1993). Vietnam report prior restraint case: *New York Times Co. v. United States*, 403 U.S. 713, 1 Media L.Rptr. 1031 (1971). Prior restraints almost always fail: *see* chapter 2, "Prior Restraint." The 1964 case that set high barriers to libel and slander suits brought by public officials: *New York Times Co. v. Sullivan*, 376 U.S. 254, 95 ALR2d 1412, 1 Media L.Rptr. 1527 (1964). Subsequent decisions that set other limits on libel and slander suits: *Gertz v. Robert Welch, Inc.*, 418 U.S. 323, 1 Media L.Rptr. 1633 (1974); *Dun & Bradstreet, Inc. v. Greenmoss Builders, Inc.*, 472 U.S. 749, 11 Media L.Rptr. 2417 (1985); *Hustler Magazine v. Falwell*, 485 U.S. 46, 14 Media L.Rptr. 2281 (1988); *Philadelphia Newspapers, Inc. v. Hepps*, 475 U.S. 767, 12 Media L.Rptr. 1977 (1986); *Milkovich v. Lorain Journal Co.*, 497 U.S. 1, 17 Media L.Rptr. 2009 (1990). Federal Freedom of Information Act: 5 U.S.C. §552 (1988). Requirement that trials and other judicial proceedings must be open: *Richmond Newspapers, Inc. v. Virginia*, 448 U.S. 555, 6 Media L.Rptr. 1833 (1980) (right of the press and the public to attend trials); *Globe Newspaper Co. v. Superior Court for Norfolk County*, 457 U.S. 596, 8 Media L.Rptr. 1689 (1982) (prohibition against mandatory closure of judicial proceedings); *Press-Enterprise Co. v. Superior Court of California, Riverside County*, 464 U.S. 501, 10 Media L.Rptr. 1161 (1984) (right to attend voir dire); *Press-Enterprise Co. v. Superior Court of California for Riverside County*, 478 U.S. 1, 13 Media L.Rptr. 1001 (1986) (right to attend preliminary hearings in criminal cases). No full press freedom to high school editors: *Hazelwood School District v. Kuhlmeier*, 484 U.S. 260, 14 Media L.Rptr. 2081 (1988).

Hate Speech, Toleration, and "More Speech"

Brandeis quotation: *Whitney v. California*, 274 U.S. 357, 377 (Brandeis, J., concurring) (1927).

The Scholarship of Press Freedom

Ralph E. McCoy, FREEDOM OF THE PRESS: AN ANNOTATED BIBLIOGRAPHY, SECOND SUPPLEMENT: 1978–1992 (S. Ill. U. Press 1994).

The British System

Archer libel suit: *see* Andrew Rawnsley, *Record Libel Damages for Archer*, MANCHESTER GUARDIAN WEEKLY, Aug. 2, 1987; Tyler Marshall, *Tabloid Accused Archer of Sex with Prostitute; British Author Awarded $800,000 in Libel Case*, LOS ANGELES TIMES, July 25, 1987. Use in parliamentary debate of statement from *Miami Herald v. Tornillo*: Comments of Mr. Knight, reported in *Parliament: Privacy Inquiry Set Up as Right of Reply Bill Fails in the Commons*, THE

DAILY TELEGRAPH, Apr. 21, 1989. *Miami Herald v. Tornillo*: 418 U.S. 241 (1974). The 1970 *Pentagon Papers* case: *New York Times Co. v. United States*, 403 U.S. 713 (1971). *Spycatcher* case: *see* Note, *The Spycatcher Cases*, 50 OHIO ST. L.J. 405 (1989); Chapman Pincher, THE SPY- CATCHER AFFAIR: A REVEALING ACCOUNT OF THE TRIAL THAT TRIED TO SUPPRESS A BOOK BUT MADE IT A BESTSELLER (St. Martin's 1987)

Most of the examples and information on British activities were taken from press ac- counts, and from personal observation of parliamentary debate, in England during April 1989. *See, e.g., Public-Interest Plea on Secrets Rejected Again*, THE TIMES, Apr. 19, 1989; *Thatcher to Repeat Attack on "Intrusive" Press*, THE TIMES, Apr. 19, 1989; *Security Service Bill: Rights Amendment Rejected*, THE TIMES, Apr. 21, 1989; *Parliament: Privacy Inquiry Set Up as Right of Reply Bill Fails in the Commons*, THE DAILY TELEGRAPH, Apr. 21, 1989; *Review on Privacy after Bill Fails: Newspapers "On Probation" to Raise Standards*, THE DAILY TELEGRAPH, Apr. 21, 1989; *Government Orders Full Review of Press Conduct*, THE TIMES, Apr. 22, 1989. *See also* Craig R. Whitney, *British Press Scandal: The British Press*, N.Y. TIMES, Apr. 17, 1989; Craig R. Whitney, *Civil Liberties in Britain: Are They under Siege by Thatcher Government?* N.Y. TIMES, Nov. 1, 1988.

2. Censorship and Prior Restraint

Textbook Censorship

Mozert v. Hawkins County Public Schools: The decisions in the trial court by Judge Hull are found at 579 F.Supp. 1051 (E.D. Tenn. 1984), 582 F.Supp. 201 (E.D. Tenn. 1984), and 647 F.Supp. 1194 (E.D. Tenn 1986). The Court of Appeals' decisions are *Mozert v. Hawkins County Public Schools*, 765 F.2d 75 (6th Cir. 1985) and 827 F.2d 1058 (6th Cir. 1987). *Smith v. Board of School Commissioners of Mobile County*: The decision in the trial court by Judge Hand is found at 655 F.Supp. 939 (S.D. Ala. 1987) and by the Eleventh Circuit Court of Appeals at 827 F.2d 684, 103 ALR Fed. 517 (11th Cir. 1987). *Minarcini v. Strongsville City School District*: 541 F.2d 577 (6th Cir. 1976). *Board of Education, Island Trees Union Free School District No. 26 v. Pico*: 457 U.S. 853, 8 Media L.Rptr. 1721 (1982). Federal court rulings that struck down the creation- science/evolution laws as unconstitutional: *Edwards v. Aguillard*, 482 U.S. 578 (1987). *See gen- erally* Michael Silence, *A Denial of Religious Freedom?* NAT'L L.J., Oct. 13, 1986; Fred M. Hech- inger, *About Education: New Fervor in School Battle*, N.Y. TIMES, Nov. 4, 1986.

Arts Censorship

Quotation regarding "least molested" arts: Morris L. Ernst and William Seagle, TO THE PURE . . . : A STUDY OF OBSCENITY AND THE CENSOR, p. 19 (Viking 1928). Ruling by Judge Kenneth Gillis of the Circuit Court of Cook County: *see* William E. Schmidt, *Ordinance on Flag in Chicago Is Held to Be Unconstitutional*, N.Y. TIMES, Nov. 1, 1989. *Rust v. Sullivan* "gag rule" case: 500 U.S. 173 (1991). *Barnes v. Glen Theater, Inc.*: 501 U.S. 560 (1991).

Arts Censorship and Political Correctness

Elaine Viets, *A Case of Black-on-Black Censorship of Art*, ST. LOUIS POST-DISPATCH, Sept. 21, 1993; Linda Eardley, *2nd Look for UMSL Painting: Controversial Parody Gets Spot in Library*, ST. LOUIS POST-DISPATCH, Sept. 25, 1993.

Radical Feminist Arguments for Censorship

Nadine Strossen, DEFENDING PORNOGRAPHY: FREE SPEECH, SEX, AND THE FIGHT FOR WOMEN'S RIGHTS (Scribner 1995). *See* Heywood Broun and Margaret Leech, ANTHONY COMSTOCK, ROUNDSMAN OF THE LORD (Albert & Charles Boni 1927); Noel Perrin, DR. BOWDLER'S LEGACY: A HISTORY OF EXPURGATED BOOKS (Atheneum 1969).

Censorship Arguments

Annie Besant's list of 175 Bible passages that could be considered obscene: *see* Morris L. Ernst and William Seagle, To THE PURE . . . : A STUDY OF OBSCENITY AND THE CENSOR, Appendix IV (Viking 1928). Shakespeare's suggestive passages: *see* Eric Partridge, SHAKESPEARE'S BAWDY: A LITERARY AND PSYCHOLOGICAL ESSAY AND A COMPREHENSIVE GLOSSARY (Dutton rev. ed. 1955). Case in which Shakespeare quotations were considered too lurid for quotation before the Supreme Court: *see* Brief of the Freedom to Read Foundation as Amicus Curiae in *Bethel School District No. 403 v. Fraser*, 478 U.S. 675 (1986). *Board of Education, Island Trees Union Free School District No. 26 v. Pico*: 457 U.S. 853, 8 Media L.Rptr. 1721 (1982). Decision upholding state laws against possession of child pornography: *New York v. Ferber*, 458 U.S. 747, 8 Media L.Rptr. 1809 (1982).

Symbolic Speech

Supreme Court rulings that burning the American flag qualifies as symbolic speech: *Texas v. Johnson*, 491 U.S. 397 (1989); *United States v. Eichman*, 496 U.S. 310 (1990). St. Patrick's Day parade case: *Hurley v. Irish-American Gay, Lesbian, and Bisexual Group of Boston*, 115 S.Ct. 2338 (1995). *See also Irish Lesbian and Gay Organization v. Bratton*, 882 F.Supp. 315 (S.D. N.Y. 1995), *aff'd Mem.* 52 F.3d 311 (2d Cir. 1995); *New York County Board of Ancient Order of Hibernians v. Dinkins*, 814 F.Supp. 358 (S.D. N.Y. 1993). For background on past protests, *see* David S. Reynolds, *Burning Flags and Barbaric Yawps*, N.Y. TIMES, July 4, 1995. *See generally* Franklyn S. Haiman, "SPEECH ACTS" AND THE FIRST AMENDMENT (S. Ill. U. Press 1993).

Prior Restraint

The *Pentagon Papers* case: *New York Times Co. v. United States*, 403 U.S. 713 (1971). Judge Hoeveler's injunction against CNN: *United States v. Noriega (In Re Cable News Network)*, No. 88-79-CR-WMH (S.D. Fla. Nov. 8, 1990). Eleventh Circuit ruling: 917 F.2d 1543, 18 Media L.Rptr. 1352 (11th Cir. 1990). Supreme Court's denial of an immediate appeal: *Cable News Network, Inc. v. Noriega*, 498 U.S. 976, 18 Media L.Rptr. 1358 (1990). *See also United States v. Cable News Network, Inc.*, 865 F.Supp. 1549, 23 Media L.Rptr. 1033 (S.D. Fla. 1994). *Nebraska Press Association v. Stuart*, 427 U.S. 539, 1 Media L.Rptr. 1064 (1976). *Near v. State of Minnesota ex rel. Olson*: 283 U.S. 697, 1 Media L.Rptr. 1001 (1931). Five 1990 prior restraint cases besides *CNN-Noriega*: *In Re Lifetime Cable*, 17 Media L.Rptr. 1648 (D.C. Cir. 1990); *In Re KingWorld Productions, Inc.*, 898 F.2d 56, 17 Media L.Rptr. 1531 (6th Cir. 1990); *State of Israel v. St. Martin's Press, Inc.*, 166 A.D.2d 251, 560 N.Y.S.2d 450 (1990); *Ernst & Young v. Bowman's Accounting Report*, No. 426/90-001 (N.Y. Sup.Ct. Jan. 1, 1990); *Corpus Christi Caller-Times v. Mancias*, 794 S.W.2d 852, 17 Media L.Rptr. 2204 (Tex. Ct. Civ. App. 1990). On the CNN-Noriega case, *see generally* Randall Rothenberg, *Noriega Tapes Case Revives Issues Once Thought Settled*, N.Y. TIMES, Nov. 14, 1990; Sandra Davidson Scott, *Noriega Ruling Sets Dangerous Precedent*,

Sᴛ. Lᴏᴜɪs Pᴏsᴛ-Dɪsᴘᴀᴛcʜ, Dec. 6. 1990; *CNN Is Sentenced for Tapes and Makes Public Apology*, N.Y. Tɪᴍᴇs, Dec. 20, 1994.

3. News Gathering

Access to Court Documents

See Tim Poor, *Number of Secret Cases Growing in U.S. Court*, Sᴛ. Lᴏᴜɪs Pᴏsᴛ-Dɪsᴘᴀᴛcʜ, Jan. 31, 1988; Tamar Lewin, *News Media Battling a Trend of Secrecy in New York's Courts*, N.Y. Tɪᴍᴇs, Feb. 8, 1988. *Gannett Co. v. DePasquale*: 443 U.S. 368, 5 Media L.Rprt. 1337 (1979). Subsequent decisions that cut back on *Gannett Co. v. DePasquale*: *Richmond Newspapers, Inc. v. Virginia*, 448 U.S. 555, 6 Media L.Rprt. 1833 (1980); *Globe Newspaper Co. v. Superior Court for Norfolk County*, 457 U.S. 596, 8 Media L.Rprt. 1689 (1982); *Press-Enterprise Co. v. Superior Court of California, Riverside County*, 464 U.S. 501, 10 Media L.Rprt. 1161 (1984); *Press-Enterprise Co. v. Superior Court of California for Riverside County*, 478 U.S. 1, 13 Media L.Rprt. 1001 (1986). Judge Gunn's decision: *Women's Health Center of West County, Inc. v. Webster*, No. 87–0050 C(6) (E.D. Mo. Feb. 5, 1988). Boesky decision: *United States v. Boesky*, 674 F.Supp. 1128, 14 Media L.Rprt. 2105 (S.D.N.Y. 1987). Decision stating that press access to pretrial materials "has never been unfettered": *Globe Newspaper Co. v. Pokaski*, 868 F.2d 497, 16 Media L.Rprt. 1385 (1st Cir. 1989). Decision regarding reporter's right to attend depositions: *Avirgen v. Hull*, 118 F.R.D. 252, 14 Media L.Rprt. 2136 (D.D.C. 1987). Cases treating audio/visual court exhibits differently than documentary exhibits: *United States v. Miller*, 579 F.Supp. 862, 10 Media L.Rprt. 1321 (S.D. Fla. 1984); *United States v. Webbe*, 791 F.2d 103, 12 Media L.Rprt. 2193 (8th Cir. 1986).

Court Protective Orders

Proposed federal act: Sunshine in Litigation Act, S. 1404, proposed by Sen. Herb Kohl, Democrat of Wisconsin, in the 103rd Congress. *See* 139 Cᴏɴɢ. Rᴇc. S10841–02 (Aug. 6, 1993) (introduction of bill); 140 Cᴏɴɢ. Rᴇc. S7702–01 (June 27, 1994) (offered as amendment); 140 Cᴏɴɢ. Rᴇc. S13041–01 (Sept. 21, 1994) (debate). Florida act: Florida Sunshine in Litigation Act, Fla. Stat. § 69.081. Texas rule: Texas R.Civ.Pro. 76(a). *See generally* Martha Middleton, *Civil Case Issue: Should a Court Keep Secrets?* Nᴀᴛ'ʟ L.J., Oct. 17, 1988; Philip H. Corboy, *Masked and Muzzled, Litigants Tell No Evil: Is This Blind Justice?* Lᴇɢᴀʟ Tɪᴍᴇs, Jan. 8, 1990; Gina Kolata, *Secrecy Orders in Lawsuits Prompt States' Efforts to Restrict Their Use*, N.Y. Tɪᴍᴇs, Feb. 18, 1992; Todd S. Swatsler and Mark A. Godsey, *An Update on the Protective Order First Amendment Debate*, Tʀɪᴀʟ Pʀᴀcᴛɪcᴇ (Newsletter of the Trial Practice Committee of the Litigation Section of the American Bar Association), Sept./Oct. 1992; *See* Jack Doppelt, *Open Justice Serves Public Interest*, ISBA [Iʟʟɪɴᴏɪs Sᴛᴀᴛᴇ Bᴀʀ Assᴏcɪᴀᴛɪᴏɴ] Nᴇᴡs, Sept. 1, 1992.

Access to Electronic Records

Decisions that have acknowledged that the federal Freedom of Information Act (FOIA) applies to computer tapes to the same extent as it does to other documents: *Long v. Internal Revenue Service*, 596 F.2d 362, 365, 5 Media L.Rprt. 1165 (9th Cir. 1979) ("[T]he FOIA applies to computer tapes to the same extent it applies to any other documents.") (Kennedy, J.); *Yaeger v. Drug Enforcement Administration*, 678 F.2d 315, 8 Media L.Rprt. 1959 (D.C. Cir. 1982); *May-*

lock v. Immigration and Naturalization Service, 714 F.Supp. 1558, 1566 (N.D. Cal. 1989); *St. Paul's Benevolent Educational and Missionary Institute v. United States*, 506 F.Supp. 822, 828 (N.D. Ga. 1980). Leading federal case that allowed an agency to refuse to produce computer tapes: *Dismukes v. Dept. of the Interior*, 603 F.Supp. 760 (D.D.C. 1984). Contrary authorities: *American Federation of State, County & Municipal Employees v. County of Cook*, 136 Ill.2d 334, 555 N.E.2d 361, 86 ALR 4th 763 (1990); *State ex rel. Margolius v. Cleveland*, 62 Ohio St.3d 456, 584 N.E.2d 665, 19 Media L.Rptr. 2122 (1992); *Brownstone Publishers, Inc. v. New York City Department of Buildings*, 146 Misc.2d 376, 550 N.Y.S.2d 564, 17 Media L.Rptr. 2237 (Sup. 1990), *aff'd* 560 N.Y.S.2d 642 (App. 1990); *Mange v. City of Manchester*, 113 N.H. 533, 311 A.2d 116 (1973); *Ortiz v. Jaramillo*, 82 N.M. 445, 483 P.2d 500 (1971); *Szikszay v. Buelow*, 107 Misc.2d 886, 436 N.Y.S.2d 558 (Sup.Ct. Erie County 1981); *Martin v. Eillisor*, 266 S.C. 377, 223 S.E.2d 415 (1976). Congressional committee statement: U.S. House of Representatives, Committee on Government Operations, *Electronic Collection and Dissemination of Information by Federal Agencies: A Policy Overview*, 99th Cong., 2d Sess., HOUSE REP. 99–560, at 10 (1986) ("Public access is a dynamic concept. If an agency has developed the ability to manipulate data electronically, it is unfair to restrain the public to paper documents. An agency cannot justify denying the public the benefits of new technology by preserving, without involvement, the same type of access that was provided in the past."). 1996 Act: Pub. L. 104–231. Decisions holding that agencies must make reasonable computer searches of computer records: *Yaeger v. Drug Enforcement Administration*, 678 F.2d 315, 321 (D.C. Cir. 1982) (different access requirements for computer records "may not be used to circumvent the full disclosure policies of the FOIA. The type of storage system in which the agency has chosen to maintain its records cannot diminish the duties imposed by the FOIA."). Decision by Justice Kennedy: *Long v. Internal Revenue Service*, 596 F.2d 362, 365, 5 Media L.Rptr. 1165 (9th Cir. 1979). Decision that refused to require the use of information-rearrangement techniques: *Yaeger v. Drug Enforcement Administration*, 678 F.2d 315 (D.C. Cir. 1982). On the subject of media access to electronic government records, *see generally* Elliot Jaspin and Mark Sableman, *News Media Access to Computer Records: Updating Information Laws in the Electronic Age*, 36 ST. LOUIS U. L.J. 349 (1991).

> *Access to Electronic Statutes*
> *Deaton v. Kidd*, No. CV193-1426CC, 1994 WL 722795 (Mo.Cir.Ct. Cole Cty. Nov. 21, 1994), *affirmed, Deaton v. Kidd*, 1996 WL 104251 (Mo. App. 1996).

> *Access to War and the Military*
> Problems relating to coverage of war: Alex S. Jones, *Editors Say Journalists Were Kept from Action*, N.Y. TIMES, Dec. 22, 1989; R. W. Apple Jr., *Correspondents Protest Pool System*, N.Y. TIMES, Feb. 12, 1991; Jason DeParle, *Keeping the News in Step: Are the Pentagon's Gulf War Rules Here to Stay?* N.Y. TIMES, May 6, 1991; Ron Dorfman, *The Use of Press Pools Severely Restricts the Media's War Coverage*, NORTHWESTERN PERSPECTIVE, Fall 1991; Paul McMasters, *Free Press Falls Victim to War*, QUILL, Oct. 1991. Decision that recognizes need for some protection for news gathering: *Branzburg v. Hayes*, 408 U.S. 665, 681 (1972). Line of cases in which the Supreme Court upheld media claims of rights of access to particular kinds of court proceedings: *Richmond Newspapers, Inc. v. Virginia*, 448 U.S. 555, 6 Media L.Rptr. 1833 (1980); *Globe News-*

paper Co. v. Superior Court for Norfolk County, 457 U.S. 596, 8 Media L.Rptr. 1689 (1982); *Press-Enterprise Co. v. Superior Court of California, Riverside County*, 464 U.S. 501, 10 Media L.Rptr. 1161 (1984); *Press-Enterprise Co. v. Superior Court of California for Riverside County*, 478 U.S. 1, 13 Media L.Rptr. 1001 (1986). Decisions that recognize the right of access to administrative hearings, local government meetings, and even areas beyond police lines at crime and accident scenes: *See, e.g., Connell v. Town of Hudson*, 733 F.Supp. 465, 17 Media L.Rptr. 1803 (D.N.H. 1990) (recognizing photographer's First Amendment rights at automobile accident scene); *Westinghouse Broadcasting v. National Transportation Safety Board*, 8 Media L.Rptr. 1177 (D. Mass. 1982) (recognizing press rights at airplane crash site controlled by National Transportation Safety Board). Cases that have held that the press is entitled to *preferred* access: *Quad-City Community News Service v. Jebens*, 334 F.Supp. 8 (S.D. Iowa 1971); *Borreca v. Fasi*, 369 F.Supp. 906 (D. Hawaii 1974); *Westinghouse Broadcasting Co. v. Dukakis*, 409 F.Supp. 895 (D. Mass. 1976). Press suit for greater access to Persian Gulf War: *The Nation Magazine v. U.S. Department of Defense*, 762 F.Supp. 1558, 19 Media L.Rptr. 1257 (S.D.N.Y. 1991). *See generally* Everette E. Dennis *et al.*, THE MEDIA AT WAR: THE PRESS AND THE PERSIAN GULF CONFLICT (Gannet Foundation Media Center 1991); Jack Landau, *Media Law Today: Excluding the Press from the Grenada Invasion: A Violation of the Public's Constitutional Rights*, EDITOR & PUBLISHER, Dec. 10, 1983.

Access to Voters and Polling Places

Florida case: *CBS Inc. v. Smith*, 681 F.Supp. 794, 15 Media L.Rptr. 1251 (S.D. Fla. 1988). Washington case: *Daily Herald Co. v. Munro*, 838 F.2d 380, 14 Media L.Rptr. 2332 (9th Cir. 1988).

Access Rights (and Hazards) Abroad

See Nicholas D. Kristoff, *Seeing Shadows Where Once There Were Leaders, Facts and Information*, N.Y. TIMES, June 9, 1989; Nicholas D. Kristoff, *Beijing Ousts 2 American Correspondents*, N.Y. TIMES, June 15, 1989; Sally Chew and Caroline Drake, *China's Repression: "Purified" Journalism*, N.Y. TIMES, Sept. 14, 1989; *China vs. Press: "Attempted Censorship,"* BROADCASTING, June 5, 1989; Leonard Zeidenberg, *China: The Weeks of Living Dangerously*, BROADCASTING, June 12, 1989. Much of the information used for this article was obtained from a private research memorandum "Reporting News from Abroad—The American Journalist and Foreign Law," prepared by Charles J. Sennet, who graciously shared it with the author.

Should Lawyers Talk to the Media?

Former prohibitions on lawyer advertising and self-promotion: ABA MODEL CODE OF PROFESSIONAL RESPONSIBILITY, Disciplinary Rules 2–101(B) (prohibiting lawyer advertising) & 7–107 (limiting statements made in connection with litigation). (This code, in effect through the 1970s, has been supplanted by the more liberal ABA Model *Rules of Professional Responsibility*. Model Rule 3.6(a) prohibits only extra-judicial statements that will have a substantial likelihood of materially prejudicing an adjudicative proceeding.) School of thought that lawyers have the *duty* to speak to the press and seek to convey their client's position to the public: *see* Clarence Jones, *When Lawyers Have a Duty to Talk to the Media*, FLORIDA BAR JOURNAL, June 1984; Weyman I. Lundquist, *Advocacy in the Public Forum*, LITIGATION, Summer 1988; Tripp

Frohlichstein, *Attorneys and the Media: A Case for "Win-Win,"* MoBar [Missouri Bar] Bulletin, Apr. 1992. Evidentiary rule that silence can be damning: *see* Fed.R.Evid. 801(d)(2)(B) and accompanying comments.

4. Confidentiality and Sources

Confidentiality Promises

Courts usually refuse to entertain suits between reporters and sources: The exception is *Cohen v. Cowles Media Co.*, 501 U.S. 663, 18 Media L.Rptr. 2273 (1991). Judy Garland suit: *Garland v. Torre*, 259 F.2d 545, 1 Media L.Rptr. 2541 (2d Cir. 1958). *Branzburg v. Hayes*: 408 U.S. 665, 1 Media L.Rptr. 2617 (1972). Expansion of the privilege to cover scholars, researchers, and professional expert witnesses: *In Re Burnett*, 22 Media L.Rptr. 1402 (N.J. Super. 1994); *In Re Grand Jury dated January 4, 1984*, 583 F.Supp. 991, 10 Media L.Rptr. 2065 (E.D.N.Y. 1984); *Farnsworth v. Proctor & Gamble Co.*, 758 F.2d 1545 (11th Cir. 1985). Hargraves case: *see Costello v. Capital Cities Communications, Inc.*, 125 Ill.2d 402, 425; 532 N.E.2d 790, 800, 15 Media L.Rptr. 2407 (1988). *Cervantes v. Time, Inc.*: 464 F.2d 986, 1 Media L.Rptr. 1751 (8th Cir. 1972).

Waiver of the Reporter's Privilege

Wheeler case: *Goulart v. Barry*, 18 Media L.Rptr. 2001 (D.C. Super. 1991), 18 Media L.Rptr. 2056 (D.C. Super. 1991), 18 Media L.Rptr. 2061 (D.C. Super. 1991), *aff'd, Wheeler v. Goulart*, 593 A.2d 173 (D.C. App. 1991); Decisions that have rejected arguments that reporters "waived" their privilege to keep sources or information confidential: *see Fischer v. McGowan*, 10 Media L.Rptr. 1651, 1657 (D.R.I. 1984) (citing cases).

Media Subpoena Cases

Los Angeles case: *Tapes and Photos of Riots Are Focus of Legal Struggle*, N.Y. Times, May 22, 1992. Senate case: Neil A. Lewis, *2 Reporters Face Subpoenas for Disclosures on Thomas*, N.Y. Times, Feb. 4, 1992; Felicity Barringer, *Newsday Refuses to Reveal Source of Leak on Anita Hill's Charges*, N.Y. Times, Feb. 14, 1992; Neil A. Lewis, *Counsel Retreats on Thomas Disclosures*, N.Y. Times, Mar. 18, 1992. *See generally* Reporters Committee for Freedom of the Press, *Agents of Discovery: A Report on the Incidence of Subpoenas Served on the News Media in 1991* (2d Report 1993); Monica Langlen and Lee Levine, *Broken Promises*, Col. Journ. Rev., July/Aug. 1988.

Agreements with Sources

Cohen v. Cowles Media Co.: 501 U.S. 663, 18 Media L.Rptr. 2273 (1991). Eighth Circuit decision that held that the promissory estoppel theory could be raised by the subject of a *Glamour* magazine article: *Ruzicka v. Conde Nast*, 939 F.2d 578, 19 Media L.Rptr. 1948 (8th Cir. 1991) and 999 F.2d 1319, 21 Media L.Rptr. 1821 (8th Cir. 1993). *See generally* Dan Oberdorfer, *Is "Burning a Source" a Breach of Contract?* Nat'l L.J., Aug. 1, 1988; Samuel Fifer, *Decision Backing Press Freedom Has Ominous Undertone*, Chicago Tribune, Aug. 17, 1990.

Interview Contract Lawsuits

Falwell suit against *Penthouse*: *Falwell v. Penthouse*, 7 Media L.Rptr. 1981 (D.W.Va. 1981). Wildmon suit over *Damned in the USA*: *Wildmon v. Berwick Universal Pictures*, 803 F.Supp. 1167, 20 Media L.Rptr. 1851 (N.D. Miss. 1992). *Cohen v. Cowles Media*: 501 U.S. 663, 18 Media L.Rptr. 2273 (1991). *Glamour* magazine case: *Ruzicka v. Conde Nast*, 939 F.2d 578, 19 Media L.Rptr. 1948 (8th Cir. 1991) and 999 F.2d 1319, 21 Media L.Rptr. 1821 (8th Cir. 1993).

Reporters Versus Sources

Janet Malcolm, THE JOURNALIST AND THE MURDERER (Knopf 1990). Deceived source suit against Malcolm: *see* chapter 5, "Fault, Semantics, and Altered Quotations." *See generally* Garry Abrams, *"Fatal Vision" Blurred by Bitter Suit*, ST. LOUIS POST-DISPATCH, Aug. 6, 1987; Karen Zappe, *"Fatal Vision" Kin Fight over Spoils of the Book*, NAT'L L.J., Feb. 6, 1989; Albert Scardino, *New Yorker in the Fray on Journalism and Ethics*, N.Y. TIMES, Mar. 21, 1989; Stuart Taylor Jr., *Janet Malcolm's License to Lie*, LEGAL TIMES, Aug. 14, 1989.

5. Libel

Fact and Opinion

"Hurling epithets" and "Copperhead to Uncle Tom" quotations: *Raible v. Newsweek*, 341 F.Supp. 808–09 (W.D. Pa. 1972). "Sleaze bag": *Henderson v. Times Mirror Co.*, 669 F.Supp. 356, 14 Media L.Rptr. 1659 (D. Colo. 1987); "con artists": *Spelson v. CBS Inc.*, 581 F.Supp. 1195 (N.D. Ill. 1984), *aff'd Mem.* 757 F.2d 1291 (7th Cir. 1985); "barbarian": *Fleming v. Benzaquin*, 390 Mass. 175, 454 N.E.2d 95 (1983); "sleazy dealings": *Anton v. St. Louis Suburban Newspapers, Inc.*, 598 S.W.2d 493, 5 Media L.Rptr. 2601 (Mo. App. 1980); "card cheat": *Muchisky v. Kornegay*, 741 S.W.2d 43 (Mo. App. 1987); "secret gratification": *Deupree v. Iliff*, 860 F.2d 300, 15 Media L.Rptr. 2225 (8th Cir. 1988). *Milkovich v. Lorain Journal* in Ohio courts: 65 Ohio App.2d 143, 416 N.E.2d 662, 6 Media L.Rptr. 2185 (1979); 15 Ohio St. 3d 292, 473 N.E.2d 1191, 11 Media L.Rptr. 1598 (1984); 46 Ohio App. 3d 20, 545 N.E.2d 1320, 17 Media L.Rptr. 1309 (1989). In the Supreme Court: 497 U.S. 1, 17 Media L.Rptr. 2009 (1990). "No false idea" statement: *Gertz v. Robert Welch, Inc.*, 418 U.S. 323, 339–40, 1 Media L.Rptr. 1633 (1974). Decisions by state courts reinstituting broader protection for opinion: *Immuno A.G. v. Moor-Jankowski*, 77 N.Y.2d 235, 566 N.Y.S.2d 906, 567 N.E.2d 1270, 18 Media L.Rptr. 1625 (1991); *West v. Thompson Newspapers*, 872 P.2d 999, 23 Media L.Rptr. 1097 (Utah 1994).

Opinion in Critical Reviews

Moldea v. New York Times Co.: 15 F.3d 1137, 22 Media L.Rptr. 1321 (D.C.Cir. 1994) and 22 F.3d 310, 22 Media L.Rptr. 1673 (D.C.Cir. 1994) (en banc).

Privileges for Witnesses and Reporters

Denise Sinner case: William C. Lhotka, *Ex-Bar President Denies Tryst with Theft Suspect*, ST. LOUIS POST-DISPATCH, Mar. 17, 1988; Karen L. Koman and Tim Poor, *Sinner's Past Is Questioned*, ST. LOUIS POST-DISPATCH, Apr. 20, 1988; William C. Lhotka, *D. Sinner Gets Fine, 18 Months*, ST. LOUIS POST-DISPATCH, Apr. 30, 1988. Witness privilege: *Murphy v. Matthews*, 841 S.W.2d 671 (Mo. banc 1992). News reporting privilege: *Hoeflicker v. Higginsville Advance, Inc.*, 818 S.W.2d 650, 19 Media L.Rptr. 1286 (Mo. App. 1991).

Trials and the Press

Tavoulareas v. Piro: 817 F.2d 762, 13 Media L.Rptr. 2377 (D.C. Cir. 1987) (en banc); *Costello v. Capital Cities Newspapers, Inc.*, 153 Ill. App. 3d 956, 505 N.E.2d 701 (1987), *rev'd* 125 Ill.2d 402, 532 N.E.2d 790, 15 Media L.Rptr. 2407 (1988).

Constitutional Privilege

Costello v. Capital Cities Newspapers, Inc.: 125 Ill.2d 402, 532 N.E.2d 790, 15 Media L.Rptr. 2407 (1988). Supreme Court's acknowledgment that "actual malice" is an "unfortunate" choice of words: *Masson v. The New Yorker Magazine, Inc.*, 501 U.S. 496, 18 Media L.Rptr. 2241 (1991). *See generally* Anthony Lewis, MAKE NO LAW: THE SULLIVAN CASE AND THE FIRST AMENDMENT (Knopf 1991).

Fault, Semantics, and Altered Quotations

Trial court's initial ruling in *Masson v. The New Yorker Magazine, Inc.*: 686 F.Supp. 1396 (N.D. Calif. 1987). Court of Appeals ruling: 895 F.2d 1535 (9th Cir. 1989). Supreme Court decision: 501 U.S. 496, 18 Media L.Rptr. 2241 (1991). First trial: *see Masson v. The New Yorker Magazine, Inc.*, 832 F.Supp. 1350 (N.D. Calif. 1993). Second trial: *see* David Margolick, *Psychoanalyst Loses Libel Suit Against a New Yorker Reporter*, N.Y. TIMES, Nov. 3, 1994. Malcolm's belated discovery of her notes: *see* David Stout, *A Child's Play and Malcolm's Missing Notes*, N.Y. TIMES, Aug. 30, 1995; Anthony Lewis, *Stranger than Fiction*, N.Y. TIMES, Aug. 25, 1995.

Libel and the Rehnquist Court

Case concerning suits brought far from defendant's home base: *Calder v. Jones*, 465 U.S. 783, 10 Media L.Rptr. 1401 (1984). Dissent from procedural vote: *Ollman v. Evans*, 471 U.S. 1127, 11 Media L.Rptr. 2015 (1985) (Rehnquist, J., dissenting from denial of certiorari). Opinion decision: *Milkovich v. Lorain Journal Co.*, 497 U.S. 1, 17 Media L.Rptr. 2009 (1990). Emotional distress case: *Hustler Magazine, Inc. v. Falwell*, 485 U.S. 46 (1988).

Reckless Disregard and the Westmoreland and Sharon Cases

Renata Adler, RECKLESS DISREGARD: WESTMORELAND V. CBS ET AL.; SHARON V. TIME (Knopf 1986).

Coals of Fire and the Alton Telegraph Case

Thomas B. Littlewood, COALS OF FIRE: THE ALTON TELEGRAPH LIBEL CASE (S. Ill. U. Press 1988).

Abuse of Libel Suits

Briggs & Stratton suit: *Briggs & Stratton Corp. et al. v. National Catholic Reporter Publishing Co. et al.*, U.S. District Court, Eastern District of Wisconsin, Civil Action No. 96-C-0641. *See generally* Brian Kaberline, *Catholic Paper's Editor Grits Teeth in the Face of $30 Million Libel Suit*, KANSAS CITY BUSINESS JOURNAL, July 5–11, 1996. California Anti-SLAPP statute: Cal. Code Civ. Pro. sec. 425.16. Suits in which California Anti-SLAPP statute has been used: *Averill v. Superior Court (the Eli Home, Inc.)*, 42 Cal. App. 4th 1170, 43 Cal. App. 4th 719, 50 Cal. Rptr. 2d 62 (1996) (critic of charity); *Beilenson v. Superior Court (Sybert)*, 44 Cal. App. 4th 944, 52 Cal. Rptr. 2d 357 (1996) (political candidate); *Church of Scientology of California v. Wollershiem*, 42 Cal. App. 4th 628, 49 Cal. Rptr. 2d 620 (1996); *Lafayette Morehouse, Inc. v. Chronicle Publishing Co.*, 37 Cal. App. 4th 855, 44 Cal. Rptr. 2d 46, 24 Media L.Rptr. 1061 (1995). Colorado decision that adopted anti-SLAPP procedures: *Protect Our Mountain Environment, Inc. v. District Court in and for the County of Jefferson*, 677 P.2d 1361 (Col. 1984).

Libel Reform Efforts

$58 million libel verdict against WFAA-TV: *Feazell v. Belo Broadcasting Corp.*, No. 86-227-1 (Waco, Tex. Dist. Ct. Apr. 19, 1991). Sprague's $34 million libel judgment against the Philadelphia *Inquirer*: *Sprague v. Philadelphia Newspapers*, No. 3644, (Phil. Ct. Com. Pleas May 3, 1990). Chicago $2.2 million verdict against the *Wall Street Journal*: *Crinkley v. Dow Jones &*

Co., (Ill. Cir. Ct. Cook Cty. May 22, 1991). Judgment in Buffalo against WKBW: *Prozeralik v. Capital Cities/ABC, Inc.*, No. 48424 (Niagara Falls N.Y. Sup. Ct. July 10, 1991), *rev'd* 82 N.Y.2d 466, 626 N.E.2d 34, 605 N.Y. Supp. 2d 218 (1993); *see also Restauranteur Gets $11 Million Libel Award*, N.Y. TIMES, Nov. 12, 1994 (second trial); *Prozeralik v. Capital Cities/ABC, Inc.*, 635 N.Y.S.2d 913 (App. Div. 1995) (affirming $6 million compensatory damages award from second trial). Pennsylvania justice's $6 million verdict against the Philadelphia *Inquirer: McDermott v. Philadelphia Newspapers*, (Phil. Ct. Com. Pleas Dec. 7, 1990). Racing promoters' $13.5 million verdict against the Cleveland *Plain Dealer: Newcomb v. Cleveland Plain Dealer*, No. 93757 (Cuyahoga Cty. Ohio Sept. 14, 1990). Texas surgeon's $31.5 million judgment against KENS-TV: *Srivastava v. Harte-Hanks Television, Inc.*, No. 85-CI-15150 (Bexar Co. Tex. Dist. Ct. May 15, 1990). 1991 study: Tom B. Kelley, *Survey of Recent Libel Cases and Identification of Common Factors* (Libel Defense Resources Center 1991). Judgment against *Food Chemical News: Reuber v. Food Chemical News*, 925 F.2d 703, 18 Media L.Rptr. 1689 (4th Cir. 1991) (en banc). Suit involving *Journal of Medical Primatology: Immuno A.G. v. Moor-Jankowski*, 77 N.Y.2d 295, 566 N.Y.S.2d 906, 567 N.E.2d 1270, 18 Media L.Rptr. 1625 (1992). Suit against insurance newsletter: *see* W. John Moore, *Full Court Presses*, NAT'L J., Feb. 16, 1991. Duluth $785,000 verdict: *Diesen v. Hessburg*, (St. Louis Cty. Minn. Dist. Ct. 1989); *see* Amy Dockser Marcus, *"False Impressions" Can Spur Libel Suits, Even If News Media Gets the Facts Right*, WALL ST. J., May 15, 1990; Alex S. Jones, *Libel Threat Is Increasing Even for Small Publications*, N.Y. TIMES, Feb. 3, 1992. $86 million St. Louis verdict: *Tanner v. Decom Medical Waste Systems* (St. Louis City Cir. Ct. Mo. 1991) *see* Judith VandeWater, *Award Tops $86 Million in Lawsuit*, ST. LOUIS POST-DISPATCH, May 14, 1991. $100 million verdict against Home Shopping Network: *GTE v. Home Shopping Network* (Pinellas Cty. Fla. Cir. Ct. 1989); *see* Calvin Sims, *$100 Million for GTE in Libel Case*, N.Y. TIMES, Aug. 3, 1989. Church of Scientology suit against Paine Webber: *Church of Scientology v. Eli Lilly & Co.*, 778 F.Supp. 661, 19 Media L.Rptr. 1593 (S.D.N.Y. 1991); *see also Church of Scientology International v. Eli Lilly & Co.*, 848 F.Supp. 1018 (D.D.C. 1994). Iowa Libel Research Project: *see* Don J. DeBenedictis, *Little Interest in Libel ADR*, ABA JOURNAL, Jan. 1992. Collapse of the Robert Maxwell media empire and Maxwell's use of libel suits to chill reporters: Steven Prokesch, *Frantic Moves Came to Light in Days before Maxwell Died*, N.Y. TIMES, Dec. 9, 1991; Anthony Lewis, *Mr. Maxwell's Lesson*, N.Y. TIMES, Dec. 9, 1991; Roger Cohen, *Charming Big Banks Out of Billions*, N.Y. TIMES, Dec. 20, 1991. *See generally* John Soloski and Randall P. Bezanson, eds., REFORMING LIBEL LAW (Guilford Press 1992); Randall Bezanson, Gilbert Cranberg, and John Soloski, LIBEL LAW AND THE PRESS (Free Press 1987); Lois G. Forer, A CHILLING EFFECT: THE MOUNTING THREAT OF LIBEL AND INVASION OF PRIVACY ACTIONS TO THE FIRST AMENDMENT (Norton 1987); Donald M. Gillmour, PUBLICITY AND THE ABUSE OF LIBEL LAW (Oxford U. Press 1992).

6. Privacy

The "Right of Privacy"

Harvard Law Review article: S. Warren & L. Brandeis, *The Right of Privacy*, 4 HARV. L. REV. 193 (1890). Prosser's refinement of the right of privacy into a four-prong right: W. Prosser,

Privacy, 48 CALIF. L. REV. 383 (1960). *Sullivan v. Pulitzer Broadcasting Co.*: 709 S.W.2d 475, 12 Media L.Rptr. 2187 (Mo. banc 1986). Federal case from Independence in which $70,000 verdict was reversed: *Deupree v. Iliff*, 860 F.2d 300, 15 Media L.Rptr. 2225 (8th Cir. 1988). North Carolina decision rejecting the false light tort: *Renwick v. News and Observer Pub. Co.*, 310 N.C. 312, 312 S.E.2d 405, 57 ALR 4th 1, 10 Media L.Rptr. 1443 (N.C. 1984).

   Journalists' Right of Privacy Primer

   The Different Laws of Privacy. Roe v. Wade: 410 U.S. 113 (1973). Forerunner to *Roe v. Wade: Griswold v. Connecticut*, 381 U.S. 479 (1965).

   Trespass and Intrusion. Consent of police as implied consent on the part of the property owner: *Florida Publishing Co. v. Fletcher*, 340 So.2d 914, 2 Media L.Rptr. 1088 (Fla. 1977) and *Wood v. Fort Dodge Messenger*, 13 Media L.Rptr. 1610 (Iowa Dist. Ct., Humbolt Co. 1986); *but see Ayeni v. CBS Inc.*, 848 F.Supp. 362, 22 Media L.Rptr. 1466 (E.D.N.Y. 1994), *aff'd in part, Ayeni v. Mottola*, 35 F.3d 680, 22 Media L.Rptr. 2225 (2d Cir. 1994). "Ambush interview" on business property open to the public: *Machleder v. Diaz*, 538 F.Supp. 1364 (S.D.N.Y. 1982), *aff'd in relevant part*, 801 F.2d 46, 13 Media L.Rptr. 1369 (2d Cir. 1986). Intrusion where reporter used a concealed camera and recording device and exceeded the subject's consent to a face-to-face interview: *Dietemann v. Time, Inc.*, 449 F.2d 245, 1 Media L.Rptr. 2417 (9th Cir. 1971). Case involving television crew barging uninvited into a dark restaurant: *Le Mistral, Inc. v. Columbia Broadcasting System*, 61 A.D.2d 491, 402 N.Y.S.2d 815, 3 Media L.Rptr. 1913 (1978). Case concerning undercover police officer filmed in massage parlor: *Cassidy v. American Broadcasting Cos.*, 60 Ill. App. 3d 831, 377 N.E.2d 126, 3 Media L.Rptr. 2449 (1978). Rejection of "necessity" defenses: *Shevin v. Sunbeam Television Corp.*, 351 So.2d 723, 3 Media L.Rptr. 1317 (Fla. 1977).

   Recording of Conversations. Federal eavesdropping statute: 18 U.S.C. §§ 2510–2520. "Criminal" or "tortious" purpose exception: 18 U.S.C. § 2511(2)(d). Rejection of theory that journalists' reporting constituted a tortious purpose: *Boddie v. American Broadcasting Cos.*, 881 F.2d 267, 16 Media L.Rptr. 2038 (6th Cir. 1989). The minority of states that have "two-party-consent" eavesdropping statutes include several large and important states such as California, Florida, Illinois, Maryland, and Pennsylvania. *See* Francis J. Flaherty, *Rules Unclear on Single-Party Taping*, NAT'L L.J., Jan. 23, 1984. Illinois eavesdropping statute: 720 ILL. COMP. STAT. 5/14. Missouri's eavesdropping statue: Mo. REV. STAT. §§ 542.400–424. Two-party consent requirement when a wireless microphone is used: Mo. REV. STAT. § 542.402.1(2).

   Public Disclosure of Private Facts. Barber v. Time: 348 Mo. 1199, 159 S.W.2d 291, 1 Media L.Rptr. 1779 (1942). Other successful private facts cases: *Deaton v. Delta Democrat Publishing Co.*, 326 So.2d 471 (Miss. 1976) (mental retardation); *Vassiliades v. Garfinkel's*, 492 A.2d 580, 11 Media L.Rptr. 2057 (D.C. 1985) (use of plastic surgery); *Y. G. v. Jewish Hospital of St. Louis*, 795 S.W.2d 488 (Mo. App. 1990) (participation in in vitro fertilization); *Daily Times Democrat v. Graham*, 276 Ala. 380, 162 So.2d 474 (1964) (photographs of a person in an embarrassing state of undress). In vitro fertilization program case from St. Louis: *Y. G. v. Jewish Hospital of St. Louis*, above. Oliver Sipple case: *Sipple v. Chronicle Publishing Co.*, 154 Cal. App. 3d 1040, 201 Cal. Rptr. 665, 10 Media L.Rptr. 1690 (1984). *See generally* Diane Zimmermann, *Requiem for a*

Heavyweight: A Farewell to the Warren and Brandeis Privacy Tort, 68 CORNELL L. REV. 291 (1983).

False Light. Missouri Supreme Court decision that prohibited use of false light claims in situations of classic defamation: *Sullivan v. Pulitzer Broadcasting Co.*: 709 S.W.2d 475, 12 Media L.Rptr. 2187 (Mo. banc 1986). Case involving story about a trained pig: *Braun v. Flynt*, 726 F.2d 245, 10 Media L.Rptr. 1487 (5th Cir. 1984). Warren Spahn case: *Spahn v. Julian Messner, Inc.*, 21 N.Y.2d 124, 286 N.Y.S.2d 832, 233 N.E.2d 840, 30 ALR 3d 196 (1967). *See generally* Diane Zimmermann, *False Light Invasion of Privacy: The Light That Failed*, 64 N.Y.U. L. REV. 364 (1989).

Right of Privacy and Gary Hart

Suits by well-known public officials: *Westmoreland v. CBS*: 596 F.Supp. 1170 (S.D.N.Y. 1984); *Goldwater v. Ginzburg*, 414 F.2d 324, 1 Media L.Rptr. 1737 (2d Cir. 1969); *Buckley v. Littell*, 539 F.2d 882, 1 Media L.Rptr. 1762 (2d Cir. 1976); *Cervantes v. Time, Inc.*, 464 F.2d 986, 1 Media L.Rptr. 1751 (8th Cir. 1972). U.S. Supreme Court comment concerning a political candidate: *Monitor Patriot Co. v. Roy*, 401 U.S. 265, 1 Media L.Rptr. 1619 (1971). Falwell's suit against Hustler: *Hustler Magazine, Inc. v. Falwell*, 485 U.S. 46 (1988); *see* Rodney A. Smolla, JERRY FALWELL V. LARRY FLYNT: THE FIRST AMENDMENT ON TRIAL (St. Martin's 1988).

Scandal, Victims' Names, and Ethical Limits

Kitty Kelley's biography of Nancy Reagan: NANCY REAGAN: THE UNAUTHORIZED BIOGRAPHY (Simon & Schuster 1991). Publication of articles about the victim in the William Kennedy Smith rape case: *see* William Glaberson, *Times Article Naming Rape Accuser Ignites Debate on Journalistic Values*, N.Y. TIMES, Apr. 26, 1991. U.S. Supreme Court decisions striking down prosecution under statutes forbidding naming of rape victims: *Florida Star v. B.J.F.*, 491 U.S. 524, 16 Media L.Rptr. 1801 (1989); *Smith v. Daily Mail Publishing Co.*, 443 U.S. 97, 5 Media L.Rptr. 1305 (1979). Kelley's prepublication legal battle with Frank Sinatra: *see* Kitty Kelley, HIS WAY: THE UNAUTHORIZED BIOGRAPHY OF FRANK SINATRA, Author's Note, pp. ix–x (Bantam Books 1986). *New York Times v. Sullivan*: 376 U.S. 254, 1 Media L.Rptr. 1527 (1964). Chief Justice Burger's quotation regarding editorial prerogative: *Miami Herald Publishing Co. v. Tornillo*: 418 U.S. 241, 258, 1 Media L.Rptr. 1898 (1974).

7. Lawbreaking, Negligence, and Unusual Claims

Reporter Deception and Lawbreaking

Missouri and Illinois eavesdropping laws: MO. REV. STAT. §§ 542.400–424; 720 ILL. COMP. STAT. 5/14. Florida case rejecting a First Amendment exception for eavesdropping: *Shevin v. Sunbeam Television Corp.*, 351 So.2d 723, 3 Media L.Rptr. 1317 (Fla. 1977). Court decisions rejecting First Amendment and journalistic "necessity" defenses to intrusion: *Dietemann v. Time, Inc.*, 449 F.2d 245, 1 Media L.Rptr. 2417 (9th Cir. 1971); *Stahl v. Oklahoma*, 9 Media L.Rptr. 1945 (Okla. Crim. App. 1983). Rules regarding surveillance: *McLain v. Boise Cascade Corp.*, 271 Or. 549, 533 P.2d 343, 346 (Or. 1975) ("If the surveillance is conducted in a reasonable and unobtrusive manner the defendant will incur no liability for invasion of privacy. On the other hand, if the surveillance is conducted in an unreasonable and obtrusive manner the defendant will be liable for invasion of privacy."). Information on photocopies viewed as private property: *Carpenter v. United States*, 484 U.S. 19, 14 Media L.Rptr. 1853 (1987).

"Negligent" Publications

Hired hit men: *Norwood v. Soldier of Fortune Magazine, Inc.*, 651 F.Supp. 1397, 13 Media L.Rptr. 2025 (W.D. Ark. 1987); *Eimann v. Soldier of Fortune Magazine, Inc.*, 880 F.2d 830, 16 Media L.Rptr. 2148 (5th Cir. 1989); *Braun v. Soldier of Fortune*, 968 F.2d 1110, 20 Media L.Rptr. 1777 (11th Cir. 1992). Teenager suffocation: *Herceg v. Hustler Magazine, Inc.*, 565 F.Supp. 802, 9 Media L.Rptr. 1959 (S.D. Tex. 1983). Kidnapper stalking victim: *Hyde v. City of Columbia*, 637 S.W.2d 251 (Mo. App. 1982). Fireworks explosion: *Yuhas v. Mudge*, 129 N.J. Super. 207, 322 A.2d 824 (1974). Food poisoning: *Cardoza v. True*, 342 So.2d 1053, 2 Media L.Rptr. 1635 (Fla. App. 1977). Investor's purchase of corporate bonds: *Gutter v. Dow Jones, Inc.*, 22 Ohio St.3d 286, 490 N.E.2d 898 (1986); *First Equity Corporation of Florida v. Standard & Poor's Corp.*, 670 F.Supp. 115, 14 Media L.Rptr. 1945 (S.D.N.Y. 1987). John Wayne Hearn case: *Eimann v. Soldier of Fortune Magazine, Inc.*, above. Richard Savage cases: *Norwood v. Soldier of Fortune Magazine, Inc.*, and *Braun v. Soldier of Fortune Magazine, Inc.*, above. Cookbook cases: *Cardoza v. True*, above. Financial advice cases: *Daniel v. Dow Jones & Co.*, 520 N.Y.S.2d 334 (City Civ. Ct. Oct. 13, 1987); *Pittman v. Dow Jones & Co.*, 662 F.Supp. 921, 14 Media L.Rptr. 1284 (E.D. La. 1987). Case involving "Mickey Mouse Club" television show: *Walt Disney Productions, Inc. v. Shannon*, 247 Ga. 402, 276 S.E.2d 580, 7 Media L.Rptr. 1209 (1981). *See generally* Jonathan M. Hoffman, *Soldiers of Misfortune: A Survey of Claims by Victims of Negligent Publishing and Broadcasting*, THE BRIEF, Summer 1991.

Failure to Publish

Blatty v. New York Times Co., 42 Cal.3d 1033, 232 Cal.Rptr. 542, 728 P.2d 1177, 13 Media L.Rptr. 1928 (1986). *See also Marc's Restaurant, Inc. v. CBS Inc.*, 730 S.W.2d 582 (Mo. App. 1987) (restaurant advertisement); *Sinn v. The Daily Nebraskan*, 829 F.2d 662 (8th Cir. 1987) (advertisement in student newspaper); *Cyntje v. Daily News Pub. Co.*, 551 F. Supp. 403, 9 Media L.Rptr. 1612 (D.V.I. 1982) (news release about governor); *Indiana Construction Corp. v. Chicago Tribune Co.*, 13 Media L.Rptr. 1863 (N.D. Ind. 1986) (contractor's suit); *Ahmad v. Levi*, 414 F.Supp. 597 (E.D. Pa. 1976) (Arab activist's suit); *Barnstone v. University of Houston, KVHT-TV*, 660 F.2d 137, 7 Media L.Rptr. 2185 (5th Cir. 1981) (refusal of television station to air controversial program).

Threats to Publishing

"Son of Sam" decision: *Simon & Schuster, Inc. v. Members of New York State Crime Victims Board*, 502 U.S.105, 19 Media L.Rptr. 1609 (1991). Fictionalization theory: *Bindrim v. Mitchell*, 92 Cal. App. 3d 61, 155 Cal. Rptr. 29, 5 Media L.Rptr. 1113 (1979). Sinatra suit against Kelley: *see* Kitty Kelley, HIS WAY: THE UNAUTHORIZED BIOGRAPHY OF FRANK SINATRA, Author's Note, pp. ix–x (Bantam Books 1986). Salinger suit: *Salinger v. Random House, Inc.*, 811 F.2d 90, 87 ALR Fed 853, 13 Media L.Rptr. 1954 (2d Cir. 1987). Other copyright holders who have attempted to use their copyrights to prevent publication of critical books: *see* chapter 8, "Copyright Lesson." First Amendment limits on RICO forfeiture remedy threatened against publishers of allegedly obscene books: *see Fort Wayne Books v. Indiana* 489 U.S. 46, 16 Media

L.Rptr. 1337 (1989) (prior judicial determination that items seized were obscene or that a RICO violation occurred necessary before allegedly obscene books can be seized).

Silly Media Lawsuits

Radio announcer "sleazy whore" suit: *Carroll v. Corcoran,* 21 Media L.Rptr. 1479 (St. Louis City Mo. Cir. Ct. 1992). "Elephant Man's disease" suit: *Kolegas v. Heftel Broadcasting Corp.,* 154 Ill. 2d 1, 607 N.E.2d 201, 20 Media L.Rptr. 2105 (1992). Ninety-seven-year-old woman's suit: *People's Bank and Trust Co. v. Globe International,* 817 F.Supp. 72 (W.D. Ark. 1993) and 978 F.2d 1065. 20 Media L.Rptr. 1925 (8th Cir. 1992). Missouri Supreme Court comment concerning "vituperative and abusive" statements: *Nazeri v. Missouri Valley College,* 860 S.W.2d 303 (Mo. banc 1993). "Old Glory Condoms" case: *In Re Old Glory Condom Corp.,* 26 U.S.P.Q.2d 1216 (T.T.A.B. 1993). Skeleton sex case: *Fashion Victim Ltd. v. Sunrise Turquoise, Inc.,* 785 F.Supp. 1302 (N.D. Ill. 1992). "Why Do Fools Fall in Love?" case: *Merchant v. Lymon,* 1995 WL 217508 (S.D.N.Y. Apr. 11, 1995). Vanna White case: *White v. Samsung Electronics America, Inc.,* 971 F.2d 1395, 20 Media L.Rptr. 1457 (9th Cir. 1992). Paul Prudhomme case: *Prudhomme v. The Proctor & Gamble Co.,* 800 F.Supp. 390, 20 Media L.Rptr. 1900 (E.D. La. 1992). Tom Waits case: *Waits v. Frito Lay, Inc.,* 978 F.2d 1093 (9th Cir. 1992). Mickey Dora case: *Dora v. Frontline Video Inc.,* 15 Cal. App. 4th 536, 18 Cal. Rptr.2d 790, 21 Media L.Rptr. 1398 (1993).

8. Copyright and Protection for Ideas

Copyright Myths and Realities

Current notice and registration requirements: 17 U.S.C. §§ 401, 411, 412. Copyright springs into existence on creation of a work: *see* 17 U.S.C. §§ 101 & 102. "Work for hire" doctrine: 17 U.S.C. § 201(b). J. D. Salinger case: *Salinger v. Random House, Inc.,* 811 F.2d 90, 87 ALR Fed 853, 13 Media L.Rptr. 1954 (2d Cir. 1987). Jeff Koons case: *Rogers v. Koons,* 960 F.2d 301, 20 Media L.Rptr. 1201 (2d Cir. 1992). Origin of "copyright": *see* L. Ray Patterson & Stanley W. Lindberg, THE NATURE OF COPYRIGHT: A LAW OF USERS' RIGHTS (U. of Ga. Press 1991). Sony Betamax case: *Sony Corp. of America v. Universal City Studios, Inc.,* 464 U.S. 417 (1984).

Fair Use and the Salinger Biography

Salinger v. Random House: 811 F.2d 90, 87 ALR Fed 853, 13 Media L.Rptr. 1954 (2d Cir. 1987).

Copyright Lesson

Copyrightability of facts and ideas: 17 U.S.C. § 102(b). *The Nation* case: *Harper & Row, Publishers, Inc. v. The Nation Enterprises,* 471 U.S. 539, 11 Media L.Rptr. 1969 (1985). The "fair use" doctrine: 17 U.S.C. § 107. The bundle of exclusive rights: 17 U.S.C. § 106. Salinger case: *Salinger v. Random House:* 811 F.2d 90, 87 ALR Fed 853, 13 Media L.Rptr. 1954 (2d Cir. 1987). Kwitny case: *Love v. Kwitny,* 706 F.Supp. 1123, 16 Media L.Rptr. 1305 (S.D.N.Y. 1989). Scientology case: *New Era Publications International, ApS v. Henry Holt & Co.,* 873 F.2d 576, 16 Media L.Rptr. 1559 (2d Cir. 1989). U.S. Constitution's intellectual property clause: Article I, Section 8, clause 8. [This copyright lesson took place in the 1980s; the situation it portrayed was ameliorated somewhat by the passage of Public Law 102–492 in 1992, which added to the fair use provision of the Copyright Act, 17 U.S.C. § 107, a sentence stating, "The fact that a work is unpublished shall not of itself bar a finding of fair use if such finding is made upon consideration of all the above factors."]

The Nature of Copyright *and Users' Rights*

L. Ray Patterson and Stanley W. Lindberg, THE NATURE OF COPYRIGHT: A LAW OF USERS' RIGHTS (U. of Ga. Press 1991). Court decisions in the 1980s restricting "fair use": see cases cited in "Copyright Lesson." Legislation sponsored by Senator Paul Simon: Pub.L. 102–492, 106 Stat. 3145 (1992). Extension of copyright to electronic "works": The electronic copyright is created by the combination of three features of the Copyright Act of 1976: the definition of copyrighted works as those works that are "fixed in any tangible medium of expression," the work for hire rule, and the acceptance of performance as equivalent to publication.

Parody and Fair Use

Campbell v. Acuff-Rose Music, Inc.: 510 U.S. 569, 22 Media L.Rptr. 1353 (1994). 1841 decision by Justice Story: *Folsam v. Marsh*, 9 F.Cas. 342 (No. 4901) (C.C.D. 1841).

Rights in Ideas

Buchwald's suit against Paramount: *Buchwald v. Paramount Pictures Corp.*, 17 Media L.Rptr. 1257 (Cal. Super. 1990); *see also* Pierce O'Donnell and Dennis McDougal, FATAL SUBTRACTION: THE INSIDE STORY OF BUCHWALD V. PARAMOUNT (Doubleday 1992). Settlement of suit: *Paramount Settles Buchwald's Compensation Suit*, N.Y. TIMES, Sept. 12, 1995. Suit concerning idea for *Fort Apache, the Bronx*: *Walker v. Time-Life Films, Inc.*, 784 F.2d 44, 12 Media L.Rptr. 1634 (2d Cir. 1986). Suit concerning idea for *Raiders of the Lost Ark*: *Zambito v. Paramount Pictures Corp.*, 613 F.Supp. 1107 (E.D.N.Y. 1985).

9. Advertising

Comparative Advertising Regulation

Statute that went into effect in 1989: The Trademark Revision Act of 1988, Pub.Law 100–667, 102 Stat. 3935, 3946. Aspirin wars: *see* Charles C. Mann and Mark L. Plummer, THE ASPIRIN WARS: MONEY, MEDICINE, AND 100 YEARS OF RAMPANT COMPETITION (Knopf 1991). Section 43(a) of the Lanham Act: 15 U.S.C. § 1125(a). "Lowest tar" case: *American Brands, Inc. v. R. J. Reynolds Tobacco Co.*, 413 F.Supp. 1352 (S.D.N.Y. 1976). Maximum Strength Anacin case: *McNeilab, Inc. v. American Home Products Corp.*, 501 F.Supp. 517 (S.D.N.Y. 1980). Jartran case: *U-Haul International, Inc. v. Jartran, Inc.*, 793 F.2d 1034 (9th Cir. 1986).

Use of Trademarks in Advertising

Ambush advertising and the 1988 Olympics: *see* Stuart Elliott, *Advertising: Companies Go for the Gold, Using Ambush Marketing*, N.Y. TIMES, Feb. 3, 1992; Stuart Elliott, *Mass-Marketer Jousting Is Newest Olympic Sport*, N.Y. TIMES, July 15, 1992. Legal framework for trademark law (consumer confusion): 15 U.S.C. § 1114. Boston Marathon case: *WCVB-TV v. Boston Athletic Ass'n*, 926 F.2d 42, 18 Media L.Rptr. 1710 (1st Cir. 1991). Other parade case: *Production Contractors, Inc, v. WGN Continental Broadcasting Co.*, 622 F.Supp. 1500, 12 Media L.Rptr. 1708 (N.D. Ill. 1985).

Publicity Rights in Advertising

Forum magazine case: *Cher v. Forum International, Ltd.*, 692 F.2d 634, 8 Media L.Rptr. 2484 (9th Cir. 1982) (advertisements that falsely implied that Cher had given *Forum* magazine an exclusive interview and that contained other ambiguous copy that tended to suggest that she endorsed the magazine were held to infringe her right of publicity). Christian Dior case: *Onassis v. Christian Dior-New York, Inc.*, 122 Misc.2d 603, 472 N.Y.S.2d 254, 10 Media L.Rptr. 1859 (1984). Bette Midler case: *Midler v. Ford Motor Co.*, 849 F.2d 460, 15 Media L.Rptr. 1620 (9th Cir. 1988); *see Y&R Ordered to Pay Midler*, N.Y. TIMES, Oct. 31, 1989. "Here's Johnny" case: *Carson v. Here's Johnny Portable Toilets, Inc.*, 698 F.2d 831, 9 Media L.Rptr. 1153 (6th Cir. 1983). Tom Waits case: *Waits v. Frito Lay, Inc.*, 978 F.2d 1093 (9th Cir. 1992). Paul Prudhomme case: *Prudhomme v. The Proctor & Gamble Co.*, 800 F.Supp. 390, 20 Media L.Rptr. 1900 (E.D. La. 1992). Efforts by heirs of Malcolm X: *see* Phil Patton, *Marketers Battle for the Right to Profit from Malcolm's 'X,'* N.Y. TIMES, Nov. 8, 1992. Rodney King: P. J. Boyer, *The Selling of Rodney King*, VANITY FAIR, July 1992. Vanna White case: *White v. Samsung Electronics America, Inc.*, 971 F.2d 1395, 20 Media L.Rptr. 1457 (9th Cir. 1992). Judge Kozinski's opinion: *White v. Samsung Electronics America*, 989 F.2d 1512, 1513, 21 Media L.Rptr. 1330 (9th Cir. 1993) (Kozinski, J., dissenting from denial of rehearing). *Masson v. The New Yorker:* 895 F.2d 1535 (9th Cir. 1989) (dissent by Judge Kozinski); 501 U.S. 496, 18 Media L.Rptr. 2241 (1991) (Supreme Court decision). 2 Live Crew decision: *Campbell v. Acuff-Rose Music, Inc.*, 510 U.S. 269, 22 Media L.Rptr. 1353 (1994). *See generally* Jane Gaines, CONTESTED CULTURE: THE IMAGE, THE VOICE AND THE LAW (U. N. Carolina Press 1991).

10. Broadcasting

Licensing of Broadcast Spectrum

Federal Communications Act: 47 U.S.C. §§ 151–926. Public interest standard: 47 U.S.C. § 307(a). Comparative hearing procedure: 47 U.S.C. § 309(a)–(f). Cellular lotteries: 47 U.S.C. § 309(i). 1993 Omnibus Budget Reconciliation Act: 47 U.S.C. § 309(j), Pub.L. 103–66, 1993 U.S.Code, Cong. & Admin. News 1988. Results of the initial spectrum auctions: Edmund L. Andrews, *Airwave Auctions Bring $833 Million for Treasury*, N.Y. TIMES, July 30, 1994; Peter Passell, *Economic Scene: Managing the Airwaves for Productivity and Profits*, N.Y. TIMES, Mar. 9, 1995. *See generally* Jonathan Blake, *FCC Licensing: From Comparative Hearings to Auctions*, 47 FED. COMM. L.J. 179 (1994); Janice Obuchowski, *The Unfinished Task of Spectrum Policy Reform*, 47 FED. COMM. L.J. 325 (1994); Kurt A. Wimmer, *Netting Federal Revenues from Thin Air*, COMM. LAWYER, Summer 1993.

Broadcasting and Press Freedoms

Red Lion Broadcasting Co. v. Federal Communications Commission: 395 U.S. 367, 1 Media L.Rptr. 2053 (1969). The personal attack rule: 47 C.F.R. § 73.1920 et seq. Political advertising requirements: Sections 315(a) & 312(a)(7) of the Communications Act, Title 47 of United States Code. Ban on "indecent programming": *Pacifica v. FCC*, 438 U.S. 726, 3 Media L.Rptr. 2553 (1978). Other content controls: *See generally Galloway v. Federal Communications Commission*,

778 F.2d 18, 12 Media L.Rptr. 1443 (D.C. Cir. 1985); *see also Hunger in America*, 20 FCC2d 143 (1969); *WBBM-TV*, 18 FCC2d 124 (1969); *Democratic National Convention Television Coverage*, 16 FCC2d 650 (1969). *Miami Herald Publishing Co. v. Tornillo*: 418 U.S. 241, 1 Media L.Rptr. 1898 (1974). *Joseph Burstyn, Inc. v. Wilson*: 343 U.S. 495, 1 Media L.Rptr. 1357 (1951). Example of five television screens displaying the same image: Robert Corn-Revere, *New Technology and the First Amendment: Breaking the Cycle of Repression*, 17 HASTINGS COMM/ENT L.J. 247 (1994). Senator James Exon's proposal to apply broadcast-style regulations to computer communications: S. 314, 104th Cong., 1st Sess.; this proposal became the Communications Decency Act of 1996, Title V of the Telecommunications Act of 1996, Pub. L. No. 104-1-4, Section 502, 110 Stat. 56, 133–35. *See generally* Lucas A. Powe Jr., AMERICAN BROADCASTING AND THE FIRST AMENDMENT (U. of Calif. Press 1987); Lee C. Bollinger, IMAGES OF A FREE PRESS (U. of Chicago Press 1991); Matthew L. Spitzer, SEVEN DIRTY WORDS AND SIX OTHER STORIES: CONTROLLING THE CONTENT OF PRINT AND BROADCAST (Yale U. Press 1986); Barbara Mc-Dowell, *The First Amendment and the Protection of Unfair Speech*, 47 FED. COMM. L.J. 85 (1994); Jerome Barron, FREEDOM OF THE PRESS FOR WHOM? (Indiana U. Press 1973). On the convergence of technologies, see Ithiel de Sola Pool, TECHNOLOGIES OF FREEDOM: ON FREE SPEECH IN AN ELECTRONIC AGE (Belknap Press 1983).

Political Television Commercials

Equal opportunities rule (Section 315 of the Communications Act): 47 U.S.C. § 315(a). Disputes regarding whether political debates are exempt news events: *Forbes v. Arkansas Educational Television Communication Network Foundation*, 22 F.3d 1423, 22 Media L.Rptr. 1015 (8th Cir. 1994); *DeYoung v. Patten*, 898 F.2d 628, 17 Media L.Rptr. 1638 (8th Cir. 1990). Disputes regarding whether documentary shows like *60 Minutes* and *20/20* and interview shows like *Donahue* qualify as news programming: *Telecommunications Research and Action Center v. FCC*, 26 F.3d 185, 22 Media L.Rptr. 1952 (D.C. Cir. 1994). Interpretation that any showing of old Ronald Reagan movies during one of Reagan's political campaign would give rise to equal opportunity rights of his opponents: *In Re Adrian Weiss (Ronald Reagan films)* 58 FCC2d 342, *review denied* 58 FCC2d 1389 (1976). No censorship, no liability rule: 47 U.S.C. § 312(a)(7); *Farmers Educ. & Co-op. Union of America, North Dakota Div. v. WDAY, Inc.*, 360 U.S. 525 (1959). Requirement that stations air commercial with graphic content: *Becker v. Federal Communications Commission*, 95 F.3d 75 (D.C. Cir. 1996). Decision that held abortion ad indecent: *Gillett Communications of Atlanta, Inc. v. Becker*, 807 F.Supp. 757, 20 Media L.Rptr. 1947 (N.D. Ga. 1992), *appeal dismissed*, 5 F.3d 1500 (11th Cir. 1993). *See* Jan Hoffman, *Picture Is Jumbled on Which Abortion Messages Can Get on TV*, N.Y. TIMES, June 11, 1992. Sponsorship identification rules: 47 U.S.C. § 317. Lowest unit charge rule: 47 U.S.C. § 315(b). Reasonable access for federal candidates rule: 47 U.S.C. § 312(a)(7). *See generally* Milton O. Gross, *Equal Time—What's the Use?* COMM. LAWYER, Spring 1988; Milton O. Gross, *Political Broadcasting II: Lowest Unit Charge, Reasonable Access, and Sponsorship Identification*, COMM. LAWYER, Summer 1988; Craig J. Blakeley and Carter G. Phillips, *Lowest Unit Charge Litigation: A Review and Analysis*, COMM. LAWYER, Summer 1991; Martin Kassman, *The Defamation You Can't Refuse: Section 315's Prohibition on Censoring Political Broadcasts*, 13 HASTINGS COMM/ENT L.J. 1 (1990).

newsletter with primarily editorial content: *Danis v. St. Louis Argyle Communications, Inc.*, St. Louis County Circuit Court, No. 676831; *Kenro, Inc. v. Fax Daily, Inc.*, 962 F.Supp. 1162 (S.D. Ind. 1997).

13. The Internet and Electronic Information

Information as Property

Winans decision: *Carpenter v. United States*, 484 U.S. 19, 14 Media L.Rptr. 1853 (1987).

Price Tags on Information

Newspaper's attempt to charge for use in a movie advertisement of quotations from the newspaper's movie review: *see* Robert Hard, *Excerpt at Your Own Risk!* SMALL PRESS, Fall 1992. Celebrity's attempt to charge for any use or republication of his image or quotations in any money-making context: *see, e.g., White v. Samsung Electronics America, Inc.*, 971 F.2d 1395, 20 Media L.Rptr. 1457 (9th Cir. 1992). Analyst of information's attempt to charge for republication of his newsworthy conclusions and A. M. Best Co.'s challenge to *The Insurance Forum*: Jane Bryant Quinn, *A. M. Best and Insurance Forum Square Off over Printing Ratings*, WASHINGTON POST, Dec. 19, 1993; *A. M. Best Sues Belth over His Use of Its Ratings*, NATIONAL UNDER-WRITER–LIFE AND HEALTH, Dec, 27, 1993; Will Higgins, *Belth Beseiged: Large Insurance Rating Service Insists Lawsuit Against Ex-Professor Is Not about Money*, INDIANAPOLIS NEWS, Mar. 15, 1994; Jane Bryant Quinn, *Tracking Insurers' Soundness Ratings*, WASHINGTON POST, Oct. 22, 1995. Attempt to control distribution of electronic Missouri statutes: *see* chapter 3, "Access to Electronic Statutes."

Who Owns Information?

Anne Wells Branscomb, WHO OWNS INFORMATION? FROM PRIVACY TO PUBLIC ACCESS (Basic Books 1994).

Law of Cyberspace Messages

Obscenity prosecution in Memphis against bulletin-board operators in California: *United States v. Thomas*, 74 F.3d 701, 24 Media L.Rptr. 1321 (6th Cir. 1996); *see* Henry J. Reske, *Computer Porn a Prosecutorial Challenge*, ABA JOURNAL, Dec. 1994. Cyber-libel suit by British scientist against researcher in Geneva: *see* Michael Smyth and Nick Braithwaite, *First U.K. Bulletin Board Defamation Suit Brought*, NAT'L L.J. Sept. 19, 1994. Ruling that English law is so one-sided and insensitive to free speech concerns that its libel judgments should not be enforced in America: *Bachchan v. India Abroad Publications, Inc.* 154 Misc.2d 228, 585 N.Y.S.2d 661 (Sup. Ct. 1992); *Abdullah v. Sheridan Square Press, Inc.*, 1994 WL 419847 (S.D.N.Y. 1994); *Matusevitch v. Telnikoff*, 877 F.Supp. 1, 23 Media L.Rptr. 1367 (D.D.C. 1995); *see also* Kyu Ho Youm, *Suing American Media in Foreign Courts: Doing an End-Run Around U.S. Libel Law?* 16 HASTINGS COMM/ENT L.J. 235 (1994). Cubby case against CompuServe: *Cubby, Inc. v. CompuServe Inc.*, 776 F.Supp. 135, 19 Media L.Rptr. 1525 (S.D.N.Y. 1991). Case brought by *Playboy*: *Playboy Enterprises v. Frena*, 839 F.Supp. 1552, 22 Media L.Rptr. 1301 (M.D. Fla. 1993). [See *Religious Technology Center v. Netcom On-Line Communication Services, Inc.*, 907 F.Supp. 1361, 24 Media L.Rptr. 1097 (N.D. Cal. 1995) for a case involving an Internet access provider's responsibility.] Prodigy case: *Stratton Oakmont, Inc. v. Prodigy Services Co.*, 23 Media L.Rptr. 1794 (N.Y. Sup.Ct. 1995); *see also* 24 Media L.Rptr. 1126 (denial of reargument). Protection for on-line services in 1996 Telecommunications Act: 47 U.S.C. § 223(e). *See generally* Eric Schlachter, *Cyberspace, the Free Market and the Free Marketplace of Ideas: Recognizing Legal Differences in Computer Bulletin Board Functions*, 16 HASTINGS COMM/ENT L.J. 87 (1993); Rex S. Heinke and Heather D. Rafter, *Rough Justice in Cyberspace: Liability on the Electronic Frontier*, THE COMPUTER LAWYER, July 1994.

Internet Jurisdiction

Blue Note case: *Bensusan Restaurant Corp. v. King*, 937 F.Supp. 295 (S.D.N.Y. 1996). Rulings finding jurisdiction: *Inset Systems, Inc. v. Instruction Set, Inc.*, 937 F.Supp. 161 (D. Conn. 1996) (jurisdiction in Connecticut); *CompuServe, Inc. v. Patterson*, 89 F.3d 1257, 24 Media L.Rptr. 2100 (6th Cir. 1996) (use of on-line service located in Ohio); *United States v. Thomas*, 74 F.3d 701, 24 Media L.Rptr. 1321 (6th Cir. 1996) (computer bulletin board based in California). Minnesota attorney general's statement: *Warning to Internet Users and Providers*, Minnesota Attorney General Hubert H. Humphrey, undated [1996]. *Playmen* case: *Playboy Enterprises, Inc. v. Chuckleberry Publishing, Inc.*, 939 F.Supp. 1032 (S.D.N.Y. 1996).

Facts and Promise of the Internet

American Civil Liberties Union v. Reno: 929 F.Supp. 824 (E.D. Pa. 1996). *Shea on behalf of American Reporter v. Reno*: 930 F.Supp. 916 (S.D.N.Y. 1996). Supreme Court decision: *Reno v. American Civil Liberties Union*, No. 96-511 (U.S. June 26, 1997).

Select Bibliography

Advertising

Baker, C. Edwin. *Advertising and a Democratic Press*. Princeton Univ. Press, 1993.

Fueroghne, Dean K. *"But the People in Legal Said": A Guide to Current Legal Issues in Advertising*. Dow Jones-Irwin, 1989.

Gartner, Michael G. *Advertising and the First Amendment*. Priority, 1989.

Kintner, Earl W. *A Primer on the Law of Deceptive Practices: A Guide for the Businessman*. Macmillan, 1971.

Mann, Charles C., and Mark L. Plummer. *The Aspirin Wars: Money, Medicine, and 100 Years of Rampant Competition*. Knopf, 1991.

Preston, Ivan L. *The Great American Blow-up: Puffery in Advertising and Selling*. Univ. of Wisconsin Press, 1975.

Broadcasting and Entertainment Media

Besen, Stanley M., et al. *Misregulating Television: Network Dominance and the FCC*. Univ. of Chicago Press, 1984.

Friendly, Fred W. *The Good Guys, the Bad Guys, and the First Amendment: Free Speech vs. Fairness in Broadcasting*. Random House, 1976.

Kronenwetter, Michael. *Free Press v. Fair Trial: Television and Other Media in the Courtroom*. Franklin Watts, 1986.

Miller, Frank. *Censored Hollywood: Sex, Sin, and Violence on Screen*. Turner, 1994.

Minow, Newton N., and Craig L. Lamay. *Abandoned in the Wasteland: Children, Television, and the First Amendment*. Hill & Wang, 1995.

O'Donnell, Pierce, and Dennis McDougal. *Fatal Subtraction: The Inside Story of* Buchwald v. Paramount. Doubleday, 1992.

Powe, Lucas A., Jr. *American Broadcasting and the First Amendment*. Univ. of California Press, 1987.

Rudell, Michael I. *Behind the Scenes: Practical Entertainment Law*. Law & Business, 1984.

Simmons, Steven J. *The Fairness Doctrine and the Media*. Univ. of California Press, 1978.

Spitzer, Matthew L. *Seven Dirty Words and Six Other Stories: Controlling the Content of Print and Broadcast*. Yale Univ. Press, 1986.

Tunstall, Jeremy. *Communications Deregulation: The Unleashing of America's Communications Industry*. Basil Blackwell, 1986.

Censorship and Obscenity

Craig, Alec. *Suppressed Books: A History of the Conception of Literary Obscenity*. World, 1963.

De Grazia, Edward. *Girls Lean Back Everywhere: The Law of Obscenity and the Assault on Genius*. Random House, 1992.

Ernst, Morris L., and William Seagle. *To the Pure . . . A Study of Obscenity and the Censor*. Viking, 1928.

Garry, Patrick. *An American Paradox: Censorship in a Nation of Free Speech*. Praeger, 1993.

Hawkins, Gordon, and Franklin E. Zimring. *Pornography in a Free Society*. Cambridge Univ. Press, 1988.

Heins, Marjorie. *Sex, Sin, and Blasphemy: A Guide to America's Censorship Wars*. New Press, 1993.

Marsh, Dave. *50 Ways to Fight Censorship and Important Facts to Know about the Censors*. Thunder's Mouth, 1991.

Strossen, Nadine. *Defending Pornography: Free Speech, Sex, and the Fight for Women's Rights*. Scribner, 1995.

Copyright and Intellectual Property

Gaines, Jane. *Contested Culture: The Image, the Voice, and the Law*. Univ. of North Carolina Press, 1991.

Goldstein, Paul. *Copyright's Highway: The Law and Lore of Copyright from Gutenberg to the Celestial Jukebox*. Hill & Wang, 1994.

Lawrence, John S., and Bernard Timberg. *Fair Use and Free Inquiry: Copyright Law and the New Media*. Ablex, 1980.

Patterson, L. Ray, and Stanley W. Lindberg. *The Nature of Copyright: A Law of Users' Rights*. Univ. of Georgia Press, 1991.

Ploman, Edward W. and L. Clark Hamilton. *Copyright: Intellectual Property in the Information Age*. Routledge, 1980.

Rose, Mark. *Authors and Owners: The Evolution of Copyright*. Harvard Univ. Press, 1993.

Sinofsky, Esther R. *A Copyright Primer for Educational and Industrial Media Producers*. Copyright Information Services, 1988.

Strong, William S. *The Copyright Book: A Practical Guide*. 4th ed. MIT Press, 1993.

First Amendment, Free Speech Theory and History

Bollinger, Lee C. *Images of a Free Press*. Univ. of Chicago Press, 1991.

———. *The Tolerant Society: Freedom of Speech and Extremist Speech in America*. Clarendon Press, 1986.

Burns, James MacGregor, and Stuart Burns. *A People's Charter: The Pursuit of Rights in America.* Knopf, 1991.

Chafee, Zechariah, Jr. *Free Speech in the United States.* Harvard Univ. Press, 1941.

Collins, Ronald K. L., and David M. Slover. *The Death of Discourse.* Westview Press, 1996.

Cox, Archibald. *Freedom of Expression.* Harvard Univ. Press, 1981.

Emerson, Thomas I. *The System of Freedom of Expression.* Random House, 1970.

———. *Toward a General Theory of the First Amendment.* Random House, 1966.

Garry, Patrick. *Scrambling for Protection: The New Media and the First Amendment.* Univ. of Pittsburgh Press, 1994.

Haiman, Franklyn S. *Freedom of Speech.* National Textbook, 1976.

Hentoff, Nat. *The First Freedom: The Tumultuous History of Free Speech in America.* Delacorte, 1980.

———. *Free Speech for Me—But Not for Thee: How the American Left and Right Relentlessly Censor Each Other.* Harper Collins, 1992.

Kalven, Harry Jr. *A Worthy Tradition: Freedom of Speech in America.* Harper & Row, 1988.

Levy, Leonard W. *Emergence of a Free Press.* Oxford Univ. Press, 1985.

———. *Legacy of Suppression: Freedom of Speech and Press in Early American History.* Belknap Press, 1960.

Lieberman, Jethro K. *Free Speech, Free Press, and the Law.* Lothrop, 1980.

McCoy, Ralph E. *Freedom of the Press: An Annotated Bibliography.* Southern Illinois Univ. Press, 1966.

———. *Freedom of the Press: An Annotated Bibliography, First Supplement: 1968–1978.* Southern Illinois Univ. Press, 1980.

———. *Freedom of the Press: An Annotated Bibliography, Second Supplement: 1978–1992.* Southern Illinois Univ. Press, 1994.

Meiklejohn, Alexander. *Free Speech and Its Relationship to Self-Government.* Oxford Univ. Press, 1948.

Monk, Linda. *The First Amendment: America's Blueprint for Tolerance.* Close Up, 1994.

Pool, Ithiel de Sola. *Technologies of Freedom: On Free Speech in an Electronic Age.* Belknap Press, 1983.

Rutland, Robert A. *The Birth of the Bill of Rights, 1776–1791.* Univ. of North Carolina Press, 1955.

Schauer, Frederick. *Free Speech: A Philosophical Enquiry.* Cambridge Univ. Press, 1982.

Siebert, Frederick S. *Freedom of the Press in England, 1476–1776: The Rise and Decline of Government Control.* Univ. of Illinois Press, 1952.

Smith, Jeffrey A. *Printers and Press Freedom: The Ideology of Early American Journalism.* Oxford Univ. Press, 1988.

Smolla, Rodney A. *Free Speech in an Open Society.* Knopf, 1992.

Sunstein, Cass R. *Democracy and the Problem of Free Speech.* Free Press, 1993.

Van Alstyne, William W. *Interpretations of the First Amendment.* Duke Univ. Press, 1984.

Wagman, Robert J. *The First Amendment Book: Celebrating 200 Years of Freedom of the Press and Freedom of Speech.* Pharos Books, 1991.

Libel and Privacy

Adler, Renata. *Reckless Disregard:* Westmoreland v. CBS, et al.; Sharon v. Time. Knopf, 1986.

Anderson, Douglas A. *A "Washington Merry-Go-Round" of Libel Actions.* Nelson-Hall, 1980.

Bezanson, Randall, Gilbert Cranberg, and John Soloski. *Libel Law and the Press.* Free Press, 1987.

Forer, Lois G. *A Chilling Effect: The Mounting Threat of Libel and Invasion of Privacy Actions to the First Amendment.* Norton, 1987.

Gillmour, Donald M. *Publicity and the Abuse of Libel Law.* Oxford Univ. Press, 1992.

Hixson, Richard F. *Privacy in a Public Society: Human Rights in Conflict.* Oxford Univ. Press, 1987.

Kane, Peter. *Errors, Lies, and Libel.* Southern Illinois Univ. Press, 1992.

Lewis, Anthony. *Make No Law: The Sullivan Case and the First Amendment.* Knopf, 1991.

Littlewood, Thomas B. *Coals of Fire: The Alton Telegraph Libel Case.* Southern Illinois Univ. Press, 1988.

Rosenberg, Norman L. *Protecting the Best Men: An Interpretive History of the Law of Libel.* Univ. of North Carolina Press, 1986.

Sack, Robert D., and Sandra S. Baron. *Libel, Slander, and Related Problems.* 2d ed. Practising Law Institute, 1994.

Smolla, Rodney A. *Jerry Falwell v. Larry Flynt: The First Amendment on Trial.* St. Martin's, 1988.

———. *Suing the Press: Libel, the Media and Power.* Oxford Univ. Press, 1986.

Soloski, John, and Randall P. Bezanson, eds. *Reforming Libel Law.* Guilford, 1992.

Prior Restraint

Friendly, Fred W. *Minnesota Rag: The Dramatic Story of the Landmark Case That Gave New Meaning to Freedom of the Press.* Random House, 1981.

Moreland, H. *The Secret That Exploded.* Random House, 1981.

Pincher, Chapman. *The Spycatcher Affair: A Revealing Account of the Trial That Tried to Suppress a Book but Made It a Bestseller.* St. Martin's, 1987.

Rudenstine, David. *The Day the Presses Stopped: A History of the Pentagon Papers Case.* Univ. of California Press, 1996.

Turnbull, M. *The Spycatcher Affair.* Heinemann, 1988.

Unger, Sanford. *The Papers and the Papers: An Account of the Legal and Political Battle over the Pentagon Papers.* Dutton, 1972.

Publishing, Access and Sources

Barron, Jerome. *Freedom of the Press for Whom?* Indiana Univ. Press, 1973.

Blue, Martha. *By the Book: Legal ABCs for the Printed Word.* Northland, 1990.

Freedman, Warren. *Press and Media Access to the Criminal Courtroom.* Quorum, 1988.

Kirsch, Jonathan. *Kirsch's Handbook of Publishing Law for Authors, Publishers, Editors, and Agents.* Acrobat, 1995.

Powe, Lucas A., Jr., *The Fourth Estate and the Constitution: Freedom of the Press in America.* Univ. of California Press, 1991.

Schmidt, Benno. *Freedom of the Press vs. Public Access.* Praeger, 1976.

Whalen, Charles W., Jr., *Your Right to Know: How the Free Flow of News Depends on the Journalist's Right to Protect His Sources.* Random House, 1973.

Yudof, Mark G. *When Government Speaks: Politics, Law, and Government Expression in America.* Univ. of California Press, 1983.

Writers' and Artists' Guides

Bunnah, Brad, and Peter Beren. *Author Law and Strategies: A Legal Guide for the Working Writer.* Nolo, 1983.

Crawford, Tad. *Legal Guide for Authors and Self-Publishers.* Allworth, 1990.

———. *Legal Guide for the Visual Artist: The Professional's Handbook.* 3d ed. Allworth, 1995.

———. *The Writer's Legal Guide.* Rev. ed. Allworth, 1996.

Dill, Barbara. *The Journalist's Handbook on Libel and Privacy.* Free Press, 1986.

DuBoff, Leonard. *Book Publisher's Legal Guide.* 2d ed. Rothman, 1991.

Fuson, Harold W., Jr., *Telling It All: A Legal Guide to the Exercise of Free Speech.* Andrews & McMeel, 1995.

Goldfarb, Ronald L., and Gail E. Ross. *The Writer's Lawyer: Essential Legal Advice for Writers and Editors in All Media.* Times Books, 1989.

Norwick, Kenneth P., and Jerry Simon Chasen. *The Rights of Authors, Artists, and Other Creative People: The Basic ACLU Guide to Author and Artist Rights.* Southern Illinois Univ. Press, 1992.

Smedinghoff, Thomas J., ed. *Online Law: The SPA's Legal Guide to Doing Business on the Internet.* Addison-Wesley, 1996.

Wilson, Lee. *Make It Legal.* Allworth, 1990.

M A R K S A B L E M A N , a former newspaper reporter and a *cum laude* graduate of Georgetown University Law Center, has practiced law in Chicago and St. Louis, concentrating in litigation and communications law. He has served as president of the American Civil Liberties Union of Eastern Missouri and as an adjunct professor of media communications at Webster University.

COLOPHON

This book is set in Adobe Caslon, a typeface with strong historical roots in the printed word. The chapter numerals are set in Snell Roundhand, chosen for its Spencerian calligraphic qualities. Combined with these typefaces is Futura, a sans-serif type that is very much a product of the twentieth century. These design elements bring to mind the communications subject matter of the book, and its modern time frame. The design of the book and jacket is the work of Gary Gore.